PLATO'S
THEAETETUS

PLATO'S THEAETETUS

Part I of *The Being of the Beautiful*

Translated and with Commentary by
Seth Benardete

The University of Chicago Press • Chicago and London

The University of Chicago Press, Chicago 60637
The University of Chicago Press, Ltd., London

95 94 93 92 91 90 89 88 87 86   5 4 3 2 1

Library of Congress Cataloging in Publication Data

Plato.
    Plato's Theaetetus.

    (The Being of the beautiful ; pt. 1)
    1. Knowledge, Theory of—Early works to 1800.
I. Benardete, Seth.   II. Title.   III. Series: Plato.
Selections.   English.   1986. pt. 1.
B358.B46   1986 pt. 1   [B386.A5] 184 s [121]   85-28863
ISBN 0-226-67031-7 (pbk.)

For Arnaldo Momigliano

Contents

Plato says: One is not even one, two is one hardly.

Theopompus fr. 15K

Introduction

I. THEAETETUS

Plato presents the *Theaetetus* in a triple frame. It is complete in itself while belonging not only to the larger setting of seven dialogues that center around Socrates' trial and death, of which it is dramatically the first (*Theaetetus, Euthyphro, Sophist, Statesman, Apology of Socrates, Crito,* and *Phaedo*), but also to a trilogy within that seven consisting of itself, the *Sophist* and the *Statesman*. The *Sophist* and the *Statesman* are themselves a closely bound pair of dialogues with the same characters as the *Theaetetus'* plus a new arrival (the Eleatic stranger), and, uniquely for the Platonic corpus, with explicit allusions to one another. The *Statesman* refers to the *Sophist,* and the *Sophist* begins with an express link to the end of the *Theaetetus*. The *Sophist* and *Statesman* seem in turn to depend on a dialogue Plato never wrote, the *Philosopher,* which would have completed the task Socrates had assigned the Eleatic stranger at the beginning of the *Sophist*. Plato thus suggests that either the three dialogues together make up somehow for the missing *Philosopher,* or the *Theaetetus* by itself is the closest he could come to writing the *Philosopher.*

The *Theaetetus* has as its theme the question, What is knowledge? That question is identified at the start with the question, What is wisdom? No answer is reached. It is by far the most skeptical of Platonic dialogues. Its skepticism would by itself seem to entitle it to be called *Philosopher,* inasmuch as the philosopher is one who loves wisdom and does not have it; but the impasse the *Theaetetus* reaches does not entail that it also contain a reflection on the reasons for its failure, and only such a reflection would exhibit philosophy as the knowledge of ignorance. Socrates has brought Theaetetus by the end of the dialogue to the point of not believing he knows what he does not know. He has not brought him to any knowledge of what he does not know, for all of Socrates' arguments tend to show that it is as impossible not to know what one knows as to know what one does not. Socrates' arguments, however, are not the same as what we may call their drift, and it is in and through their drift that the despairing skeptic of the arguments yields to the philosopher with self-knowledge.

The drift of an argument is seized upon most readily when one can apply the argument to the situation in which that argument is embedded. Socrates presents from 172c to 177c a picture of the philosopher in his difference from the man who is caught up in the business of the law court; and if we were not warned by Socrates' telling Theodorus that he is speaking of one whom Theodorus calls a philosopher, we might believe that Socrates, too, subscribed fully to it. It is not, however, the interpretation of a single phrase that compels us to disassociate Socrates from the picture. Socrates begins the dialogue in such a way as to make it clear that he has a far greater resemblance to the pettifogger than to the would-be philosopher. Low things like his own hometown, money, and genealogy interest Socrates; they do not interest Theodorus. Socrates knows his way to the marketplace; Theaetetus and Theodorus do not. Indeed, they do not know that Socrates brought philosophy into the marketplace from its former place above the heavens and below the earth, where they themselves still dwell. It is of a piece with this ignorance that they are as unaware of the necessity for evil to be coeval with good as of Socrates' imminent trial. The extreme skepticism of the *Theaetetus* proves to be a consequence of their lofty ignorance of such things. They face Socrates' arguments and overlook Socrates.

The *Theaetetus,* however, is not so constructed that if one does take Socrates into account, one has at once the solutions to the difficulties Theaetetus recognizes; rather, the initial correction of the arguments in order to include Socrates only deepens the very same difficulties. The version of Protagoras' argument that Socrates makes up applies especially to the conversation that Theaetetus and Socrates are having. Socrates' own midwifery, in which Theaetetus is supposed to trust, turns out to look the same as Protagorean relativism, since they both imply that whatever is true is relative to the being together of Socrates and Theaetetus; so whatever they produce jointly belongs solely to their being together and does not admit of any critical detachment from itself. Socrates then is found to be testing the possibility of midwifery in the context of, on the one hand, an interlocutor unaware of even the need for the testing, and, on the other, Socrates himself being fully aware that the test he has to conduct depends on the conditions that are to be tested. That Socrates' perspective does not coincide with either Theaetetus' or Theodorus' leads to the double movement of the dialogue: Up to the middle of the dialogue, where Theodorus drops out, there is a progressive convergence of Socrates with Protagoras as the representative sophist, which Theaetetus and Theodorus take to be a progressive divergence of Socrates from Protagoras; and from the middle to the end there is a progressive divergence of Socrates from Protagoras, which Theaetetus takes to be a progressive convergence of Socrates with Protagoras. It is this apparent convergence that makes it necessary to appeal to the Eleatic stranger. He is to show whether or not Socrates is really a sophist.

The first part of the *Theaetetus* discusses the question of knowledge in light of the difficulty of bringing Theaetetus' initial understanding of knowledge—to know is to count or measure—together with what he now learns is Socrates' peculiar knowledge, midwifery or the knowledge of man. Socrates develops for him a way to do this by proposing an improved Protagoreanism that understands all things as products of arbitrarily designated agents and patients. Theaetetus' universe of numberable things comes to light as a universe of measures relative to man. Socrates then convinces Theodorus of the falseness of his own construction; but he can do so only by appealing to an understanding of philosophy that denies Socrates' own understanding of philosophy for which man and the horizon of man constitute the necessary beginning of philosophy while Theodorus and Theaetetus are susceptible to Protagoreanism precisely because man is for them wholly unproblematic. Their indifference to the human things (the just, the noble, and the good) leads to their inadvertent absorption of the political perspective; but Socrates thinks through the political to a perspective that is truly philosophic.

The second half of the *Theaetetus* begins promisingly enough. Theaetetus acknowledges that perception cannot be knowledge, since soul alone examines the beings; but he ruins that insight by denying that the soul has any instruments other than itself for their examination. Theaetetus accordingly, in denying that his own speaking with Socrates in dialogue is that instrument at work, denies that the knowledge of false opinion is part of Socrates' midwifery and constitutes his knowledge of ignorance. Socrates thus proves the being of false opinion and its necessity for philosophy across the arguments Theaetetus accepts for its impossibility. We are given then in the *Theaetetus* a split between the two elements that make up Socrates' midwifery— his knowledge of man and his knowledge of ignorance—for the former looks like any other kind of specialized knowledge, and the latter, while being global in scope, seems to be self-contradictory. Prior, however, to any rethinking of their inner unity, it turns out to be necessary to burst these two kinds of knowledge completely apart without the help of their mysterious bonding in Socrates himself. The *Sophist* and the *Statesman* represent that total separation argumentatively and their unity dialogically. Plato thus suggests that through their weaving together there would come to be once more the *logos* of dialogue that is philosophy.

II. SOPHIST

The *Sophist* seems to be concerned with two things: being and nonbeing, on the one hand, and true and false speech, on the other. If speech is either true or false speech, it seems not even plausible for being to be either being or nonbeing, since we would then be compelled to say that nonbeing is as much being as false speech is speech. If nonbeing, however, is being, then nonbeing cannot be nonbeing, for otherwise the falseness of false speech would not consist in its saying "nonbeing." And, in turn, if nonbeing is nonbeing, the falseness of false speech again cannot consist in its saying "nonbeing," for it would then not be saying anything. If we then say that nonbeing is appearing, and appearing is not unqualified nonbeing, being is being and appearing, and we want to distinguish between the strict identity which belongs to being and the likeness of nonbeing to the strict identity of being. We say, then, "Here is Socrates himself" and "Here is a likeness of Socrates." Everything in the likeness of Socrates that is a likeness of Socrates himself will generate a true speech of Socrates identical to another speech true of Socrates himself. Everything, however, in the likeness of Socrates that is not a likeness of Socrates himself yields a false speech of Socrates. Among the false speeches of Socrates would be, for example, the paint on Socrates' portrait but not the color of the paint that is true of Socrates himself. The paint, then, without the color (*per impossibile*), is not true of Socrates, but it certainly is not a likeness of Socrates either. The paint must be together with its color in order for it to be both a likeness of Socrates and nonbeing, but it seems to be utterly mysterious how by being together it can be that and by being apart it ceases to be anything of the sort. If everything then is just what it is and nothing else, it is impossible for there to be any speech, either true or false, for speech is impossible unless something can be put together with something else. The conditions for speech are the same as the conditions for nonbeing, and we can have speech if there is always falsehood or being if there is never truth. Parmenides must and cannot be right.

If this is the gist of the sophist's argument, it is hard to see how the Eleatic stranger shows its incoherence and thereby distinguishes between sophistry and philosophy. He leads us to believe that inasmuch as *logos* comes to be through the weaving together of kinds, the problem of nonbeing has been solved; but he goes on to characterize *logos,* insofar as it can be said to be true or false, as the weaving together of verb and noun (action and actor) without ever showing how these two kinds of *logos* are related to one another. The stranger himself even says that he has always failed to solve the problem of nonbeing, and in the dialogue he proves that the problem of being is no less baffling. He proposes then that his own *logos,* even if it fails to solve either problem, will be as far as it goes adequate for both; but since he also asserts that being and nonbeing are as different as light and dark, he implies that no single *logos* can be adequate for both unless it is indifferent to that difference. The argument, then, that the sophist mounts against philosophy is reinforced by the stranger's own self-contradictory account. That Theaetetus believes by the end that the problem has been solved only goes to show the degree to which the stranger in tracking the sophist has become indistinguishable from the sophist.

At the beginning of the *Sophist,* Socrates asserts that the sophist and the statesman are each an apparition of the real philosopher; but the stranger says that the Eleatic circle holds the sophist, the statesman, and the philosopher to be three. The stranger's "three" means either that each of the three "is" as much as any other, and he is denying what Socrates says, or that number is indifferent to the difference between being and nonbeing, and to count is not necessarily to count the beings. Now the stranger accepts the necessity to abandon Parmenides and grant some being to nonbeings. So he implies that to be, though it means to be something, does not mean to be countable, and that there cannot be an arithmetic of being. The division of things into kinds, then, by means of which he determines the nature of the sophist both before the problem of nonbeing arises and after he has settled the issue, can only appear to be based on the premise that each thing is what it is and nothing else. The analysis of nonbeing must be an analysis of the nonarithmetical basis of division. It must be an analysis of appearance at the same time that it is an analysis of the stranger's practice of dichotomy. The name for this double analysis is "the other." It is by no means obvious how "the other" saves both the stranger's divisions and the being of nonbeing. Theaetetus certainly does not understand the solution, for the stranger is forced to alter the very terms of the problem in order to gain Theaetetus' assent. Theaetetus accepts God as the maker of the beings and rejects any account in terms of irrational nature, and the stranger praises him for his choice on the basis of his nature that does not need any reasons.

The obscurity of "the other" as the stranger's own solution and the self-contradiction in the solution Theaetetus accepts combine to make one wonder whether any approach to the *Sophist* that separates its dialogic form from its arguments can yield more than a series of riddles. The *Sophist's* dialogic form presents us with another riddle: Either Socrates is just another sophist, or all philosophers prior to Socrates were sophists. The first half of the dialogue, in which the stranger traps Socrates in progressively narrower definitions until the sophist can be only Socrates, is balanced by its second half, in which the stranger proceeds to condemn all earlier philosophers for not understanding the necessity of Socrates' so-called second sailing. Inasmuch as the second sailing is inseparable from Socrates' discovery of political philosophy, the *Sophist's* companion dialogue, the *Statesman*, in which the stranger brings about a complete identity of dialogic form and argument, needs to be put together with the *Sophist* before the *Sophist* can be understood by itself. It is because the *Statesman* is essentially prior to the *Sophist* that it follows it of necessity. The *Sophist* then requires a double reading. But even such a double reading does not suffice, for its problem is initiated by the *Theaetetus*, in which the joint failure of Socrates and Theaetetus to answer the question, What is knowledge?, prompts them to appeal to the Eleatic stranger. His answer is contained in the *Sophist* and the *Statesman;* it is not contained in either of them separately. It is therefore another question whether his twofold answer differs from the answer to be found in the *Theaetetus*.

III. STATESMAN

No dialogue seems to be less well conceived than the *Statesman*. It discusses briefly what interests us politically, and it discovers at length what holds no interest for philosophy. The Eleatic stranger cannot even digress without violating the measure of the mean, for his digressions either go on too long and still fall short, or they come to an end before he has said enough to justify his digressing in the first place. He copies from the *Sophist* a way of dividing by twos even though he comes to admit its inadequacy for political things. In a conversation between an ex-Parmenidean and Socrates' namesake, the *Statesman* looks as if it is condemning political philosophy in the presence of its founder. The theme of the dialogue, however, is not political philosophy, but political science; so perhaps it vindicates political philosophy by holding political science up to ridicule.

The *Statesman* seems to show that political philosophy must come to light almost entirely through misconceptions. The bewildering way in which the stranger begins turns out to be the model he follows throughout. He proposes to find the two kinds of science, of which one is political science, and the other every other science. His proposal seems to be of the same order as young Socrates' later mistake, for which the stranger rebukes him severely, of asserting that there are two kinds of animals, of which one is man, and the other all beasts. The stranger never admits that his own proposal was a mistake. He convinces young Socrates that political science is as theoretical as arithmetic through winning his assent to three propositions: (1) the knowledge of rule makes one a ruler regardless of whether one rules or not; (2) a city and a household do not differ in kind; (3) strength and intelligence of soul are the most effective ways for a king to maintain his rule. The third of these propositions seems to be against the intention of the first, and the second denies that there is anything distinctly political in political science. A science that is fully known without its ever being exercised is proved to be a theoretical science because in its being exercised it relies on something nonscientific; and this something is not brute force even though an appropriate name for the science characterizes the relation between master and slave. The stranger seems to be saying by way of these paradoxes that political science is against the grain of both politics and science, even if, in its exhibition of the unity of action and argument (or, as the stranger puts it, "The rule of the king is one of the sciences"), it comes the closest philosophy can to the Socratic identity of virtue and knowledge. Political philosophy is necessarily a latecomer to both the city and philosophy.

The sheer contrariness of the *Statesman* is not just due to the manly simplicity of young Socrates, who finds nothing to object to in the statesman's killing of his fellow citizens provided that it conforms with the law, but also to the double intention of the stranger. The discovery of political science is meant to be exemplary for the dialectical science, whose theme is the highest and greatest of the beings; but political science cannot be exemplary unless it is brought together with things alien to it, or, as the stranger suggests, those alien things are already present in political science and make it the only natural paradigm for dialectics. Young Socrates' simplicity thus combines with the true character of political science to distort political things while it reveals political things. In order, however, for it to be fully exemplary, it is necessary that political science be seen in its coming to be exemplary, for there is no procedure outside of political science which can guide political science. The broken surface of the *Statesman* is a reflection of the self-knowledge of political science.

The *Statesman*, like its companion dialogues, the *Theaetetus* and the *Sophist*, is in two parts. The first examines the conditions which would make political life unnecessary. Those conditions are the same as what, according to the *Republic*, the city has as its primary aim (the satisfaction of all bodily needs), and from which it is distracted by the unwelcome necessity of war. The stranger strongly implies that the frustration of this aim is the condition for the possibility of philosophy.

No Socrates without evil. In the second half, the stranger argues that the city understands itself of necessity in light of what would, if realized, make the city dispensable. The law is a sign of this necessary misunderstanding. The stranger thus vindicates the city over against the city. He vindicates both Athens and Socrates.

Guide for the Reader

The numbers and letters in the margins of the dialogues refer to the pages and sections of Stephanus' edition of Plato. In the commentaries, and in the notes, the references are to Burnet's edition which numbers each line within each letter section.

Parentheses in the translation give: (1) the transcription of the Greek word, for example, account (*logos*); (2) the literal or alternative meaning of the word, for example, "simply" (artlessly); or (3) an omission in the Greek which English cannot dispense with and which seems important, for example, Perception (is) knowledge. In some cases, therefore, (art) could be (science).

The following rules are adhered to as strictly as possible. Hyphenated words that are not standard in English represent compound words, for example, "animal-hunting" is used for *zôiothêrikê*. Contracted forms imply that the Greek lacks something, uncontracted that it is present in the Greek and is to receive some emphasis. For example, "that's so" means that "is" does not occur, "that is so" means that it does. "We've" means that the Greek omits the pronoun, "we have" that it does not, and "we are" that the pronoun is present though possibly not the verb.

To on is always translated as "that which is," *ta mê onta* "the things which are not," and when necessary they are put in single quotes. But in order not to lose sight of their participial form in Greek, the commentary speaks of being and nonbeings. "Being" in the translation is always for *ousia*. *Genesis* is either "becoming" or "coming-to-be." *Gignesthai* is "become," "come to be," "prove to be," "occur," "happen," or "arise."

Eidos is always translated "species" and *genos*, "genus," for the first is cognate with the verb "see" and the second with "become." The distinction has nothing to do with Aristotle's betwen species and genus. *Idea,* which is almost equivalent to *eidos* but rarer (particularly in the plural) and which suggests a whole that is not subject to division, is always "look," with its transcription in parenthesis. "Kind" never translates a Greek substantive but is used either for the indefinite pronoun or to complete the sense in English. "Things" also does not translate for the most part any Greek substantive; when it does, it is *pragmata,* which is always put afterward in parenthesis. *Pragmata* are things with which we deal and are of concern to us.

The phrase "simply true" translates *alêthinos* and is used to distinguish it from *alêthês* ("true"); *alêthinos* implies that something is genuine. "Proper part" is for *morion,* "part" for *meros.*

Although consistency has been aimed at, it has not always been possible to achieve it. The most important variations are these. The three verbs for know, *gignôskô* (know by acquaintance), *oida* (the perfect of "see"), and *epistamai* (connected by Plato with "supervise," "be in charge," *epistatô, ephistamai*) have not always been kept distinct. But "know how to" never translates either of the first two; the aorist of *gignôskô* is "come to know," the present almost always "recognize" or "be familiar with" but sometimes "cognize." The first two, moreover, are used with a personal object more frequently than *epistamai* is, and, in the latter half of the *Theaetetus,* in those sentences in which *gignôskô* and *oida* both occur, the participial form will be the former and the finite the latter (with the exception of 203D). *Agnoô,* which is mostly translated "be ignorant," can also at times be "fail to recognize," or "fail to understand." "Knowledge" or "science" is always for *epistêmê,* "cognition" for *gnôsis,* and "intelligence" and "intelligent" for *phronêsis* and *phronimos* respectively, though "prudence"/"prudent" and even "wisdom"/"wise" might on occasion have seemed more appropriate.

The verb *dokô* is translated in several ways. When it occurs without a personal pronoun, it is translated "seem," "resolve," or "decide." If it is with a pronoun, it is usually either "impression" or "opinion." "Impression" is used when the context suggests that it is an opinion of the moment, "opinion" when it seems to be longstanding. The reader is free to judge each case differently. The noun *doxa* is "opinion," "impression," or "reputation." Parenthetical "it seems," or "it seems that," always translates *eoiken,* which is otherwise "resembles." In replies it is always, "it seems likely." The cognate noun *eikôn* is "semblance," whereas *eidôlon* is "image."

The verbal system for "speak" is complex in Greek, and "speak," "mean," "say," "talk," "mention," "remark," and "state" are all used to convey different tenses, aspects, and nuances. *Logos,* however, is as far as possible always "speech" and never, for instance, "argument."

"To say something" (*legein ti*) means to say something significant or to make sense, and "to say nothing" (*legein ouden*) means to make no sense, as does the adjective *alogon*. Only when the context calls for a literal translation is the idiomatic sacrificed, but it should of course always be kept in mind.

PLATO'S
THEAETETUS

Theaetetus

EUCLIDES

TERPSION[1]

EUCLIDES: Just now, Terpsion, or a long time ago from the country?

TERPSION: Fairly long. And I was in fact looking for you throughout the marketplace and was surprised that I couldn't find you.

EUCLIDES: That's because I wasn't anywhere in the city.

TERPSION: Well, where then?

EUCLIDES: On going down to the harbor I met Theaetetus as he was being carried out of Corinth from the army camp to Athens.[2]

TERPSION: Alive or dead?

EUCLIDES: Alive, barely. He's in a bad way also from some wounds, *B* but the outbreak of the illness in the army affects him more.

TERPSION: Don't you mean dysentery?

EUCLIDES: Yes.

TERPSION: What a man you say's in danger.

EUCLIDES: Beautiful and good, Terpsion, and, you know, I was listening even now to some people highly praising his conduct in the battle.

TERPSION: Well, there's nothing strange in that, but far more surprising if he were not of that sort. But how come he refused to *C* take lodgings here in Megara?

EUCLIDES: He was pressing for home, though I begged and advised him, but he wasn't willing. And then, when I sent him on his way, on my way back I recalled with amazement how prophetically Socrates had spoken about him as well as different things. My impression is that Socrates met him shortly before his death when

Theaetetus was a lad, and on the basis of his association and conversation with him expressed great admiration for his nature. And when I came to Athens he narrated to me the speeches of

D his conversation with him—they're well worth hearing—and he said there was every necessity that he become renowned if he reached maturity.

TERPSION: Yes, and he did, it seems, tell the truth. But what were the speeches? Could you be their narrator?

143 EUCLIDES: No, by Zeus, not at any rate straight off from memory, but I did write down reminders just as soon as I returned home, and later, in recalling it at my leisure, I proceeded to write them up. And as often as I returned to Athens, I questioned Socrates repeatedly about whatever I hadn't remembered, and then on my return here I made corrections. So pretty nearly the entire speech has been written by me.

TERPSION: True. I've heard you mention it before, and though you know I always intended to urge you to show it, I've delayed doing so up till now. Well, what prevents us from going through it now? As for myself, I really need a rest in any case, since I've come from the country.

B EUCLIDES: But of course, I myself escorted Theaetetus up to Erineos;[3] so I wouldn't take a rest without pleasure. Well, let's go, and while we're resting, the boy will read.

TERPSION: A good suggestion (What you say's right).

EUCLIDES: Here's the book, Terpsion. And I wrote the speech down on these terms, not with Socrates narrating them to me as he did, but with Socrates conversing with those with whom he said he conversed. He said they were the geometer Theodorus and Theaetetus. In order that the narrations between the speeches

C might not cause trouble (*pragmata*) in the writing, whenever either Socrates spoke about himself, for example, "And I said" or "And I spoke," or in turn about whoever answered, "He consented" or "He refused to agree," it's for these reasons that I removed things of this sort and wrote it as if he himself were conversing with them.

TERPSION: And there's nothing wayward in that, Euclides.

EUCLIDES: Well, boy, take the book and read.[4]

SOCRATES

THEODORUS

THEAETETUS[5]

SOCRATES: If I were to care, Theodorus, more for those in Cyrene, I *D* would be asking you about the state of affairs there and whether any of the young there make geometry or something else of philosophy their concern. But as it is I don't, for I'm less a friend to those there than to these here, and I'm more desirous of knowing who of our young are expected to prove good and able. Now I myself examine this on my own, to the extent that I can, and I ask everyone else with whom I see the young are willing to associate. Now it's not the smallest number who consort with you, *E* and it's just that they do so, for you deserve it on account of geometry as well as for everything else. So if you did meet anyone worth speaking of, I would hear about it with pleasure.

THEODORUS: As a matter of fact, Socrates, it's certainly worth it for me to tell and for you to hear about the sort of lad of your fellow citizens I met. And if he were beautiful, I'd be afraid to speak of him with intensity, should anyone in fact get the impression that I'm desirous of him. But as it is—please don't get annoyed with me—he is not beautiful, but he resembles you in the snubness of his nose and the bulging of his eyes, but he has them less than you do. I'm speaking fearlessly. Know well, of all whom I've ever *144* met—and I've consorted with very many—I'm aware of no one yet whose nature is as wonderfully good. For to be as good a learner as he is, in a way that's hard for anyone else to match, and yet to be exceptionally gentle, and on top of this to be manly beyond anyone whatsoever, I would have suspected that it doesn't occur and I don't see it occurring, for those who are as sharp as he is, quick witted, and with good memories are for the most part also quickly inclined to bursts of anger, and in darting about *B* they're swept along like unballasted ships, and they grow up rather more manic than more manly, whereas those in turn who are more grave face up to their lessons somewhat sluggishly and are full of forgetfulness. But he goes so smoothly, so unfalteringly, and so effectively to his lessons and investigations, and all with so much gentleness, just as a stream of olive-oil flows without a sound, as for it to be a cause of wonder that someone of his age behaves in this way.

SOCRATES: You report well. But which citizen is his father?

THEODORUS: Though I've heard the name, I don't remember. But as a matter of fact, of those here approaching us, he's the one in the middle. He as well as some of his comrades were just now oiling themselves in the course outside, and it's my impression that with the oiling over they're coming here. But do consider whether you recognize him.

SOCRATES: I recognize him. He is the son of Euphronius from Sunium, a man, my friend, who's very much of the sort you describe him to be, otherwise well thought of and moreover who left, you know, a great deal of property. But I don't know the name of the lad.

THEODORUS: Theaetetus, Socrates, is his name. But it's my impression that some guardians of his have wasted the property, though all the same, Socrates, he's of an amazing liberality when it comes to money.

SOCRATES: How grand a nobleman you speak of. Please urge him to sit alongside me here.

THEODORUS: It shall be done. Theaetetus, come over here to Socrates.

SOCRATES: Yes, please do, Theaetetus, so that I too may examine myself as to what sort of face I have. Theodorus says I have one similar to yours. Still, if each of the pair of us had a lyre and he said they had been similarly tuned, would we straight off trust him, or would we go on to examine whether he's speaking as one who is skilled in music?

THEAETETUS: We would go on to examine.

SOCRATES: Isn't it the case that if we found him to be of that sort we would be persuaded, but if unmusical, we would distrust him?

THEAETETUS: True.

SOCRATES: Yes, and now, I suspect, if our concern was at all for the similarity of faces, we would have to examine whether he speaks as one who is a skilled draftsman or not.

THEAETETUS: That's my opinion.

SOCRATES: Is Theodorus really then a skilled painter?

THEAETETUS: No, not as far as I know.

SOCRATES: And not skilled in geometry either?

THEAETETUS: There's really no doubt that he is, Socrates.

SOCRATES: As well as skilled in astronomy, logistics, music, and everything connected with education?

THEAETETUS: That's my opinion at least.

SOCRATES: So whereas, in something of the body, if in praising or blaming us in some respect, he says we are similar, it's scarcely worthwhile to pay him any mind—

THEAETETUS: Perhaps not.

SOCRATES: But what if he should praise the soul of either one of us in point of virtue and wisdom? Isn't it then worthwhile for him who hears it to be eager to examine the one praised, and for the latter as eagerly to display himself?

THEAETETUS: Yes, of course, Socrates.

SOCRATES: Well then, it's time, my dear Theaetetus, for you to display and for me to examine, since, know well, though Theodorus has praised many to my face, strangers as well as fellow townsmen, he did not yet praise anyone as he did you just now.

THEAETETUS: That would be all to the good, Socrates, but look and   C
see whether he was not speaking in jest.

SOCRATES: This is not Theodorus' way. But don't back out of what has been agreed upon by pretending that he was speaking in jest, in order that he may not be compelled actually to bear witness— no one will in any case denounce him for false evidence—but stand by your agreement with confidence.

THEAETETUS: Well, I must do it, if that's your opinion.

SOCRATES: So tell me. You're surely learning from Theodorus something of geometry?

THEAETETUS: Yes I am.

SOCRATES: And of that which pertains to astronomy, harmony, and   D
calculations?

THEAETETUS: Yes, and I'm certainly eager.

SOCRATES: Why, I am too, my boy, from him and everyone else who I suspect has a professional competence in any of these things. But still and all, though everything else about them I have down to a fair degree, there's a small point about which I'm perplexed that has to be examined with you and these here. Tell me. To learn, isn't it to become wiser in whatever one learns?

THEAETETUS: Of course.

SOCRATES: Yes, and the wise, I suspect, (are) wise by wisdom.

THEAETETUS: Yes.

SOCRATES: And this doesn't differ at all, does it, from knowledge   E
(science)?

THEAETETUS: What sort of thing?

SOCRATES: Wisdom. Or isn't it in just those things in which they (are) knowledgeable that they (are) wise?

THEAETETUS: Why certainly.

SOCRATES: So knowledge and wisdom (are) the same?[6]

THEAETETUS: Yes.

SOCRATES: Well, this is the very point about which I'm perplexed, and I'm incapable of grasping it adequately by myself, whatever knowledge is. Can we really say it? What do you all say? Who would   *146*
be the first of us to speak? The one who makes a mistake, and

whoever at any time makes a mistake, will, as children playing
ball say, take his seat, an ass; but whoever prevails without a
mistake, he'll be our king and enjoin us to answer whatever he
wants.[7] Why are you all silent? It surely can't be, Theodorus, that
in my love of speeches I am being boorish, eager as I am to make
us converse and become friends and mutually agreeable?[8]

B THEODORUS: Not in the least, Socrates, nothing of the sort would be
boorish, but urge any of the lads to answer you. I am unused to
conversation of this sort, and I'm not of an age to get used to it
either. But it would be fitting for these here, and they would
improve much more, for youth truly is open to improvement in
everything. But, just as you began, don't let go of Theaetetus but
ask away.

SOCRATES: Do you hear, Theaetetus, what Theodorus is saying? He's
C not one, I suspect, that you'll be willing to disobey, and it's not
sanctioned either for a younger to disobey a wise man who enjoins
things of this sort. But in a good and noble fashion speak out.
Knowledge is what in your opinion?

THEAETETUS: Well, I must, Socrates, since you all urge it, for if I do
make any mistake, you'll all in any case correct it.

SOCRATES: Yes of course, if, that is, we can.

THEAETETUS: Well, then, it's my opinion that whatever one might learn
from Theodorus are sciences (knowledges)—geometry and those
D you just now went through and, in turn, shoemaking and the arts
of the rest of the craftsmen—all and each of them, are nothing
else than knowledge.

SOCRATES: That's noble and lavish, my dear, when you're asked for
one, you offer many and complex instead of simple.

THEAETETUS: Just how do you mean this, Socrates?

SOCRATES: Perhaps it's nothing, but what I suspect, however, I'll point
out. Whenever you say leathermaking, you're not pointing out
anything else, are you, than a knowledge of the making of shoes?

THEAETETUS: Nothing else.

E SOCRATES: And what about when you say carpentry? Are you pointing
out anything else than a knowledge of the making of wooden
utensils?

THEAETETUS: Just this.

SOCRATES: Isn't it that in the case of both, of whatever each of the two
is a knowledge, this is what you are determining?

THEAETETUS: Yes.

SOCRATES: Yes, but the question, Theaetetus, was not this, of what
things there's knowledge, nor how many sciences there are either,

for we didn't ask because we wanted to count them but to get to know knowledge whatever it itself is. Or am I making no sense?

THEAETETUS: Yes, that's right of course.

SOCRATES: Then examine this as well. If someone should ask us about   *147* something trifling and ready at hand, for example, about mud (clay) whatever it is, if we should answer him that there's the mud of potters, the mud of furnace makers, and the mud of brick-makers, wouldn't we be ridiculous?

THEAETETUS: Perhaps.

SOCRATES: First of all, for one thing, because we surely must believe that the questioner understands our answer whenever we say mud, re-gardless of whether we add that of dollmakers or of all the rest of   *B* the craftsmen whatsoever. Or do you believe that someone under-stands some name of something if he doesn't know what it is?

THEAETETUS: In no way.

SOCRATES: So whoever does not know science does not understand the science of shoes either.

THEAETETUS: No, he doesn't.

SOCRATES: So whoever's ignorant of science does not understand the leatherworking (science), or any different art either?

THEAETETUS: That is so.

SOCRATES: So the answer to the question "What is science?" is laugh-able, whenever one answers with the name of some art, for though one's not been asked this, one answers with the science of something.   *C*

THEAETETUS: It seems likely.

SOCRATES: And in the second place, though it surely must be possible to answer trivially and briefly, one goes round on an endless road. For example, in the case of the question of mud, it's surely trivial and simple to say that should earth be kneaded with a liquid there would be mud and to dismiss whatever it is of.

THEAETETUS: Yes, Socrates, it now appears easy in this way. And you're probably asking the sort of thing that recently occurred also to ourselves as we were conversing, I mean myself and your hom-onym here, Socrates.   *D*

SOCRATES: What sort of thing, exactly, Theaetetus?

THEAETETUS: Theodorus here was giving us some proof (drawing) about powers (roots), about the three-foot (line) and the five-foot (line)—that they're not commensurable in length (*mêkos*) with the one-foot (line)—and in this way he went on choosing each (line) one by one up to the seventeen-foot (line), where for some reason or other he got stuck.[9] Then something of the following sort occurred to us, since the powers (roots) appeared infinite in mul-

E   titude, to attempt to gather them together into one, by whatever
we'll address all these powers (roots).

SOCRATES: And did you really find something of the sort?

THEAETETUS: My impression is that we did, but you too examine it.

SOCRATES: Speak.

THEAETETUS: We took all of number in two, and the number that has
the power of coming to be by the multiplication of an equal by
an equal we made a semblance of its figure to a square and ad-
dressed it as a square and equal-sided number.

SOCRATES: That's really good.

THEAETETUS: Then again, the number between this—of which there
148   is the three, the five, and every one which does not have the power
of coming to be by the multiplication of an equal by an equal, but
its becoming is either by the multiplication of a greater number
by a less, or a less by a greater, and a larger and a less side always
comprehend it—we made a semblance of it in turn to the oblong
figure and called it an oblong number.

SOCRATES: Most beautifully. But what next?

THEAETETUS: All lines that make a square of the equal-sided and plane
number, we determined as length (mêkos), and all that make a
square of the other-lengthed number, we determined them as
B   powers (roots), on the grounds that they are not commensurable
in length with the former lines but with the planes of which they
are the powers. And something else of the sort about solids (cubes).

SOCRATES: That's really the best that human beings can do, boys. So
my impression is that Theodorus will not be found guilty of false
evidence.

THEAETETUS: And yet, Socrates, as to what you're asking about knowledge, I wouldn't be capable of answering it as I did about length
(rational root) and power (root), even though it's my impression
that you are seeking for something of the same sort, and so once
more Theodorus appears false.

C   SOCRATES: But what of this? Suppose he had said in praising you for
running that he had not met any youngster who was so skilled in
running, and then in running the course, you had been defeated
by the fastest at his peak, do you believe he would have praised
any less truly?[10]

THEAETETUS: No, I don't.

SOCRATES: But knowledge, as I was speaking of it just now—do you
believe that to find out about it is something small, and it's not a
job for the all-round tip-top?

THEAETETUS: Yes, by Zeus, I do, it's certainly for the topmost.

SOCRATES: Well, then, be confident about yourself and believe that

Theodorus is making sense, and be eager in every way both about   D
everything else as well as about knowledge to grasp a speech as
to whatever in fact it is.

THEAETETUS: As far as eagerness goes, Socrates, it will come to light.

SOCRATES: Come then—you just now led the way beautifully—in imitation of your answer about powers (roots), just as then you comprehended them, though they were many, in one species, so now
try to address the many sciences too with one speech.

THEAETETUS: But know well, Socrates, it's often that I tried to make   E
an examination of it, in hearing the questions that are reported
as coming from you. But for all of that, I am myself incapable of
either persuading myself that I say anything adequately or hearing
some one else speaking in just the way you urge, and I'm incapable
as well of getting rid of my concern with it.

SOCRATES: The reason is, my dear Theaetetus, that you're suffering
labor pains, on account of your not being empty but pregnant.

THEAETETUS: I don't know, Socrates, what, however, I've experienced
I say.

SOCRATES: And then, you most ridiculous fellow, you've not heard   149
that I am the son of a midwife, very noble and farouche,
Phaenarete?[11]

THEAETETUS: Yes, I've heard it before now.

SOCRATES: And you've not heard as well that I practice the same art?

THEAETETUS: In no way.

SOCRATES: Well, know well that's the case. Don't, however, denounce
me before the rest. They have not been aware, comrade, that I
have this art, and so, because they do not know, they don't say
this about me, but they say I'm most strange and make human
beings perplexed.[12] Have you heard this too?

THEAETETUS: Yes I have.   B

SOCRATES: Am I then to tell you the cause?

THEAETETUS: Yes, of course.

SOCRATES: Do reflect, then, about that which in its entirety characterizes midwives, and you'll more easily understand what I want to
say. You know surely that none of them is still conceiving and
giving birth when she acts as midwife to anyone else, but it's those
who by that time are incapable of giving birth.

THEAETETUS: Yes, of course.

SOCRATES: And they do say that Artemis is the cause of this, because
unallied her lot has lain with lying-in.[13] Now she does not after   C
all grant the barren to be midwives, because human nature is too
weak to grasp an art of whatever it is inexperienced, and so, in

honor of their similarity to herself, she charged those who do not bear on account of their age.

THEAETETUS: It's likely.

SOCRATES: Then isn't the following as likely as it is necessary,[14] that those who are pregnant and those who are not are recognized by the midwives rather than by anyone else?

THEAETETUS: Certainly.

D SOCRATES: And, what's more, the midwives by giving drugs and singing incantations are capable of arousing labor-pains or, if they want, of making them milder, and getting those who are having a hard time of it to give birth, and if it's decided to abort at an early stage,[15] they abort.

THEAETETUS: That is so.

SOCRATES: Have you further perceived this, that the following thing is theirs—they also are the most uncanny go-betweens, since they are all-wise when it comes to getting to know what sort of woman must be with what sort of man to give birth to the best possible children?

THEAETETUS: I don't know that at all.

E SOCRATES: Well, know that they take greater pride in this than in the cutting of the umbilical cord. Reflect. Do you believe that the care and harvesting of the fruits from the earth and the recognition, in turn, of what sort of plant and seed must be cast into what sort of earth are of the same or a different art?

THEAETETUS: No, but of the same.

SOCRATES: And into woman, my dear, do you believe there's a different art of something of this sort, and a different one of harvesting?

THEAETETUS: It's unlikely at any rate.

150 SOCRATES: Yes it is. But on account of the unjust and artless bringing together of man and woman—its name is pimping—the midwives, because they are august, shun even the art of go-between, in fear that they may fall into the former charge on account of it, since it's surely suitable for only those who are in their being midwives also to act as go-betweens correctly.[16]

THEAETETUS: It appears so.

SOCRATES: Well, then, that which characterizes midwives is of this extent, but it's less than my own action, for it's not the case that

B sometimes women give birth to images and sometimes to the simply true, and that it's not easy to gain recognition of the difference. For if it were the case, it would be the greatest and most beautiful work for midwives to discriminate whatever's true and whatever's not. Or don't you believe it?

THEAETETUS: Yes I do.

SOCRATES: Yes, but to my art of midwifery everything else belongs just as it does to them, and it differs as much by the fact that it midwifes men and not women as by the fact that it examines their souls in giving birth and not their bodies. But this is the greatest thing in our art, to be capable of assaying in every way whether   C
the thought of the young is giving birth to an image and a lie or something fruitful and true. Since this too belongs to me as it does to midwives, I am sterile of wisdom, and that for which many before now reproached me—that I ask everyone else but I myself don't declare anything about anything because I don't have anything wise—this reproach of theirs is true. The cause of this is the following. The god compels me to midwife and prevented me from generating. Now I myself therefore am obviously hardly wise at all, and I have not had a discovery of this sort as an   D
offspring of my soul. But whoever associate with me, some appear at first as even very foolish, but all—whomever the god allows— as the association advances, make an amazing lot of progress. It's their own opinion and everyone else's too. And this too is as plain as day, that they never learnt anything from me, but they on their own from themselves found and gave birth to many beautiful things. Now of the midwifery the god and I (are) responsible, and it's plain in the following way. Many before now who failed to   E
recognize this and held themselves responsible and despised me, either on their own or persuaded by someone else departed earlier than they should have. And after their departure, they aborted the rest on account of a poor association, and in bringing up badly the things that I midwifed, they lost them, and made more of false things and images than of the truth, and finally they got to be of the opinion (and everyone else was too) that they were fools.   *151*
Aristides the son of Lysimachus has been one of them, and there have been very many different ones too, and whenever they come back, begging for my association and doing amazing things, the *daimonion* that comes to me checks me from associating with some and allows me to associate with some, and it's these who once more improve.[17] And whoever associate with me undergo this same thing as women in giving birth do. They suffer labor-pains and are filled with perplexity for nights and days far more than women are, and my art is capable of arousing this kind of labor-   B
pain and putting it to rest. Now this is the way it is for these. But sometimes, if I somehow get the impression, Theaetetus, that they're not pregnant, in recognition of the fact that they don't need me, I very kindly act as go-between and, with allowance made for a god's help, guess very adequately by whose association

they would be benefited. And many of them I gave in marriage to Prodicus, and many to different wise and divinely-speaking men.[18] Now I lengthened this out for you, my excellent fellow, for the sake of the following. I suspect that you, just as you yourself believe, are pregnant with something within and are suffering from labor pains. Therefore apply yourself to me as to the son

C   of a midwife and myself skilled in midwifery too, and whatever I ask be eager to answer in just the way you can. And if, after all, on examining something of whatever you say, I believe it an image and not true, and then take it out and throw it away, don't be angrily savage as those who give birth for the first time are about their children. Many before now—my wonderful fellow!—have got so disposed toward me as to be simply (artlessly) ready to bite, whenever I remove any nonsense of theirs, and they don't believe I'm doing this out of goodwill. They are far from knowing that

D   no god is ill-disposed to human beings, and I don't do anything of the sort either out of ill-will, but it's in no way sanctioned for me to make a concession to falsehood and wipe out truth. Accordingly, once more from the beginning, Theaetetus, try to say whatever is knowledge, and never say you can't, for if a god's willing and you're manly, you'll be able.

THEAETETUS: Well, Socrates, when you're encouraging me in this fashion, it's shameful not in every way to be eager to say whatever

E   one has. My opinion is then that whoever knows something perceives that which he knows, and as it now appears, knowledge is nothing else than perception.

SOCRATES: That's good and noble, my boy. One ought to speak in this way when one makes a declaration. But come, let's examine it in common, whether it's in fact fruitful or a wind-egg.[19] Perception, you say, (is) knowledge?

THEAETETUS: Yes.

SOCRATES: Well, you've probably not spoken a trivial speech about

152   knowledge, but the one Protagoras too used to say. He's said these same things in a somewhat different way. He says somewhere, "Of all things (*khrêmata*) (a) human being is the measure, of the things which are, that (how) they are, and of the things which are not, that (how) they are not."[20] Surely you've read it?

THEAETETUS: I've read it, and often.

SOCRATES: Isn't this more or less the sense of what he says, that of whatever sort things severally appear to me, that's the sort they are for me, and of whatever sort to you, they're of that sort in turn for you, and you and I (are) human being?

THEAETETUS: Indeed, he is speaking in this way.

SOCRATES: Well, it's likely you know for a wise man not to talk non- *B*
sense, so let's follow him up. Isn't it sometimes the case when the
same wind's blowing one of us is cold and one not? And one is
slightly cold and one intensely?

THEAETETUS: Indeed so.

SOCRATES: Are we to say that at that time the wind itself in itself is
cold or not cold? Or are we to obey Protagoras that it's cold for
whoever's cold and not for whoever's not?

THEAETETUS: It seems likely.

SOCRATES: Doesn't it then appear thus to each of the two?

THEAETETUS: Yes.

SOCRATES: Yes, but this "appear" is "perceive"?

THEAETETUS: Yes it is.

SOCRATES: So appearance and perception (are) the same in hot things *C*
and everything of the sort. For whatever sort each perceives, it's
that sort that they probably are for each.[21]

THEAETETUS: It seems likely.

SOCRATES: So perception is, after all, always of that which is, and it's
without falsehood inasmuch as it is knowledge.

THEAETETUS: It appears so.

SOCRATES: Was Protagoras really then, by the Graces, someone all-
wise, and did he make this an enigma for us, the vast refuse-heap,
but was he telling the truth as if it were a forbidden secret to his
pupils?

THEAETETUS: How exactly are you saying this, Socrates? *D*

SOCRATES: I shall speak actually a not trivial speech. It says, "After
all, nothing is one alone by itself, and you would not address
anything correctly or of any sort whatsoever, but if you address
it as big, it will also appear small, and if heavy, light, and all things
in this way, on the grounds that nothing is one, neither something
nor of any sort whatsoever. But all things—it's those we say are
the things which are (not addressing them correctly)—come to be
from locomotion and motion and mutual mixing; for nothing
ever is, but (everything) always becomes." And about this let all *E*
the wise in succession except Parmenides converge,[22] Protagoras
and Heraclitus, and Empedocles, as well as the tip-top poets of
each kind of poetry, Epicharmus of comedy and Homer of tragedy.[23] Homer with the line "Ocean and mother Tethys, the becoming (*genesis*) of gods"[24] has said that everything is the offspring
of flowing and motion. Or doesn't he seem to mean this?

THEAETETUS: Yes, to me he does.

SOCRATES: Who, then, would still be capable, should he dispute against *153* so large an army and so great a general as Homer, of not proving himself to be ridiculous?

THEAETETUS: It's not easy, Socrates.

SOCRATES: No, it isn't, Theaetetus. Since, actually, the following kinds of things are adequate signs for the speech that says that motion supplies that which seems to be and the fact of becoming, and rest the fact of nonbeing and perishing. For the hot and fire—it's that which both generates and manages everything else—is itself generated from locomotion and rubbing, and these are a pair of motions. Or aren't these the comings-into-being of fire?

B THEAETETUS: Yes, they are indeed.

SOCRATES: And what's more, the genus of animals gets born out of these same things?

THEAETETUS: Of course.

SOCRATES: And what of this? Doesn't the condition of bodies get destroyed by quiet and idleness, but get preserved for the most part by exercises and motion?

THEAETETUS: Yes.

SOCRATES: And doesn't the condition in the soul acquire learnings by learning and practice, which are motions, and get saved and become better, but by quiet, which is lack of practice and folly, it does not learn anything at all and forgets whatever it does learn?

C

THEAETETUS: Indeed it does.

SOCRATES: So the good is motion both in terms of soul and in terms of body, and the (bad) the contrary?

THEAETETUS: It seems likely.

SOCRATES: Am I then further to tell you of occasions of windlessness and calm seas and everything of the sort, that quiet conditions rot and destroy, but the other things preserve? And am I to add to them as their summit the golden chain, by which Homer means nothing else than the sun, and he makes plain that as long as the sun and its orbiting are in motion, all things are and are preserved both among gods and human beings, but if this should stop as if it were bound, all things (*khrêmata*) would be corrupted, and, as the saying goes, everything would become topsy-turvy?[25]

D

THEAETETUS: Well, Socrates, my opinion is that he's making plain just those things you mean.

SOCRATES: Make then the following kind of supposition, my excellent fellow. First, in connection with the eyes, that which you call white color—don't appoint it to be itself as something other outside your eyes any more than in your eyes or any place for it at all, for otherwise it would surely be in order and abiding and not be becoming in becoming.

E

THEAETETUS: Well, how?

SOCRATES: Let's follow the speech of the moment, and set down nothing alone by itself as being one. And in this way black and white and any color whatsoever will come to light for us as having come to be from the application (*prosbolê*) of the eyes onto the suitable local motion (*phora*), and precisely that which we say each color to be will be neither that which applies (strikes against) nor that *154* to which there is application (struck against), but something in between that has become private (peculiar) for each. Or would you insist that what sort each color appears to you, it's that sort for a dog and any animal whatsoever?

THEAETETUS: No, by Zeus, I wouldn't.

SOCRATES: And what of this? Does anything at all appear similar to a different human being and you? Do you have (know) this strongly, or is it much more the case that not even for you yourself (is there) the same thing, on account of the fact that you yourself are never in a condition similar to yourself?

THEAETETUS: I'm rather of this opinion than of that.

SOCRATES: Isn't it the case, then, that if that against which we're mea- *B* suring ourselves or which we're touching were great or white or hot, it would never, in its fall on something else, have come to be something else, if, that is, it itself does not at all alter. And if, in turn, that which is doing the measuring against or the touching were each of these things, it would not have become, if itself were not affected in any way, different when a different thing approached it or underwent something. Since as it is now, my dear, we're being compelled somehow or other to say without qualms amazing and laughable things, as Protagoras would say and everyone who tries to say the same as he does.

THEAETETUS: How do you mean it exactly, and what sort of things?

SOCRATES: Take a small paradigm, and you'll know everything I want. *C* We say surely that six dice, if you apply four to them, are more than the four and one and a half times as much, and if you apply twelve, they're less and half as much, and it's insupportable to speak in a different way. Or will you put up with it?

THEAETETUS: No, I won't.

SOCRATES: What then? If Protagoras or someone else asks you, "Theaetetus, is it possible that anything become bigger or more in a different way than by increase?" what will you answer?

THEAETETUS: Well, Socrates, if I answer in light of the present question *D* that which is my opinion, I'll answer that it's impossible, but if in light of the former, being on guard lest I say contrary things, I'll answer that it's possible.

SOCRATES: Gosh, that's good, by Hera, my dear, and divine. But, it seems, if you answer that it is possible, something Euripidean will result, for our tongue will be irrefutable, but our mind (*phrên*) not free from refutation.[26]

THEAETETUS: True.

SOCRATES: Then if you and I were dreadfully canny and wise, having scrutinized all the things of our minds (*phrenes*), we would then for the future be testing one another out of a superabundant

E store and, engaged in sophistic fashion in a battle of this sort, we would proceed to strike and ring the speeches of one against the speeches of the other. But as it is, because we're laymen, we'll want to observe them in relation to themselves, as to whatever they are which we're thinking, whether in our view they are consonant with each other or not in any way whatever.

THEAETETUS: Yes, of course I would want this.

SOCRATES: And I would too no less. And since this is so, shall we do anything else than calmly go back over the examination, on the

155 grounds that we're very much at our leisure, without feeling peevish, but truly scrutinize ourselves as to whatever these hallucinations in us are?[27] The first of which we'll say in our reexamination is, I suspect, that nothing would ever become greater or less, either in bulk or number, as long as it is equal to itself. Isn't this so?

THEAETETUS: Yes.

SOCRATES: Yes, and a second: To whatever there should be neither addition nor subtraction, this never either increases or decreases but is always equal.

THEAETETUS: Yes, certainly.

B SOCRATES: And isn't there a third too: Whatever was not before, this is incapable of being later without having come to be and becoming?

THEAETETUS: Yes, it seems so anyhow.

SOCRATES: It's precisely these three agreements, I suspect, that fight against themselves in our soul whenever we speak of the agreement about the dice or whenever we say that I, in being the size I am, without increasing or undergoing the contrary, am within a year now taller than you the youngster but later smaller, though

C nothing of my bulk has been removed but when you increased. For I am later what I was not before without having come to be, for without becoming it's impossible to come to be, and if I lose nothing of my bulk I would never be becoming less. And there are moreover thousands upon thousands of things in this state, provided we shall accept this case. Surely you're following, Theaetetus; it's my impression at any rate that you're not inexperienced in things of this sort.

THEAETETUS: Yes indeed, by the gods, Socrates, I wonder exceedingly as to why (what) in the world these things are, and sometimes in looking at them I truly get dizzy.

SOCRATES: The reason is, my dear, that, apparently, Theodorus' guess *D* about your nature is not a bad one, for this experience is very much a philosopher's, that of wondering. For nothing else is the beginning (principle) of philosophy than this, and, seemingly, whoever's genealogy it was, that Iris was the offspring of Thaumas (Wonder), it's not a bad one.[28] But do you understand by now why these things are of this sort on the basis of which we say that Protagoras speaks, or not yet?

THEAETETUS: Not yet, in my opinion.

SOCRATES: Then you'll be grateful to me if I join with you in ferreting *E* out the hidden-away truth of the thought of a renowned man, or rather, of renowned men.

THEAETETUS: Of course I'll be grateful, and not a little either.

SOCRATES: Take a look around then and make sure no one of the uninitiated can overhear. They are those who believe that nothing else is except whatever they are capable of getting a tight grip on with their hands, but actions, becomings, and everything invisible they don't accept as in the class (part) of being.

THEAETETUS: Why, it's of stiff and repellent human beings, Socrates, *156* that you're speaking.

SOCRATES: The reason, my boy, is that they are without the Muses to a large degree, but the rest are far cleverer, whose mysteries I'm about to tell you. Their principle (beginning), from which everything is attached—even what we were just now speaking of—is this: the all was motion and there (is) nothing else beyond this, but there (are) two species of motion, and each of the two (is) infinite in multitude, and one (is) with a power to affect (make) and one with a power to be affected. And out of the association and rubbing of these against one another, there come to be offspring, infinite in multitude but twins (double)—that which (is) *B* perceived and that which (is) perception—which (the latter) (is) always falling out together with and (is) getting generated with that which (is) perceived. Now the perceptions have for us the following sorts of names: sights and hearings and smellings and freezings and burnings and, yes, pleasures certainly and pains and desires and fears (are) their designations and different ones as well, the nameless of which (are) without limit, and the named very many. And the perceived genus in turn (is) cogenerated with each of these, omnifarious colors with omnifarious sights, and *C* likewise sounds with hearings, and all the rest of the things per-

ceived which come to be congeners with all the rest of the perceptions.[29] Now what exactly, in light of the former assertions,
does this myth of ours want, Theaetetus? Do you have it in mind?

THEAETETUS: Hardly, Socrates.

SOCRATES: Well, look and see whether it may be here brought to
completion in some sense. It just wants to say that all these are in
motion, as we're saying, and speed and slowness are in their motion. Now everything slow conceives its motion in the same and

D relative to the things consorting with it and precisely in this way
generates, and the things precisely so generated are faster, for
they are born(e) and their motion is by nature in bearing (moving
locally).[30] Whenever, then, an eye and something else of the things
commensurate with it consort and generate the whiteness and
perception cognate with it, which would never have come to be
if each of the two of them had come to anything else, it's precisely
at that time when they are being born(e) between—the sight from

E the side of the eyes and the whiteness from the side of that which
(is) giving birth along with sight to the color—that the eye, lo
and behold, becomes full of sight and precisely at that time sees
and becomes not sight but an eye seeing. And that which cogenerated the color gets filled all round with whiteness and becomes
in turn not whiteness but white, whether it (is) wood or stone or
whatever thing (khrêma) turns out to get colored with a color
(khrôma) of this sort. And for all the rest in precisely this way, stiff

157 and hot and everything, it must be supposed in the same way,
nothing is itself by itself—it's what we were saying even then—
but in the association with one another, all things become and
become of all sorts from the motion, since actually it's impossible
in any single case to think fixedly, as they say, on that which affects
(makes) as being something and that which gets affected as being
by itself separately. For there's neither anything affecting before
it comes together with that which (gets) affected, nor anything
affected before it comes together with that which affects, and so
that which comes together with something and affects, if it falls
in turn on something else, comes to light as being affected. Consequently, on the basis of all this, just as we were saying at the
beginning, there is to be nothing that is one itself by itself, but

B always to become for something, and "be" must be removed from
everywhere—not that we've not been often compelled even now
by habituation and lack of knowledge to use it. But, as is the speech
of the wise, one must make no concessions: to be is neither a something nor of something nor of me nor this nor that nor any different
name that makes for stoppage, but one must make utterances

in accordance with nature—becomings and makings and perishings and alterings—since if one stops something in one's speech, whoever does (makes) it is easily refutable. One must also speak in this way piecemeal (part by part) and about many things collected together; it's to this aggregate that they lay down for themselves the names human being and stone and each animal and species. Are you then of the opinion, Theaetetus, that these things are pleasing to you, and would you enjoy the taste of them as satisfying? *C*

THEAETETUS: I do not know, Socrates, for I'm not even capable of understanding how it is with you, whether you're speaking your very own opinions or you're testing me.

SOCRATES: You don't remember, my dear, that it's I who neither know nor adopt (produce) anything of the sort as mine, for I am incapable of generating them. But I midwife you and for the sake of this I sing incantations and serve up for you to get a taste of the several wise things until I may help to lead out into the light *D* your very own opinion. And then, when it is led out, I'll go ahead and examine whether it will show up as a wind-egg or fruitful. But be confident and persistent, and in good and manly fashion answer whatever appears to you about whatever I ask.

THEAETETUS: Ask then.

SOCRATES: Well, say once more whether it satisfies you that there not be anything, but good and beautiful and everything we were just now going through (be) always becoming.

THEAETETUS: Well, to me at least, when I listen to you explicating it in this way, it surprisingly appears to make sense, and one has to suppose it to be in just the way you've gone through it.

SOCRATES: Then let's not leave out anything that's missing from it. *E* What's missing is the stuff about dreams and illnesses—madness as well as everything else—and everything said to be a mishearing or misseeing or any different misperceiving. You know surely that, in all these cases, it seems to be widely agreed upon that the speech which we were just now going through gets refuted, since it's as certain as can be that false perceptions come to be for us *158* here. And far from it being the case that the things appearing to each also are these things, but, wholly the contrary, none of the things which appears is.

THEAETETUS: What you say, Socrates, is most true.

SOCRATES: Then precisely what speech, my boy, is left for him who's laying down perception as knowledge, and that the things appearing to each also are these things for him to whom they appear?

THEAETETUS: Well, I, Socrates, am reluctant to say that I don't know what I'm to say, because you just now rebuked me when I said it, *B* since truly to this extent I would be incapable of disputing that the crazy or the dreamers are not opining false things, whenever some of them believe they are gods and some feathered and they're thinking of themselves in their sleep as flying.

SOCRATES: Then you really don't have in mind the following sort of disputation about them, and especially about dreaming and waking?

THEAETETUS: What sort?

SOCRATES: That which I suspect you've often heard from questioners—what evidence could one have to prove, if someone should ask now on these terms at the present moment, whether we're

C   asleep and dreaming everything we're thinking, or we're awake and conversing with one another while awake.

THEAETETUS: That's it, Socrates, it is perplexing as to what evidence one must use for showing it, for all the same things follow in parallel as if they were correlative. For just as there's nothing to prevent that what we've now conversed about also be dreamt as (seem) a conversation with one another in sleep, so whenever in a dream what we dream we're explaining (what we seem to be explaining) are dreams, the similarity of these to those is strange.

SOCRATES: You do see, then, that it's not the possibility of disputation

D   which is difficult, when it's even open to dispute as to whether it is in waking or in dreaming, and when indeed the time we spend in sleeping is equal to that when we're awake. In each of the two times, our soul insists that whatever its opinions are at the moment cannot be more certainly true, so for an equal time we say these things are the things which are, and for an equal time those, and we insist with a similar vehemence in each time.

THEAETETUS: That's altogether so.

SOCRATES: Doesn't, then, the same speech hold as well for bouts of illness and fits of madness, except for the time, which isn't equal?

THEAETETUS: Right.

SOCRATES: What then? Will the truth be determined by the length and brevity of the time?

E THEAETETUS: But that would be laughable in many ways.

SOCRATES: Well, do you have anything else that's a clear pointer as to which sorts of these opinions (are) true?

THEAETETUS: No, not in my opinion.

SOCRATES: Well, in that case, listen to me as to what sort of things they would say about them, those who determine that the opinions at any moment are true for him who is of that opinion. I suspect that they speak, by questioning, in this way: "Theaetetus, whatever is altogether other, will it have in any respect any power the same as the other? And let's not suppose that our question is about that which is in some respect the same and in some respect other, but suppose it wholly other."

THEAETETUS: Well, then it's impossible for it to have anything the same either in power or in anything else whatsoever, whenever it is utterly other.   *159*

SOCRATES: Isn't it then necessary to agree that something of the sort is also dissimilar?

THEAETETUS: Yes, that's my opinion at least.

SOCRATES: So if it turns out that something is becoming similar or dissimilar to something, either to itself or to something else, shall we say that in becoming similar, it's becoming the same, and in becoming dissimilar, other?

THEAETETUS: It's a necessity.

SOCRATES: Weren't we saying before that the things which affect are many and infinite, and likewise too the things that are affected?

THEAETETUS: Yes.

SOCRATES: And further that if something else mingles with something else, it will not generate the same things but others if it then mingles with something else?

THEAETETUS: Yes of course.   *B*

SOCRATES: Let's speak then from now on of me and you and everything else in accordance with the same speech, Socrates healthy and, in turn, Socrates sick. Are we to say that this is similar to that or dissimilar?

THEAETETUS: Do you mean the sick Socrates, this as a whole, is similar or dissimilar to that as a whole, the healthy Socrates?

SOCRATES: You've got it most beautifully. That's the very thing I mean.

THEAETETUS: Surely dissimilar then.

SOCRATES: So he's other too in just the way in which he's dissimilar.

THEAETETUS: It's a necessity.

SOCRATES: And you'll speak similarly of his sleeping and everything we just now went through?   *C*

THEAETETUS: Yes, I will.

SOCRATES: Then for each of the things whose nature is to affect something, will anything else be the case than that whenever it gets a healthy Socrates, it will use me as other, and whenever sick, as an other?

THEAETETUS: Why of course it won't.

SOCRATES: And so I, the affected, and that, the affecting, will generate others in each of the two cases?

THEAETETUS: Why certainly.

SOCRATES: Whenever, being healthy, I drink wine, it appears to me pleasant and sweet?

THEAETETUS: Yes.

SOCRATES: The reason is that, precisely on the basis of what has been previously agreed upon, that which affects and that which is affected generate a sweetness and a perception, both being born(e) together. And the perception, being from the side of that which is affected, renders the tongue perceiving, and the sweetness born(e) about it from the side of the wine makes the wine both be and appear sweet to the healthy tongue.

D

THEAETETUS: Yes, of course. The prior things had been agreed upon by us in this way.

SOCRATES: But whenever it gets me being ill, is anything else the case than that first of all in truth it does not take the same me. That's precisely because it approaches a dissimilar.

THEAETETUS: Yes.

E SOCRATES: The Socrates of this sort and the drinking of the wine generate, when paired, other things, about the tongue a perception of bitterness, and about the wine a bitterness coming to be and being born(e), and the wine is not bitterness but bitter, and I'm not perception but perceiving.

THEAETETUS: Yes, certainly.

SOCRATES: And just as I shall never become in just this way if I'm perceiving anything else—for a different perception is of the different, and it makes the perceiver a different sort and different—so that which affects me shall never generate the same and become of the same sort if it comes together with a different thing. For if it generates a different thing from a different thing, it will become a different sort.

160

THEAETETUS: That is so.

SOCRATES: Nor again shall I become of the same sort as myself anymore than that will become of the same sort as itself.

THEAETETUS: No indeed.

SOCRATES: Yes, and it's just as much a necessity that I become of something (perceiving something) whenever I become perceiving—for it's impossible to become perceiving and perceiving nothing—as for that to become for someone whenever it becomes sweet or bitter or anything of the sort. For it's impossible to become sweet and sweet for no one.

B

THEAETETUS: That's altogether so.

SOCRATES: Then I believe the only thing thing left is for us to be for one another if we are, or if we become, to become for one another, since necessity binds our being together and it binds it to nothing else of all the rest, not even to ourselves, so it's only left that it has become bound with one another. Consequently, regardless of whether it's for being or becoming, if someone gives a name to something, he must state that it is or becomes for someone (something) or of something or relative to something. But neither he himself must say that there's something in itself which is or becomes, nor must he accept it from anyone else who says it, as the   *C* speech we've gone through indicates.

THEAETETUS: That's altogether so, Socrates.

SOCRATES: Isn't it the case, then, that it's precisely inasmuch as that which is affecting me is for me and not for anyone else, that I in fact perceive it and anyone else does not?

THEAETETUS: Of course.

SOCRATES: My perception's after all true for me—for it is of my being on every occasion—and I (am) the judge according to Protagoras of the things which are for me that (how) they are, and of the things which are not that (how) they are not.

THEAETETUS: It seems likely.

SOCRATES: How, then, if I am without falsehood and do not stumble   *D* in my thought, would I not be a knower of the things which are or become of which I'm the perceiver?

THEAETETUS: In no way is it possible that you're not.

SOCRATES: So after all, it has been said by you very beautifully that knowledge is not anything else than perception, and there has been a coincidence to the same point of the assertion, according to Homer and Heraclitus and the entire tribe of this sort, that all things are in motion like streams; of the assertion, according to Protagoras the most wise, that (a) human being is the measure of all things (*khrêmata*); and of the assertion, according to Theaetetus,   *E* that since these things are so, knowledge comes to be perception. Is it really so, Theaetetus? Are we to say this is yours, a newborn child as it were, and mine the delivery? Or how do you say?

THEAETETUS: It's a necessity in just this way, Socrates.

SOCRATES: Well this, it seems, we have at last generated with difficulty, whatever in fact it is. But after its birth, on its name-day, it truly has to be run around in a circle by the speech, as we examine it, lest, without our being aware of it, that which is coming to be be unworthy of rearing but be a wind-egg and a falsehood.[31] Or do   *161* you believe that in any case, regardless, you must rear that which is your own just because it is yours and you must not expose it, or will you in fact put up with seeing its being tested, and will you not be vehemently distressed if someone slips it away from you though you are giving birth for the first time?

THEODORUS: Theaetetus will put up with it, Socrates, for he's not in any way peevish. But by the gods speak, and say in turn in what respect it's not in this way.

SOCRATES: You are simply (artlessly) a lover of speeches, Theodorus—yes, you are—and good, because you suspect that I am a kind of

B sack of speeches. And I would with ease take one out and say, "On the other hand, these things are not in this way." But you don't understand that which is happening (coming to be), that not one of the speeches comes out of me but always from whoever is conversing with me. And I, I know nothing of a superior kind, except a little bit, as much as to take a speech from another who's wise and accept it in a measured way. And now I'll try to take it from him here and not at all speak myself.

THEODORUS: What you say's more beautiful, Socrates. And do it in this way.

SOCRATES: Do you know, then, Theodorus, what I wonder at (admire) in your comrade Protagoras?

C THEODORUS: What sort of thing?

SOCRATES: All the rest of what he has said pleases me a lot, that that which is the opinion of each this also is for each. But I've been in a state of wonder at the beginning of his speech, that he did not say in beginning his Truth, "Pig is the measure of all things (*khrêmata*)" or "Dog-faced baboon," or anything else of those with perception that's stranger, in order that he could have begun to speak to us in a magnificent and very contemptuous way, by showing that though we admired him as if he were a god for his widsom, he is, after all, not at all better in point of intelligence than a

D tadpole, let alone than anyone else of human beings. Or how are we to speak, Theodorus? For if it will be true to each whatever each opines through perception, and if neither someone else will discriminate the experience of someone else better nor will another be more competent to examine the opinion of an other whether it's correct or false, but as it has been said many times, each one alone by himself will opine his own things, and all these

E (are) correct and true, however can it be, comrade, that Protagoras (is) wise, so as actually to claim for himself that he justly deserves to be the teacher—with great wages—of everyone else, and we (are) more foolish and have to frequent his school, since each of us is the measure for himself of his own wisdom? How are we to deny that Protagoras says these as a wooer of the public? As for myself and that which characterizes my own art, the maieutic—I keep silent about it and all the laughter we incur—but I suspect that the entire business of conversation is also open to ridicule.

For to examine and try to refute the appearances and opinions
of one another, when those of each are correct—isn't that a long *162*
and immense piece of nonsense, if the Truth of Protagoras (is)
true and she did not make her utterances in jest out of the inner
sanctum of the book?

THEODORUS: Socrates, the man's a friend, as you just now said. I
wouldn't choose then through an agreement of my own for Protagoras to be refuted, any more than I would choose to resist you
against my opinion. So take Theaetetus back. He appeared in any
case just now to comply with you harmoniously.

SOCRATES: Would you really, Theodorus, should you go to Sparta, to *B*
the palaestras there, would you claim it as your right, on observing
everyone else naked, and some in poor shape, not to display in
turn your looks (species) by stripping alongside them?

THEODORUS: Well, what's your impression, if they were going to leave
it up to me and obey me (be persuaded by me)? Just as in the
present case I suspect I'll persuade you to allow me to observe
and not to drag me, stiff as I already am, to the stripping-place,
and to wrestle against the younger and more supple.

SOCRATES: Well, if that's to your liking, Theodorus, it's no skin off my
nose, as the proverbialists say.[32] Then I have to go back to the *C*
wise Theaetetus. Do say, Theaetetus, first in regard to what we
just now went through, aren't you really surprised if so suddenly
you'll show up as in no way worse in point of wisdom than anyone
whatsoever of human beings or maybe gods? Or do you believe
the Protagorean measure is spoken less pertinently for gods than
for human beings?

THEAETETUS: No, by Zeus, I don't. And as to what you're asking, I'm
very surprised. For while we were going through in what way they
were saying that of whatever opinion each is, this also is for him *D*
whose opinion it is, it appeared to me to be very well said. But
now it has quickly changed around to the contrary.

SOCRATES: That's because you are young, my dear boy. You therefore
comply too keenly with demagogery and are persuaded. For Protagoras or someone else on his behalf will say in reply to this:
"Noble children and elders, you're sitting down together and making a public speech, and you bring gods into the middle, though
I except them from my speaking and writing, that they are or *E*
that they are not, and you say just what the many would welcome
hearing—'It's just dreadful if each human being will not differ at
all in point of wisdom from any kind of cattle whatever.' But you
don't speak any demonstration and necessity of any kind, but you
employ the likely, which if Theodorus or anyone else of the ge-

163

ometers should be willing to use in geometry, he wouldn't even be worth a single pip.[33] So you and Theodorus consider whether you'll accept speeches about matters of so great an importance that are spoken by way of plausibility and likelihoods (semblances)."[34]

THEAETETUS: But it's not just, Socrates, as either you or we would say.

SOCRATES: Then it has to be examined in a different way, it seems, as is your speech and the speech of Theodorus.

THEAETETUS: Yes, of course, in a different way.

SOCRATES: Let's then examine in the following way whether knowledge and perception are after all the same or other, for surely our entire speech was tending toward this point, and for its sake we set in motion these many strange things. Isn't that so?

THEAETETUS: That's altogether so.

B SOCRATES: Shall we really then agree that whatever we perceive by seeing or by hearing, all these we also at the same time know? For example, before we understand the language of the barbarians, shall we either deny that we hear whenever they speak or assert that we hear and know what they're saying? And if in turn we do not know letters but we're looking at them, shall we insist that we don't see them or we know them if we see them?

THEAETETUS: Yes, Socrates, we'll say we know that very thing of them which we see and hear. For we see and know, we'll say, the shape and color of the letters, and we hear and at the same time know C the sharpness and flatness of the sounds. But what the letter-experts and the interpreters teach about them, we neither perceive by seeing or hearing nor know.

SOCRATES: That's excellent, Theaetetus, and it's not worthwhile to dispute with you on these points, in order that you may grow. But look! Here's something else on the attack, and consider at what point we'll repel it.

THEAETETUS: What sort of thing exactly?

D SOCRATES: It's of the following sort. If someone should ask, "Is it possible, in the case of whatever one should become a knower, while still having a memory of this very thing and keeping it safe, not to know this very thing which one remembers at the moment when one remembers it?" I'm being long-winded, it seems, in wanting to ask whether someone if he gets to know (learn) something does not know it when he remembers it.

THEAETETUS: But how could that be, Socrates? What you're saying would be a monster.[35]

SOCRATES: I am uttering nonsense, you mean? But consider. Don't you say seeing's perceiving and sight perception?

THEAETETUS: Yes, I do.

SOCRATES: Isn't it the case then that, according to the speech of the *E* moment, whoever saw something has become a knower of that which he saw?

THEAETETUS: Yes.

SOCRATES: And what of this? Now memory, don't you say it's something?

THEAETETUS: Yes.

SOCRATES: Of nothing or something?

THEAETETUS: Of something, doubtless.

SOCRATES: Isn't it of whatever one learnt and whatever one perceived, of some sorts of things like this?

THEAETETUS: Why certainly.

SOCRATES: Then precisely that which one saw, one surely remembers sometimes?

THEAETETUS: One remembers.

SOCRATES: Even with one's eyes shut? Or if he does this he forgets?

THEAETETUS: But it's dreadful, Socrates, to assert that.

SOCRATES: Yes, but we must, however, if we're to save the former *164* speech, and if not, it's lost and gone.

THEAETETUS: I too, by Zeus, suspect it, yet I don't quite adequately understand. Say in what respect.

SOCRATES: In the following. Whoever sees, we say, has become a knower of that which he sees, for sight and perception and knowledge have been agreed to be the same.

THEAETETUS: Certainly.

SOCRATES: Yes, but whoever sees and has become a knower of what he was seeing, if he shuts his eyes, he remembers but does not see it. Isn't that so?

THEAETETUS: Yes.

SOCRATES: Yes, but "he doesn't see" is "he doesn't know," if "he sees" *B* is also "he knows."

THEAETETUS: True.

SOCRATES: So it turns out, of whatever someone becomes a knower, that though he's still remembering, he doesn't know, since he doesn't see. And we said it would be a monster should that prove to be the case.

THEAETETUS: What you say is most true.

SOCRATES: So it appears that something impossible results if one says knowledge and perception are the same.

THEAETETUS: It seems likely.

SOCRATES: So one must say each of the two (is) different.

THEAETETUS: Probably.

SOCRATES: What then would knowledge be? We have to speak again *C* from the beginning, it seems. But, Theaetetus, what in the world are we about to do?

THEAETETUS: About what?

SOCRATES: It appears to me that we jumped away from the speech and just like an ignoble cock we're crowing before we've won.

THEAETETUS: How's that exactly?

SOCRATES: We seem in the contentious way of contradiction to have gained an agreement in light of agreements about words (names) *D* and to be satisfied with our prevailing over the speech by something of the sort. And though we say we're not competitors but philosophers, we are, without our being aware of it, doing the same things as those dreadful men.

THEAETETUS: I don't yet understand how you're speaking.

SOCRATES: Well, I shall try to make plain about them just exactly what I have in mind. We asked whether someone doesn't know something if once he's learnt it he remembers, and we proved that whoever saw it and shut his eyes was remembering and not seeing, and we then proved that he did not know at the same time he was remembering, but this was impossible. And it was precisely in this way that the Protagorean myth got lost and perished, as well as your own at the same time, that knowledge and perception are the same.

E THEAETETUS: It appears so.

SOCRATES: It wouldn't have, I suspect, my dear, if the father of the other myth were still alive, but he would now be defending it in lots of ways. But as it is, we're casting reproaches on a lone orphan, for not even its guardians, whom Protagoras left behind—and Theodorus here is one of them—are willing to take the field; but, more to the point, we'll probably have to go to its assistance ourselves for the sake of the just.

THEODORUS: That's because it's not I, Socrates, but rather Callias the *165* son of Hipponicus who's the guardian of his things,[36] but we for some reason or another inclined rather early away from bare speeches and toward geometry. Still and all, we'll be grateful to you if you do assist it.

SOCRATES: You speak beautifully, Theodorus. Consider then my assistance, such as it is. If one should not pay attention to words, on whose terms for the most part we've got accustomed to affirm or deny, one would agree to more dreadful things than those just now. As to what the terms are, am I to tell you or Theaetetus?

B THEODORUS: No, rather in common, but let the younger answer, for if he makes a slip he'll cut a less disgraceful figure.

SOCRATES: Then I speak the most dreadful question, and it is, I suspect, something of the following sort. "Is it possible for the same person in knowing something not to know this which he knows?"

THEODORUS: Then what shall we answer, Theaetetus?

THEAETETUS: Impossible, surely, I suspect.

SOCRATES: No, not, that is, if you're to set down seeing as knowing. For how will you handle an inescapable question, when you're stuck, as the saying goes, in a well and an unflappable man asks, once he's covered your other eye with his hand, whether you see the cloak with the covered eye? *C*

THEAETETUS: I suspect that I'll deny that I see with this one of course but I'll affirm, however, that I do with the other.

SOCRATES: Then aren't you seeing and not seeing the same thing at the same time?

THEAETETUS: Yes, this is somehow the case.

SOCRATES: I'm not at all ordering this, he'll say, nor did I ask as to the how, but only whether what you know this you also do not know, and it's now evident that you're seeing what you do not see. And you've in fact agreed that seeing's knowing and not seeing not knowing. Then on the basis of this, figure out what's the result for you.

THEAETETUS: Well, I figure that it's the contrary to what I just laid *D* down.

SOCRATES: Yes, and perhaps—my wonderful fellow!—you would have experienced several more of the sort if someone went on to ask you whether it is possible to know sharply, and is it possible bluntly, and to know close at hand but not far away, and to know intensely the same thing and slightly. There are thousands of different things with which—had a light-armed mercenary in speeches asked them as he lay in ambush, when you set down knowledge and perception as the same, and with an assault on hearing, smelling, and perceptions of that sort—he would now be pressing his refutative attack and not let up before in amazement at his much *E* prayed-for wisdom you had been hobbled by him, and exactly where he had worsted you and bound you hand and foot, he would then be holding you for as big a ransom as you and he decided on. Now perhaps you would say, what kind of speech will Protagoras speak as an auxiliary to his own? Are we to try to say?

THEAETETUS: Yes of course.

SOCRATES: There are not only all these things—as many as we say in defending him—but, I suspect, he'll come and engage in close combat (with that mercenary) out of contempt for us and say: *166* "Here's that good Socrates of yours! He's responsible for a mere child getting a fright, when he was asked whether it was possible for the same person to remember and at the same time not know the same thing, and in his fright denied it on account of his incapacity to see ahead, and thus in his speeches showed up poor little me as a laugh. But, most slovenly Socrates, this is the way it is: whenever you're examining any of my things through questioning, if the one to whom the question is put slips up in answering it in just the sort of terms that I would answer, then I am refuted, but if the terms are different, then the one to whom the question is put is alone refuted. For instance, is it your impression that anyone will concede to you that a memory of what one experienced, if it is present to one, is an experience of just the sort that it was when he experienced it, if he is no longer experiencing it? Far from it. Or is your impression that he will, in turn, be reluctant to agree that it's possible for the same person to know and not to know the same thing? Or if he is frightened of this, that he'll ever grant that whoever is getting to be dissimilar is the same as the one who he is before he is getting to be dissimilar? And, if he'll really have to take precautions against the spoils of the chase of each other's words, he'll prefer to grant that someone is he but not *he*s, and, what's more, these *he*s keep on becoming infinite, provided that dissimilarity keeps on becoming? But," he'll say, "You blessed innocent!—Approach what I'm saying in a nobler and grander way, if you're capable, and prove straight out that to each of us there do not come to be private (peculiar) perceptions, or that though they do come to be private, it would not any the more follow that that which appears becomes for him alone, or—if 'be' has to be the name used—is for just him to whom it appears. But in speaking—of all things!—of swine and dog-faced baboons, not only are you yourself a swine, but you're convincing also your auditors to do this against my writings. There's nothing beautiful in doing (making) that. I assert the truth is as I've written: each of us is the measure of the things which are and are not, and another differs from an other in thousands of things by this very fact, that to one different things are and appear, and to one different. And I'm far from denying that wisdom and a wise man are, but I'm saying that he's the very one who's wise, whoever by inducing a change makes appear and be good things for anyone of us to whom they appear and are bad. So don't prosecute again the speech by my phrasing, but learn with still greater clarity in the following way what I'm saying. Recall the sort of thing that was being said in the previous remarks, that whatever he eats appears and is bitter to whoever is ill, but to whoever is healthy the contrary is and appears. Now one must

B

C

D

E

not make either of these the wiser—for it's not at all possible— *167*
nor deliver the accusation that the ill (is) a fool because he opines
those sorts of things, and the healthy (is) wise because he opines
different sorts of things, but one has to change the former to the
other things, for the other condition (is) better. And this holds as
well in education—one has to effect a change from another condition to the better. But the physician effects a change by drugs,
the sophist by speeches. Since it's not at all the case that one makes
someone who's opining false things later opine true things, for
it's impossible to opine either the things which are not or different
things beyond whatever one experiences, but these things (are)
always true. But, I suspect, whoever is opining by a poor condition *B*
of soul things akin to itself, a good condition makes him opine
other things of the sort. It's these that some out of inexperience
call the apparitions that are true, but I call the others better than
the others, but in no way truer. And I'm far from saying, my dear
Socrates, that the wise (are) frogs, but I am saying they're phy-
sicians in terms of bodies and farmers in terms of plants, for I
assert that they too make good and healthy perceptions and truths
be in plants in place of poor perceptions,[37] whenever any of them *C*
is ill. But it's wise and good public speakers who make cities be
of the opinion that the good things in place of the poor things
are just. Since no matter what sorts of things these are that are
just and beautiful in the opinion of each city, these also are for
it as long as it holds them to be so, but the wise makes good things
be for it and be so in its opinion in place of the several poor things
it has. And in accordance with the same speech, the sophist too,
if he's capable in this way of tutoring those who are being edu- *D*
cated, (is) wise and deserves a lot of money in the eyes of the
educated. And so others are wiser than others and no one opines
false things, and you have to put up with being a measure, whether
you want to or not, for it's in these terms that this speech gets
saved. If you can dispute it from the beginning, then go ahead
and range a counterspeech against it and dispute it; or if you want
to do it through questions, do it through questions, for this in no
case must be avoided, but anyone of sense must pursue it most
of all. Act (make), however, in this way; don't be unjust in your
questioning. For it makes little sense to claim to care for virtue *E*
and then to go ahead and continually be unjust in speeches. And
to be unjust in a situation of this sort is to fail to separate, whenever
one's engagements are of this kind, competition and conversation,
and in the former be playful and trip up one's opponent to the
extent that one is capable of it, but in conversation be in earnest

168

and put one's interlocutor on his feet again, pointing out to him only the slip-ups in which he had been led astray by himself and his former associations. For if you act (make) in this way, those who spend their time with you will blame themselves for their own confusion and perplexity, and they won't blame you, and they'll pursue you and love you; they'll hate themselves and flee from themselves into philosophy in order that, once they've become different, they may be rid of who they were before. But if, just as the many do, you do the contrary of this, the contrary will befall you and instead of as philosophers you'll reveal your as-

B

sociates as loathers of this business (*pragma*) whenever they become older. If you obey me then—and this was stated even before—if not in a spirit of enmity or contention, but with gracious condescension in thought, you will truly examine what we're saying, in declaring that all things are in motion, and that which is the opinion of each, this also is for a private person and a city. And on this basis, you'll go on to examine whether knowledge and perception (are) the same or maybe different, but not as you're doing it now on the basis of the habitual usage of words and

C

phrases: it's these that the many, by dragging and pulling in any which way, make the occasion for mutual perplexities of all sorts.

I offer this, Theodorus, to your comrade by way of assistance to the best of my capacity, a small bit from a small store. But if he were still alive himself, he would have gone to the assistance of his own things in a more magnificent way.

THEODORUS: You're joking, Socrates. You've assisted the man in a very lively way.

SOCRATES: It's good of you to say so, comrade. Tell me. You surely noticed that when Protagoras was speaking just now and reproaching us because in conducting our speeches before a mere

D

child we competed against his own things by means of the boy's fear, and in his calling off in disparagement any kind of charming whimsy, while setting off the measure of all things with august majesty, he urged us to be in earnest about his own speech?

THEODORUS: Of course I noticed it, Socrates.

SOCRATES: What then? Do you urge obedience to him?

THEODORUS: Yes, exactly.

SOCRATES: Do you see then that all these here are mere children except for you? So if we'll obey the man, then it's you and I who must,

E

in asking and answering one another, prove to be in earnest about his speech, in order that he cannot bring this charge at least, that in being playful before lads we examined his speech.

THEODORUS: But what of it? See here. Wouldn't Theaetetus better follow an examination of a speech than many who have long beards?

SOCRATES: Well, not at all better than you at least, Theodorus. So don't suppose that I must defend your dead comrade in every way and *169* you in none. But come—my excellent fellow!—do follow just a little way, up to this very point, when we know whether you, after all, must be the measure of geometrical theorems (drawings) or all are as competent for themselves as you are in astronomy and everything else in which you are charged with excelling.

THEODORUS: It's not easy, Socrates, to sit beside you and not give an account (*logos*), and I was just now distracted into uttering nonsense when I said that you'd leave it up to me not to strip and wouldn't use compulsion as the Spartans do. But my impression is that you tend rather toward Sciron, for Spartans order one *B* either to go away or to strip, but my impression is that your act is rather on the model of Antaeus, for you don't release anyone who approaches before you compel him to strip and go to the mat in speeches.[38]

SOCRATES: Yes, Theodorus, it's an excellent semblance that you made of my disease; I am however more stubborn than they. Thousands of Heracleses and Theseuses, mighty in speaking, have before now met and thrashed me roundly, but I none the less do not stand aside and withdraw—it's to that extent that a dreadful love of exercise in *C* matters of this kind has slipped into me. So don't you begrudge a drubbing and a benefit of yourself and me at once.

THEODORUS: I no longer speak of resisting, but lead wherever you want, for I must in any case be refuted and endure whatever fate you spin out for me in these matters.[39] I'll not, however, be able to submit myself to you beyond what you propose.

SOCRATES: Well, it's enough even to go so far. Now please watch the following sort of thing very closely, lest at some point we slip unawares into conducting a childish species of speeches, and *D* someone once more reproach us for it.

THEODORUS: Well, I'll try of course, to the extent that I'm able.

SOCRATES: Well, then, let's get our grip back on this at just the same point as before, and let's see whether we were correctly or incorrectly annoyed when we faulted that speech that was making each one self-sufficient in point of intelligence. And Protagoras did concede to us that some are superior when it comes to the better and worse, and it's these he granted were the wise. Isn't that so?

THEODORUS: Yes.

SOCRATES: Now if he were present and was making the agreement himself, and it was not we who had in taking the field conceded *E* it on his behalf, there would now be no need to take it up again and confirm it; but as it is, someone might cancel our authority to make an agreement on his behalf. It's for this reason that it's more beautiful to come to an agreement of greater clarity about this very point, for it's not just a slight variance whether it's in this or a different way.

THEODORUS: What you say is true.

SOCRATES: Let's not then through different (speeches) but on the basis of his speech gain the agreement as briefly as possible.

170

THEODORUS: How?

SOCRATES: In this way. He surely says that whatever is the opinion for each, this also is for him whose opinion it is?

THEODORUS: Yes, he says so indeed.

SOCRATES: Then aren't we too speaking, Protagoras, the opinions of (a) human being, or rather of all human beings, and we assert that there's no one who's not convinced that he's wiser than everyone else in some things but in some things different people are wiser than he is. And in the greatest dangers, whenever they are foundering on campaigns, in illnesses, or at sea, their relation to

B

the rulers on these several occasions is as to gods, in the expectation that they're their saviors, and they don't differ by anything else than by the fact that they know. And all human affairs surely are as full of people seeking teachers and rulers of themselves, of the rest of the animals, and their occupations, as they are of those who believe in turn that they're competent to teach and competent to rule? And in all these matters what else shall we say than that human beings themselves are convinced that wisdom and folly are at home among them?

THEODORUS: Nothing else.

SOCRATES: They're convinced that wisdom (is) true thought and folly false opinion?

C

THEODORUS: Why certainly.

SOCRATES: How then shall we handle the speech, Protagoras? Are we to assert that human beings always opine what is true, or at times true and at times false? For it surely turns out on the basis of both that they don't always opine what is true but both. Consider, Theodorus, whether anyone of Protagoras' circle or you yourself would be willing to insist that no other is convinced that an other is foolish and opines what is false.

THEODORUS: Well, it's unbelievable, Socrates.

D

SOCRATES: And yet the speech that says (a) human being (is) the measure of all things (*khrêmata*) has come to the point of submitting to this necessity.

THEODORUS: How's that exactly?

SOCRATES: Whenever you judge something by yourself and declare in front of me an opinion about something, then in accordance with his speech let this be true for you. But is it not possible for all the rest of us to come to be judges of your judgment, or are we always deciding that you opine what's true? Or don't thousands battle you on each occasion with counteropinions, convinced that you judge and believe what is false?

THEODORUS: Yes, by Zeus, Socrates, it's indeed thousands, Homer says,   *E* and it's they who give me all the trouble (*pragmata*) that I have from human beings.[40]

SOCRATES: What then? Do you want us to say that you at that time are opining what is true for yourself and false for the thousands?

THEODORUS: It seems on the basis of the speech at least to be a necessity.

SOCRATES: And what of Protagoras himself? Isn't it a necessity that if not even he were to believe that (a) human being was the measure, or the many either—just as they don't at all believe it—this truth   *171* which he wrote is strictly for no one? And if he were to believe it, and the multitude do not share his belief, you know that first of all, to the extent that more are of the opinion that it's not than that it is, to that extent it is not more than it is.

THEODORUS: It's a necessity, provided, that is, it will be and will not be in accordance with each opinion.

SOCRATES: Yes, and, in the second place, this is the cleverest thing about it. He surely concedes that the belief of those who have a counteropinion to his own about his own belief—in which they're convinced that he's speaking what is false (lying)—is true, since he agrees that everyone opines the things which are.

THEODORUS: Yes, of course.

SOCRATES: Would he then concede his own is false if he agrees that   *B* the belief of those convinced he's speaking falsely (lying) is true?

THEODORUS: It's a necessity.

SOCRATES: Yes, but everyone else does not concede that they themselves are speaking falsely?

THEODORUS: Indeed they don't.

SOCRATES: Yes, but he's agreeing that this opinion too is true on the basis of what he has written?

THEODORUS: It appears so.

SOCRATES: So will there be after all a dispute from all who take their start from Protagoras, or rather won't there be an agreement at least by him, whenever he concedes to the one contradicting him that he's opining what is true, and at that time Protagoras himself   *C* will also concede that neither a dog nor the chance human being is a measure about even one thing which he does not understand (learn)? Isn't that so?

THEODORUS: Just so.

SOCRATES: Isn't it the case then that since it's disputed by all, the Truth of Protagoras would not be true for anyone, neither anyone else nor himself?

THEODORUS: We're running down my comrade too much, Socrates.

SOCRATES: Well, you know, my friend, it's not plain whether we're not in fact running right past the right, for it's likely that he, since he is older, be wiser than us. And if he should for instance pop up here on the spot and just up to his neck, he would, as is likely, once he charged me with talking a lot of nonsense and you with agreeing, slip down out of sight and be off and running. But I suppose it's a necessity for us to deal with ourselves as the sort we are, and to say whatever are our own opinions on each and every occasion. And so, now in this particular case, are we to assert that anyone whatsoever would agree to this at least, the fact of another being wiser than an other and similarly more foolish?

THEODORUS: It's my opinion at any rate.

SOCRATES: Are we also to say that the speech would especially take its stand in the region we outlined when we were going to the assistance of Protagoras, that the many things in which, in whatever way one's opinion is, it's in that way that they are for each—hot things, dry things, sweet things, all things of this cast? But if it's anywhere that he'll concede that in some things someone differs from someone else, he would be willing to say it's about the healthy and the sick things that not every mere woman and child, let alone every beast, is competent to cure itself, because it recognizes what is healthy for itself, but it's exactly here if anywhere that someone differs from someone else.

THEODORUS: I'm of the opinion, at least, that this is the way it is.

SOCRATES: Isn't it the case about political things too, that though for beautiful and ugly things, just and unjust, and holy and not, of whatsoever sort they are that each city in its belief lays down for itself as lawful, these also are in truth for each, and in these things neither layman than layman nor city than city is in any way wiser? Still, in the case of laying down for itself things that are to its own advantage or not to its own advantage, it's here, if anywhere, that he'll agree again that adviser differs from adviser and another opinion of a city from an other in light of truth. And he would scarcely have the nerve to assert that whatever a city lays down for itself in the belief they're to its advantage, it's as certain as can be that these things will be to its advantage. But it's in the former

case, I mean in the just and unjust, holy and unholy things, that they're willing to insist that none of them is by nature with a being of its own, but the opinion resolved on in common, this becomes true at that time, whenever it's resolved on and for as long a time as it's so resolved. And everyone who does not altogether speak the speech of Protagoras,[41] leads wisdom in one way or another to this. But a greater speech, Theodorus, from a lesser speech is   C
overtaking us.

THEODORUS: Aren't we at leisure, Socrates?

SOCRATES: It appears we are. And though I often realized it at other times of course—you extraordinary being![42]—it's striking now as well how likely it is that those who passed much time in the practices of philosophy show up as laughable public speakers when they enter the courts.[43]

THEODORUS: How exactly do you mean that?

SOCRATES: It's probable that those who since youth knock about courts and places of the sort are, in comparison with those who have been reared in philosophy and that sort of engagement, like domestics in comparison to free.   D

THEODORUS: In what respect exactly?

SOCRATES: In the sense that they always have available that which you said—leisure—and they conduct their talks in peace and at their leisure. And just as we at the present moment are now taking for a third time a speech in exchange for a speech, so they do too, if the speech that comes along pleases them more than that which lies in front of them, just as it did us. And it's of no concern to them whether they talk at length or briefly, if only they hit upon 'that which is'. But *they* are always speaking in the press of busi-   E
ness—water in its flow is bearing down on them[44]—and there's no room to have their talks about whatever they desire, but the plaintiff stands over them holding necessity and an outline that is read alongside as they speak and outside of which they must not speak.[45] And their speeches are always about a fellow-slave before a seated master, who holds some kind of suit (justice) in his hand, and the contests are never indifferent, but he's always   *173*
the case in point, and the course is often in fact about his life (soul): as a result of all this, they become sharp and shrewd, knowing how to cozen their master in speech and beguile him in deed, but they become small and not upright in their souls, for their enslavement since their youth on has deprived them of the possibility of growth, straightness, and liberality. It compels them to do crooked things, imposing on their still tender souls great dangers and fears which they're incapable of supporting with the just

and true, and so turning at once to the lie and mutual injustice

B they often get bent and stunted, and from lads they end up as men with nothing healthy and sound in their thought. They have become, they believe, dreadfully uncanny and wise. And here you have the sort that they are, Theodorus. But as for those of our chorus, do you want us to go through it or dismiss it and turn once more to the speech, in order that we may not in fact abuse too much in excess the freedom and possibility of exchanging speeches that we were just now speaking of?

C THEODORUS: In no way, Socrates, but let's go through it. You've made a very good point, that we who are choristers in this sort of thing are not subservient to the speeches, but the speeches are as it were our domestics, and each of them waits around to be completed whenever we decide. No judge and no observer supervises us as he does poets to rebuke and rule.

SOCRATES: Let's speak then, since, it seems, you're of the opinion that we are to, about those at the top—for why should one speak of those who spend their time in philosophy so poorly?—it's surely these who since their youth, first of all, don't know the way to the

D marketplace, or where's a court, councilhouse, or anything else that's a common assembly of the city. And laws and decrees, spoken or written, they neither see nor hear, and the serious business of clubs for gaining office, and meetings, banquets, and revelries with flute girls—it doesn't even occur to them to do them in their dreams. And whether someone has been well-born or base-born in the city, or whether someone has incurred some evil from his ancestors, on the men's or women's side—he's less aware of it than

E of the proverbial pitchers of the sea.[46] And he doesn't even know that he does not know all these things, for he's not abstaining from them for the sake of good repute, but in truth his body alone is situated in the city and resides there, but his thought, convinced that all these things are small and nothing, dishonors them in every way and flies, as Pindar puts it, "deep down under the earth"[47] and geometricizes the planes, "and above heaven"

174 star gazing, and in exploring everywhere every nature of each whole of the things which are and letting itself down to not one of the things nearby.

THEODORUS: How do you mean this, Socrates?

SOCRATES: Just like Thales, Theodorus, while star gazing and looking up he fell in a well, and some gracefully witty Thracian servant girl is said to have made a jest at his expense—that in his eagerness to know the things in heaven he was unaware of the things in front of him and at his feet. The same jest suffices for all those

who engage in philosophy. For someone of this sort has truly *B*
become unaware of his neighbor next-door, not only as to what
he's doing but almost to the point of not knowing whether he is
a human being or some different nursling. But what (a) human
being is and in what respect it's suitable for a nature of that sort
to act or be acted on that's different from all the rest—he seeks
that, and all his trouble (*pragmata*) is in exploring it. Surely you
understand, Theodorus, or don't you?

THEODORUS: Yes I do, and what you say is true.

SOCRATES: It's precisely for this reason, my friend, that whoever is of
this sort in associating with each in private and in public, just as *C*
I was saying at the beginning, whenever he's compelled in a court
or anywhere else to converse about the things at his feet and things
before his eyes, he gives not only Thracian girls but the rest of
the crowd a laugh, falling into wells and every kind of perplexity
by inexperience, and his lack of deportment is dreadful as he
gives the impression of plain silliness. For just as on occasions of
abuse he has nothing peculiar to revile anyone with, because he
knows of no evil of anyone from his failure to have practiced it
(and so in his perplexity he's evidently laughable), so no less on *D*
occasions of praise and the boastings of everyone else when he's
not in any feigned way but truly and openly laughing, he seems
to be nonsensical. For when a tyrant or a king is praised, he's
convinced he's hearing that one of the herdsmen is deemed to be
happy—a swineherd, for example, a shepherd, or some cow-
herd—for milking a lot of cattle. But he holds that they are grazing
and milking a more peevish and conspiratorial animal than the
herdsmen are, but it's necessary that a ruler of this sort become
by lack of leisure no less boorish and uneducated than the herdsmen, with his wall cast around him as a sheepfold on a mountain. *E*
And whenever he hears of someone in possession of ten thousand
acres of land or still more—"Oh! he possesses an amazing quan-
tity"—his impression is that he's hearing of a very small amount,
accustomed as he is to look at the entire earth. And when people
harp on families—"How grand and noble so-and-so is; he can
show seven wealthy ancestors"—he's convinced the praise is from
those whose sight is altogether dim and limited, who are incapable,
by lack of education, of looking over all eternity and calculating
that each and every one has had countless thousands of grand- *175*
fathers and ancestors, and anyone whatsoever has had among
them many thousands of rich men and beggars, kings and slaves,
barbarians and Greeks. But for those who make themselves august
in a recitation of twenty-five ancestors and refer themselves to

B   Heracles the son of Amphitryon, their petty calculation seems strange to him; and because whoever was the twenty-fifth further back from Amphitryon was the sort he was as chance befell him, and the fiftieth further back from him no less, he laughs when they're incapable of calculation and release from the vanity of a foolish soul. And on all these occasions whoever is of this sort is laughed at by the many, since he seems to be partly arrogant and partly ignorant of the things at his feet and is perplexed in particular.

THEODORUS: You altogether speak, Socrates, of the way it happens.

SOCRATES: Yes, but whenever he himself gets to drag someone up,
C   my friend, and he's responsible for someone being willing to leave off from "How am I wronging you, or you me?" and turns to the examination of justice itself and injustice, what each of the pair (is) and in what respect they differ from everything or each other, or from "Whether a king's happy in possession of mickle gold,"[48] and turns to an examination of kingship and of human happiness and misery in general, of what sort the pair is and in what way it's suitable for the nature of (a) human being to acquire one and
D   avoid one of the pair—whenever that one who's small in his soul and shrewd and a shyster has to give an account (*logos*) of all these things, then he pays back the converse. Hung up on high he's dizzy and looking from high above he's in dismay by his unfamiliarity, he's perplexed and stutters, and he does not give Thracian girls a laugh, or anyone else who's uneducated either—for they don't perceive it—but all those who have been reared in a fashion contrary to slaves. So here you have the way of each of the two, Theodorus: the way of him who has been truly nurtured
E   in freedom and leisure—he's the one you call a philosopher—it's no matter of indignation for him to seem to be naive and nothing, whenever he falls into slavish services (it's as if he does not know how to pack up bedding or flavor a relish or fawning speeches); and the way of him in turn, who's capable of serving in all things of this sort keenly and sharply, but who doesn't know how to arrange his cloak on the right in a free man's way or for that
176   matter get a harmony of speeches and hymn correctly a life of gods and happy men.

THEODORUS: If you should persuade everyone, Socrates, of what you're saying as you did me, peace would be more widespread and evils less among human beings.

SOCRATES: But it's not possible for the evils either to perish, Theodorus—it's a necessity that there always be something contrary to the good—or for them to be established among gods, but of necessity they haunt mortal nature and this region here; it's for this reason that one ought to try to flee from here to there as soon as possible. Flight (is) assimilation to a god as far as possible, and *B* assimilation (is) to become just and holy with intelligence. But as a matter of fact, it's hardly at all easy—my excellent fellow!—to persuade that it's not after all for the sake of which the many say one should avoid wickedness and pursue virtue, that it's for this sake that one must practice virtue and not vice, in order that, of all things, one may seem to be good and not bad. For all this is, as the saying goes, the drivel of old women, as it appears to me. But let's tell the truth as follows. A god (is) in no way unjust in *C* any respect, but he's the most just that it's possible to be, and there is nothing more similar to him than whoever of us becomes in turn as just as possible. It's in his dealing with this that there's the truly dreadful uncanniness of a man or his nothingness and unmanliness, for the cognition of this (is) wisdom and simply true virtue, and its ignorance folly and manifest vice, and all the rest of seeming uncanniness and wisdom that occur in the practice of political power (is) vulgar, and what occurs in the arts common. As for whoever, then, is doing an injustice and saying or doing *D* unholy things, it's best by far in his case not to make the concession that he is uncanny by his criminal willingness to stop at nothing, for they glory in the reproach and believe they're hearing that they're not utter nonsense, merely burdens of the earth,⁴⁹ but that they're men as they ought to be in a city—those who will get themselves to safety. So one must tell the truth, that they are by so much more the sort they suspect they're not because they don't suspect it, for they're ignorant of the penalty for injustice, and it's what they least ought to be ignorant of. For it's not what it is in their opinion, beatings and executions—people who do no injustice undergo them on occasion—but it's what's impossible to avoid. *E*

THEODORUS: What exactly do you mean?

SOCRATES: Paradigms stand in 'that which is', my friend, of the divine which is most happy and of the godless which is most miserable, and they don't see that this is the way it is, but by their folly and extreme foolishness they unawares make themselves similar to the *177* latter on account of their unjust actions, and make themselves dissimilar to the former. So they pay the penalty for exactly this by living the life that resembles that to which they make themselves similar. And if we say that unless they get rid of their uncanniness, even when they're dead that region clear of the bad won't receive them, but it's here they'll always have their own similarity of a way of life; bad in association with bad, they'll listen to this as altogether the talk of some mindless people, uncanny and criminally willing to stop at nothing as they are.

THEODORUS: Indeed they will, Socrates.

B SOCRATES: I know it, be sure, comrade. There's one thing, however, that has befallen them. Whenever they have to give and receive in private an account (*logos*) of the things they blame, and they're willing in a manly fashion to put up with it for a long time and not to take flight in an unmanly way, then strangely—you extraordinary being!—they end up as not being satisfied with themselves about what they're saying, and that rhetorical (art) of theirs somehow or other shrinks up, so as for them to seem to be no different from children. Now let's stand apart and withdraw from

C these things—they were in fact said as by-products—for if we don't, always more will keep on flowing in and choke up the speech with which we began, and let's go to the previous remarks, if you're of that opinion too.

THEODORUS: As for me, Socrates, things of this sort are less unpleasant to listen to, for they're easier for someone of my age to follow. If, however, it's been resolved on, let's go back.

SOCRATES: Weren't we then at some point hereabouts of the speech, in which, we claimed, those who speak of that sweeping being,[50] and whatever is the opinion of each on any occasion also is for him whose opinion it is, are willing in everything else to insist upon this and not least in the case of the just things, that it's as

D certain as can be that whatever a city lays down for itself, once the city has got an opinion about them, these also are just for the city which laid them down for as long as they are laid down. But about the good things, there is no one still so manly as to have the nerve to fight it out that whatever a city lays down for itself in the belief they're beneficial, then these things also are, for as long a time as they are laid down, beneficial—unless one should give it the name, but it would surely be a jest in light of what we're saying. Or isn't it?

THEODORUS: Certainly.

E SOCRATES: The reason is that he is not to say the name but to observe the matter (*pragma*) that is named.

THEODORUS: Don't let him then.

SOCRATES: But whatever a city names this, surely it's aiming at that in its legislation, and all the laws, to the extent that it believes and is capable, it lays down for itself as beneficially as possible. Or does the city legislate by looking at anything else?

178 THEODORUS: In no way.

SOCRATES: Does it really then also always hit upon it, or doesn't each often fail too?

THEODORUS: I suspect there's failure too.

SOCRATES: Well, it's still more the case that everyone would agree to these same things from the following viewpoint, should one ask about the species in its entirety in which the beneficial also happens to be. And that surely is in fact about future time. For whenever we legislate for ourselves, we're laying down the laws on the grounds that they will be beneficial in later time, and this we would correctly speak of as "future."

THEODORUS: Certainly.   *B*

SOCRATES: Come then, let's ask in just this way Protagoras or anyone else of those who say the same things as he does. "Of all things (a) human being is the measure," as you all assert, Protagoras— of white things, heavy things, light things, everything of the sort without exception—for with his own tribunal for them in himself, believing they're the sort as he experiences them, he believes they're true for him and are the things which are. Isn't that so?

THEODORUS: That's so.

SOCRATES: Shall we really assert, then, Protagoras, that he does have   *C*
the tribunal in himself also for the things that will be, and whatever sort he believes they will be, these things also become to him who conceived the belief? For example, a feverish heat. Whenever some layman believes he'll get a fever and this hotness will be, and another, but a physician, holds the counterbelief, in accordance with the opinion of which of the two are we to assert how the future will turn out? Or will it be in accordance with the opinion of both, and he won't be hot for the physician and won't be feverish, while to himself there'll be both?

THEODORUS: In that case it would be laughable.

SOCRATES: Well, I suspect in regard to the future sweetness and dryness of wine, the opinion of the farmer is authoritative and not   *D*
that of the lyre-player.

THEODORUS: Why certainly.

SOCRATES: Nor, in turn, about what will be out of tune and in tune, would a trainer's opinion prove to be better than a musician's, since later, too, the trainer himself will be of the opinion that it is in tune.

THEODORUS: In no way.

SOCRATES: And isn't it also the case for the future feaster, whoever's not an expert cook, when a banquet is being got ready, his judgment is less authoritative than the relish-maker's about the future pleasure. Let's not yet fight it out with the speech about the pleas-   *E*

ant that is now or has been for him, but about that which will in
the future be for each and be the opinion of each—is he himself
his own best judge? Or you, Protagoras? Would your anticipatory
opinion prove to be better, at least in the case of what will be
persuasive in speeches for each of us in court, or any layman's
whatsoever?

THEODORUS: Yes, indeed, Socrates, it was in exactly this that he used
to promise to surpass everyone.

179 SOCRATES: Yes, by Zeus, my good man,[51] or else no one would converse
with him and offer him a lot of money, if he were not persuading
his associates that neither a soothsayer nor anyone else would
better judge that which will be and will seem than he himself.

THEODORUS: Most true.

SOCRATES: Isn't it the case, then, that both acts of legislation and the
beneficial are concerned with the future, and everyone would
agree that it is often a necessity for a city in legislating for itself
to fail to hit upon the most beneficial?

THEODORUS: Yes indeed.

SOCRATES: So it will be stated by us in a measured way before your
B   teacher that it's a necessity for him to agree that someone is wiser
than someone else, and that whoever is of that sort is the measure,
and there is no necessity whatsoever for me the nonknower to
become the measure, as the speech on his behalf was just now
compelling me to be of that sort, whether I was wanting to or not.

THEODORUS: It's my impression, Socrates, that the speech particularly
gets convicted in the former way (though it's also convicted in
this), in which it makes the opinions of everyone else authoritative,
and these opinions believe, evidently, that his speeches are in no
way true.

C SOCRATES: There're many different ways, Theodorus, in which a conviction of the sort might be gained against the view that every
opinion of everyone is true. But in regard to the experience each
has in the present, out of which the perceptions and the opinions
in conformity with these perceptions come to be, it's harder to
gain the point that they're not true. But perhaps I'm making no
sense, for maybe they are unconvictable, and those who assert
they are as plain as day and are sciences would perhaps be saying
the things which are, and the speech of Theaetetus here has not
been way off the mark when he set down perception and knowl-
D edge as the same. We have to approach it more closely, then, as
the speech on behalf of Protagoras prescribed, and give this
sweeping being a sharp tap and see whether it rings sound or

hollow. Now, whichever way it is, there has been a battle about it, not a trivial one, and it has involved not a few.

THEODORUS: It's far from being trivial, but it's been very much on the increase around Ionia, for the comrades of Heraclitus are the very vigorous choral leaders of this speech.

SOCRATES: That's all the more reason, my dear Theodorus, you see, to examine it, and from the beginning, just as they themselves E present it.

THEODORUS: That's altogether so. About these Heraclitean opinions, Socrates, or, as you say, Homeric and still more ancient, it's no more possible to converse with all who pretend to be experienced with them—the members of the Ephesian circle—than with those driven to madness by the gadfly. They simply (artlessly), in accordance with their own writings, sweep along. And as for the possibility of staying by a speech and question, and quietly an- *180* swering and asking in turn, there is less than nothing in them of that, or rather even nothing does not surpass these men when it comes to the small degree of quietness in them.⁵² But if you ask any of them anything, they send off shots as if they were drawing up enigmatic shaftlets from a quiver, and if you seek to get an account (*logos*) of this, as to what he has said, you'll be struck by another freshly altered name.⁵³ And you'll never get anywhere with any one of them, any more than they themselves will with one another, but they take very good care to permit nothing to be stable either in speech or in their own souls, convinced as they B are, in my opinion, that that is to be stationary. And they are wholly at war against that, and as far as they are capable, they throw it out from everywhere.

SOCRATES: Perhaps, Theodorus, you've seen the men fighting, but you've not been with them when they are at peace, for they are not your comrades. But, I suspect, they point out things of this sort (i.e., the stable things) to their pupils at their leisure, whomever they want to make similar to themselves.

THEODORUS: What do you mean, pupils? You extraordinary being! C For this sort there's not another who becomes the pupil of another, but they grow up spontaneously, from whatever source each of them happens to get a god in him, and the other is convinced that the other knows nothing. Now from these, as I was going to say, you would never get an account (*logos*) regardless of whether they're willing or unwilling. But we must take it off their hands and examine it by ourselves as if it were a problem.⁵⁴

SOCRATES: And there's a measure of sense in what you say. And as for the problem, have we taken on anything else than this—from D the ancients who were concealing it from the many with poetry,[55] it was that the becoming (*genesis*) of everything else happens to be streams, Oceanus and Tethys, and nothing is at rest, and from those later who, because they were wiser, were revealing it openly, in order that even the shoemakers, once they heard it, may understand their wisdom and stop believing in their foolishness that some of the things which are are at rest and some in motion, but once they understand that everything is in motion they may honor them? But I almost forgot, Theodorus, that different people, on *E* the other hand, declared the contrary to this—"As the sort that is immoveable, there is 'to be' as the name for the all"[56]—and all the different things that the Melissuses and Parmenideses in opposing all of them insist on, that all things are one and it is at rest in itself without a place in which it moves. How shall we handle all of these, Theodorus? For in advancing little by little, we have, without being aware of it, fallen into the middle of both, and *181* unless we somehow manage to defend ourselves and escape, we'll pay the penalty, as those do in gymnasia who play at tug-of-war, whenever they are seized by both sides and dragged in contrary directions.[57] Now I'm of the opinion that we must examine the others first, toward whom we started out, the streamers. And if it's evident they're making sense, we'll drag ourselves off with them, and try to avoid the others, but if the arresters of the whole seem to be saying truer things,[58] we'll flee over to them and away *B* from those who set the immoveable things in motion.[59] And if it's evident that there's no measure of sense in what both are saying, we'll be laughable, convinced that we're making sense though we're nobodies, and have repudiated in the scrutiny very ancient and all-wise men.[60] See, then, Theodorus, whether it's profitable to advance into so great a danger.

THEODORUS: Rather it's unendurable, Socrates, not to examine thoroughly what each of the two groups of men is saying.

SOCRATES: If you of all people are that eager, we must make the *C* examination. Now it's my impression that the start of our examination is about motion—what sort of thing are they saying after all, those who assert that all things are in motion? I want to say the following sort of thing. Do they say there's some one species of motion, or, as it appears to me, two? Don't, however, let it only be my opinion, but you too share in it, in order that we may, if in fact we have to, suffer in common. Tell me. Do you call it motion whenever something changes from place to place or even when it's revolving in the same?

THEODORUS: Yes I do.

SOCRATES: Well, then, let this be one species. But whenever it is in the   *D*
    same but grows old, or becomes black from white or stiff from
    soft, or alters in any different alteration, isn't it worthwhile to
    declare it another species of motion?

THEODORUS: It's necessary rather.

SOCRATES: I mean, then, by the two species of motion this pair, alter-
    ation and locomotion.

THEODORUS: And it's right to say so.

SOCRATES: Well, then, now that we made this kind of division, let's
    converse with those who assert that all things are in motion, and
    let's ask: Do you assert that everything's in motion in both ways,   *E*
    moving locally and altering, or some move in both ways, and some
    in one of the two?

THEODORUS: But, by Zeus, I for one cannot say. But I suspect they
    would say in both ways.

SOCRATES: Yes, for if not, comrade, it will be evident that for them
    things are both in motion and at rest, and it will be no more
    correct to say that all things are in motion than that all things are
    at rest.

THEODORUS: What you say is most true.

SOCRATES: Then, since they must be in motion, and nonmotion must
    not be in anything, it's all things without exception that are always   *182*
    in motion with every kind of motion.

THEODORUS: It's a necessity.

SOCRATES: Please examine the following point of theirs. In the case
    of the becoming of hotness, or of whiteness, or of anything what-
    soever, weren't we saying that they assert somehow in this way,
    that each of these is born(e) along with a perception between that
    which affects and is affected, and that which is affected becomes
    capable of perceiving (it does not become perception), and that
    which affects becomes a certain sort (it does not become sortness)?
    Perhaps "sortness" appears an odd name, and you don't under-
    stand it when spoken of collectively.[61] Listen, then, part by part.   *B*
    That which affects is neither hotness nor whiteness, but it becomes
    hot and white—and so for all the rest. You surely remember we
    were speaking in this way previously, that as nothing is itself one
    by itself, so neither is that which affects or is affected, but from
    both of them becoming mutually together, the perceptions and
    the things perceived come to be and give birth to some as certain
    sorts and some as perceiving?

THEODORUS: Of course I remember.

SOCRATES: Now let's dismiss everything else, whether they speak in a   *C*
    different way or in this way. But for the sake of which we're

speaking, let's only guard this, and ask: All things are in motion and flow, as you say? Don't they?

THEODORUS: Yes.

SOCRATES: In respect, then, to both the motions we divided, they move locally and they alter?

THEODORUS: Yes, of course, provided that it's in the strict sense they are to move completely.

SOCRATES: Now if there was only local motion but not alteration, we could surely say what sort of things are the things that move locally in their flow. Or how are we saying?

THEODORUS: It's in this way.

D SOCRATES: But since not even this abides, that it's the white that's flowing which flows, but it changes, so as for there to be a flowing even of just this, of whiteness, and a change into a different color, in order that it may not in this way be convicted of loitering, is it ever possible to address it as some color so as really to be addressing it correctly?

THEODORUS: But what possibility is there, Socrates? Or for that matter anything else of the things of this sort, if it's always slipping out and away while one's speaking and precisely because it's flowing?[62]

SOCRATES: And what are we to say about any sort of perception what-

E ever, for example, of seeing or hearing? Does it ever abide in just seeing or hearing?

THEODORUS: It ought not, at any rate, if all things are in motion.

SOCRATES: So one must address it no more as seeing than as not-seeing, nor any different perception either rather than not, since all things in all ways are in motion.

THEODORUS: Indeed one must not.

SOCRATES: And yet perception (is) knowledge, as Theaetetus and I said.

THEODORUS: That was so.

SOCRATES: So on being asked what knowledge is, we no more answered after all about knowledge than about nonknowledge.

183 THEODORUS: It seems that's what you did.

SOCRATES: The correction of our answer would turn out to be for us a beauty if, in order that that answer may appear, of all things, correct, we should be eager to prove that all things are in motion. For this is what comes to light, it seems, if all things are in motion—every answer, about whatever one answers, is similarly correct. Or if you want, in order that we may not put a stop to them in the speech, every answer becomes correct[63]—to say "This is so" and "This is not so."

THEODORUS: What you say's correct.

SOCRATES: Yes, Theodorus, except that I did say "so" and "not so." But one must not even say "so," for "so" would no longer be in *B* motion, nor in turn "not so," for not even this is a motion. But those who speak this speech must set down some different language, since now at least they don't have the words for their own hypothesis, unless, after all, "not even so" would most particularly fit them, since it is spoken without a limit.

THEODORUS: This is at any rate a dialect they're most at home with.[64]

SOCRATES: Are we then quit of your comrade, Theodorus, and do we not as yet concede to him that every man is the measure of all *C* things (*khrêmata*), unless someone is intelligent? And we'll not concede knowledge (is) perception, at least in terms of the quest for all things to be in motion, unless Theaetetus here has something different to say?

THEODORUS: What you've said is excellent, Socrates. For with this brought to an end, I too must be quit of answering you, in accordance with the contract that specified it as the completion of Protagoras' speech.

THEAETETUS: Don't, Theodorus, not before you and Socrates go *D* through those who assert in turn that the all is at rest, as you just now proposed.

THEODORUS: So young, Theaetetus, and you teach your elders to be unjust and violate agreements? But get yourself ready to give Socrates an account (*logos*) of that which remains.

THEAETETUS: Yes, if, that is, he wants to. I would have listened in any case with the greatest pleasure about those whom I'm speaking of.

THEODORUS: "Horsemen to the plain" is your challenge to Socrates in inviting him to speeches.[65] Ask and you'll hear.

SOCRATES: But, Theodorus, it's my impression that I'll not obey Theaetetus, at least about what he's urging. *E*

THEODORUS: Why exactly won't you obey him?

SOCRATES: Although I'm ashamed before Melissus and everyone else, who speak of the all as one at rest, lest our investigation be vulgar and common, I'm less ashamed before them than before Parmenides who is one. Parmenides appears to me at once, in the saying of Homer, "as awesome to me as uncanny."[66] In fact, I once got together with the man when I was very young and he very old, and he appeared to me to have some altogether grand *184* and noble depth.[67] So I'm afraid that we'll fail as much to understand what he was saying as we'll fall far short of what he thought when he spoke, and—this is the greatest thing—that for whose sake the speech has started out, about knowledge, whatever it is, that that will prove to be unexamined under the press of the speeches that are bursting in like revellers, if anyone will obey them. And this is all the more the case now, since the speech we now awaken makes it impossible to handle by its immensity, regardless of what one will do. For if one will examine it incidentally, it would undergo what it does not deserve, and if one will do it adequately, it will by its lengthening wipe out the issue of knowledge. We must do neither, but we must try by means of the

B maieutic art to deliver Theaetetus from whatever he's pregnant with in regard to knowledge.

THEODORUS: Well, if it's so resolved, we must do it in this way.

SOCRATES: Well, then, Theaetetus, go on and examine still further this much of the following sort about what has been said. You answered that knowledge (was) perception. Didn't you?

THEAETETUS: Yes.

SOCRATES: If then someone should ask you as follows, "By what does (a) human being see the white and black things, and by what does he hear the high and low notes?" You would, I suspect, say, "By eyes and ears."

THEAETETUS: Yes, I would.

C SOCRATES: To be accommodating when it comes to words and phrases and fail to examine them with precision is in many cases not an ignoble trait, but rather, the contrary to it is illiberal. But sometimes it is necessary, just as now it's necessary to get a handle on the answer you give, in what way it's not correct. Consider. Which answer's more correct? By which we see, this is eyes, or through which we see; and by which we hear, ears, or through which we hear?

THEAETETUS: It's my opinion, Socrates that it's rather through which we perceive each several thing than by which.

D SOCRATES: That's because it's surely dreadful, my boy, if many kinds of perceptions sit in us as if in wooden horses, but all these do not strain together toward some single look (*idea*), regardless of whether it's soul or whatever one must call it, by which we perceive through these as if they're tools all the perceived and perceptible things.

THEAETETUS: Well, it's my impression that it's more in the latter way than in the former.

SOCRATES: It's for the following reason, you see, that I'm being such a stickler for precision with you about them—is it by some same kind of thing of ourselves that we attain through eyes white and black things, and through the rest, in turn, some other things?

E And will you be able, on being questioned, to refer all things of the sort to the body? But perhaps it's better for you to speak and answer the question yourself rather than for me to meddle on your behalf. Tell me. Hot things, stiff things, light things, and sweet things—those through which you perceive them, do you set them down severally as belonging to the body? Or is it to something else?

THEAETETUS: Nothing else.

SOCRATES: Will you also be willing to agree that those things which you perceive through another power, it is impossible to perceive *185* them through a different power? For example, what through hearing, through sight, or what through sight, through hearing?

THEAETETUS: Of course I'll be willing.

SOCRATES: Then if you think something about both, you would not have any more through the other tool than through the other a perception of both.

THEAETETUS: Indeed I wouldn't.

SOCRATES: So about sound and about color, first, do you think this very thing about both, that both of the pair are?

THEAETETUS: Yes, I do.

SOCRATES: And each of the two (is) other than each of the two, but the same as itself?

THEAETETUS: Why certainly.   *B*

SOCRATES: And that both of the pair (are) two, and each of the two one?

THEAETETUS: This too.

SOCRATES: And you are further capable of examining whether as a pair they (are) similar or dissimilar to one another?

THEAETETUS: Perhaps.

SOCRATES: So through what do you think all these things about the pair? For it's possible neither through hearing nor through sight to grasp the common thing about them. And there's still this as a piece of evidence for what we're saying. If it should be possible to conduct an examination as to whether both of the pair are salty or not, you know you'll be able to say by what you'll examine it, and this appears as neither sight nor hearing but something else.   *C*

THEAETETUS: Of course it does, it's the power through the tongue.

SOCRATES: What you say is beautiful. But the power through what exactly makes clear to you that which is common in all things as well as that which is common in these, by which you apply the name "is" and "is not," and what we were just now asking about them? What sort of tools will you assign all these through which the perceiving element of us perceives each thing severally?

THEAETETUS: You mean being and to be not and similarity and dissimilarity and "the same" and other[68] and, further, one and the

D   rest of number about them. It's plain that you're asking about both even and odd as well, and everything else that follows them, through which of the things of the body do we perceive them by means of the soul.

SOCRATES: You're following exceedingly well, Theaetetus, and these are the very things I'm asking about.

THEAETETUS: But, by Zeus, Socrates, I for one could not say, except that I'm just of the opinion that there's no private (peculiar) tool of that sort at all for these things as there is for those, but

E   the soul itself through itself, it appears to me, examines the common things about all of them.

SOCRATES: It's because you *are* beautiful, Theaetetus, and not, as Theodorus was saying, ugly. For whoever speaks beautifully (is) beautiful and good. And besides being beautiful you did me a favor and freed me from a very large speech, if it appears to you that the soul itself through itself examines some things, and some things through the powers of the body. For this, which was my opinion too, I wanted it to get to be your opinion as well.

186 THEAETETUS: Well, it does appear to be so.

SOCRATES: In which of the two do you place being? This most particularly follows along in all cases.

THEAETETUS: Well, I place it in those things which the soul by itself aims at (desires).[69]

SOCRATES: And the similar too and the dissimilar and "the same" and other?

THEAETETUS: Yes.

SOCRATES: And what of this? Beautiful and ugly, good and bad?

THEAETETUS: It's my opinion that it's the being of these things in their mutual relations which the soul most especially examines, calcu-

B   lating in itself the past and the present things relative to the future.

SOCRATES: Hold it. Whereas one will perceive the stiffness of the stiff

190 through one's touch, and the softness of the soft likewise—

THEAETETUS: Yes.

SOCRATES: Still, their being, and that the pair of them is, and their contrariety to one another, and the being in turn of the contrariety—does the soul itself go back over them and compare them with each other and try to judge them for us?

THEAETETUS: Yes, of course.

SOCRATES: Aren't there some things that are just there by nature to

C   be perceived for human beings and beasts as soon as they are born—and these are all the experiences that stretch to the soul through the body? But the calculations about these things in regard to being and benefit come about, to whomever they do come about, with difficulty and in much time through a lot of trouble (*pragmata*) and education?

THEAETETUS: That's altogether so.

SOCRATES: Is it possible, then, for him to hit upon truth if he does not even hit upon being?

THEAETETUS: Impossible.

SOCRATES: But if one will fail to hit upon the truth of anything, will one ever be a knower of this?

THEAETETUS: But how could that be, Socrates? *D*

SOCRATES: So in the experiences, after all, there is no knowledge, but there is in reasoning about them; for in this case, it seems, it's possible to touch upon being and truth, but in that case it's impossible.

THEAETETUS: It appears so.

SOCRATES: Do you really then call this and that the same, though the pair of them has so many differences?

THEAETETUS: It's certainly not just, at any rate.

SOCRATES: What name then do you give to that, to seeing, hearing, smelling, feeling cold, feeling hot?

THEAETETUS: I for one name it perceiving. What else?

SOCRATES: So you call it in its entirety perception? *E*

THEAETETUS: It's a necessity.

SOCRATES: For which, we say, there is no share in the possibility of touching on truth, for it cannot on being either.

THEAETETUS: It cannot indeed.

SOCRATES: And so it has no share in knowledge either?

THEAETETUS: No, it doesn't.

SOCRATES: So perception and knowledge, Theaetetus, would never after all be the same.

THEAETETUS: It appears not, Socrates. And it has moreover now become most manifest that knowledge is different from perception.

SOCRATES: Well, it certainly wasn't at all for this purpose that we began *187* conversing, in order that we may find whatever knowledge is not, but what it is. But still and all, we've advanced so far at least, so altogether not to seek it in perception but in that name, whatever the soul has, whenever it alone by itself deals with the things which are.

THEAETETUS: Well, this is called, Socrates, as I believe, to opine.

SOCRATES: Yes, it's right for you to believe it. But wipe out everything before, and now, once more from the beginning, look and see *B* whether you can spy out any better, since you've come so far. And say again whatever is knowledge.

THEAETETUS: Now it's impossible, Socrates, to say it's every kind of opinion, since there is also false opinion, but it's probable that true opinion is knowledge, and let this be stated as my answer, for if it appears to us as we go on not to be so, we'll try, just as we did now, to say something else.

SOCRATES: Yes, that's really the way you must speak Theaetetus, eagerly

C rather than as at first when you hesitated to answer. For if we act in this way, it's one or the other of a pair of things that will follow, either we'll find that toward which we're going, or we'll less believe we know what we in no way know. And for all of that, a wage of this sort is not to be despised. And now in particular what do you assert? When there is of opinion a pair of looks (*ideai*), and one is of the simply true, and one is of the other false, are you defining true opinion as knowledge?

THEAETETUS: Yes I am, for this now appears to me so.

SOCRATES: Is it then still worth it to resume once more about opinion—

THEAETETUS: What sort of thing exactly are you speaking of?

D SOCRATES: It's something that in a sense disquiets me now and often at different times has done so, so as to have got me into a lot of perplexity before myself and before everyone else, when I'm not able to say whatever is this experience we have and in what manner it comes to be in us.

THEAETETUS: What sort of thing exactly?

SOCRATES: The fact of someone opining false things. So I'm considering and I'm still even now in doubt whether we're to let it go, or are we to go on to examine it in a somewhat different way than a little while ago.

THEAETETUS: Why not, Socrates, provided that it appears we should in any sense whatsoever? For just now you and Theodorus were making a good point about leisure—there's nothing urgent in matters of this sort.

SOCRATES: You rightly recalled it, for perhaps it's not inopportune to

E track it, as it were, once more, for it's surely a better thing to accomplish a little well than a lot inadequately.

THEAETETUS: Why certainly.

SOCRATES: How then? What exactly are we saying? We do assert on several occasions there's false opinion, and someone of us is opining false things, and one, in turn, true things, and all on the grounds that it is this way by nature.

THEAETETUS: Yes, we do indeed assert it.

188 SOCRATES: In the case of all things and individually, doesn't this hold for us, either to know or not to know? I dismiss for the moment

learning and forgetting on the grounds that they are between them, for nothing is pertinent there for our speech.

THEAETETUS: Well, Socrates, there's nothing left in the case of each except to know or not to know.

SOCRATES: Isn't it a necessity now that whoever opines, opines either something of the things which he knows or does not know?

THEAETETUS: It's a necessity.

SOCRATES: And yet it's just impossible, if one knows, not to know the same thing, or if one does not know, to know.   *B*

THEAETETUS: Of course.

SOCRATES: Is it the case then that whoever is opining the false believes these things not to be those things which he knows, but some other things of those which he knows, and though he knows both he is in turn ignorant of both?

THEAETETUS: But it's impossible, Socrates.

SOCRATES: Well, does he then believe that whatever he does not know are some other things of whatever he does not know, and this is possible, for him who knows neither Theaetetus nor Socrates to take into his thought that Socrates (is) Theaetetus or Theaetetus Socrates?

THEAETETUS: But how could that be?   *C*

SOCRATES: Well, it's surely not the case that whatever one knows, one believes they are what one does not know, nor in turn whatever one does not know, what one knows.

THEAETETUS: It will be a monster.

SOCRATES: How then would one still come to opine false things? For outside of these, it's surely impossible to opine, inasmuch as either we know or we don't know all things, and in these cases it nowhere appears possible to come to opine false things.

THEAETETUS: Most true.

SOCRATES: Are we then not to examine what we're looking for along these lines by proceeding in terms of knowing and not knowing, *D* but in terms of being and not?

THEAETETUS: How do you mean?

SOCRATES: Maybe it's this simple, that whoever is opining the things which are not about anything whatsoever cannot possibly not opine false things, regardless of whatever different conditions may hold for the state of his thought.

THEAETETUS: Yes, it's likely, Socrates.

SOCRATES: How then? What shall we say, Theaetetus, if someone quizzes us, "But is that which is being said possible for anyone whatsoever, and will any human being opine that which is not, whether about any of the things which are or itself by itself?" And then we shall

E   say, it seems, in reply to this, "Yes, whenever in believing he does not believe what is true." Or how shall we speak?

THEAETETUS: In this way.

SOCRATES: Is there something of this sort also anywhere else?

THEAETETUS: What sort of thing?

SOCRATES: Can someone see something but see nothing?

THEAETETUS: But how?

SOCRATES: But if he sees some one thing at least, he sees something of the things which are. Or do you believe that the one is ever among the things which are not?

THEAETETUS: No, I don't.

SOCRATES: So whoever sees some one thing at least, sees something which is.

THEAETETUS: It appears so.

189   SOCRATES: And so whoever hears something, hears some one thing at least and hears something which is.

THEAETETUS: Yes.

SOCRATES: And besides, whoever touches something, touches some one thing at least and which is, since (it is) one?

THEAETETUS: This too.

SOCRATES: Then whoever opines, doesn't he opine some one thing at least?

THEAETETUS: It's a necessity.

SOCRATES: But whoever's opining some one thing, isn't he opining something which is?

THEAETETUS: I concede it.

SOCRATES: So whoever opines that which is not, opines after all nothing (not even one thing).

THEAETETUS: It appears he does not.

SOCRATES: But whoever then opines nothing is altogether not opining at all.

THEAETETUS: Plainly, it seems.

B   SOCRATES: So it's not possible after all to opine that which is not, either about the things which are or itself by itself.

THEAETETUS: It appears not.

SOCRATES: So to opine what is false is something else than to opine the things which are not.

THEAETETUS: It's something else, it seems.

SOCRATES: So neither in this way nor as we were examining it a little while ago is there false opinion in us.

THEAETETUS: No, there isn't in fact.

SOCRATES: Well, do we then address it with this name when it comes to be in the following way?

THEAETETUS: How?

SOCRATES: It's by being a certain kind of else-opining that we claim there is false opinion. It's whenever someone makes an exchange   C
in his thought of some one of the things which are for something else of the things which are and says it is that. For in this way he's always opining that which is, but it's another instead of an other, and in mistaking that which he was aiming at, he would be justly spoken of as opining false things.

THEAETETUS: It's my opinion that you've now spoken most correctly. For whenever anyone opines (something as) ugly instead of (as) beautiful or beautiful instead of ugly, then truly he's opining false things.

SOCRATES: It's plain, Theaetetus, you despise me and do not fear me.

THEAETETUS: Why exactly?

SOCRATES: You're of the opinion, I suspect, that I would not attack   D
your "truly false," and ask whether slowly swift is possible or heavily light, or it's possible for anything else that's a contrary to become contrary to itself, not in accordance with its own nature, but in accordance with the nature of its contrary. Now as for this, I let it go, so that you may not have gained confidence to no purpose. But it's satisfactory, you say, to opine what is false is to else-opine?

THEAETETUS: It satisfies me at any rate.

SOCRATES: So it is possible, according to your opinion, to set down in one's thought something other as an other and not as that (i.e., other)?

THEAETETUS: Of course it is possible.

SOCRATES: Then whenever the thought of someone does this, isn't it   E
also a necessity that it by itself think either both or the other?

THEAETETUS: Yes, it's a necessity, and either together or in turn.

SOCRATES: Most beautiful! But do you call thinking just what I do?[70]

THEAETETUS: What do you call it?

SOCRATES: A speech which the soul by itself goes through before itself about whatever it is examining. As one who does not know, of course, I'm declaring it to you. Soul thinking looks to me as nothing else than conversing, itself asking and answering itself, and affirming and denying. But whenever it has come to a determi-   *190*
nation, regardless of whether its sally was on the slow or keen side, and then asserts the same thing and does not stand apart in doubt, we set this down as its opinion. Consequently, I for one call opining speaking, and opinion a stated speech; it's not, however, before someone else any more than it's with sound, but in silence before oneself. But what of you?

THEAETETUS: I too.

SOCRATES: So whenever someone opines the other as an other, he then asserts before himself, it seems, the other is an other.

B THEAETETUS: Why certainly.

SOCRATES: Then go ahead and recall whether you ever said before yourself, "It's as certain as can be, you see, the beautiful is ugly," or, "The unjust is just." Or even, and this is the chief point, consider whether you ever did try to persuade yourself, "It's as certain as can be, the other is an other." Or it's wholly the contrary, that not even asleep did you ever yet get the nerve to say before yourself, "It's altogether so after all, the odd is even," or anything else of the sort.

THEAETETUS: What you say is true.

C SOCRATES: But do you believe that anyone else, whether healthy or crazy, had the nerve to speak before himself in all seriousness in persuading himself that it's a necessity for the ox to be a horse or the two one?

THEAETETUS: No, by Zeus, I do not.

SOCRATES: Then if to speak before oneself is to opine, no one, in speaking and opining both, would come to say and opine, in touching on both with his soul, "The other is an other." Now you too must disregard my wording, for I mean it in the following way: no one opines that the ugly (is) beautiful or anything else of the sort.

THEAETETUS: Well, Socrates, I disregard it, and it's my opinion that it is as you say.

SOCRATES: So it's impossible in opining both to opine the other as an other.

THEAETETUS: It seems likely.

SOCRATES: And further, if it's only the other one's opining and in no way the other, one will never opine the other to be an other.

THEAETETUS: What you say is true, for otherwise he would be compelled to touch on that which he is not opining.

E SOCRATES: So there's no room, after all, in opining either both or the other to else-opine. Consequently, if one will define to other-opine as false opinion, one would not be making any sense, and that's because it's evident that neither in this way nor in terms of the former is there false opinion in us.

THEAETETUS: It seems likely that there's not.

SOCRATES: But, Theaetetus, if it will be evident that it is not, we'll be compelled to agree to many strange things.

THEAETETUS: What sorts of things exactly?

SOCRATES: I shan't tell you before I try to examine it in every way, for I would be ashamed on our behalf, in the perplexity in which we are, if we're compelled to agree to the sorts of things I'm speaking of. But if we find a way out and get ourselves free of it, it's then that we'll speak about everyone else as if they're suffering from it, while we stand free and clear of ridicule. But if we turn out to be perplexed in every way, then, I suspect, in all humility we'll hand ourselves over to the speech to be trampled on like the seasick and be handled in whatever way it wants. So listen to the kind of way out I still find for our inquiry. *191*

THEAETETUS: Just speak.

SOCRATES: I'll deny we agreed correctly when we agreed that it's impossible to opine what one does not know to be what one knows and to be deceived, but it's possible in a sense. *B*

THEAETETUS: Do you mean what I even then suspected, when we said it to be of this sort, that sometimes I, being familiar with Socrates, but seeing someone else from a distance with whom I'm not familiar, came to believe he was Socrates whom I know? For in a situation of that sort, there occurs the sort of thing you say.

SOCRATES: Didn't we stand apart and withdraw from it because what we know was making us, though we know, not to know?

THEAETETUS: That's altogether so.

SOCRATES: Then let's not set it down in this way but as follows. Perhaps one will make us some concession, and perhaps one will resist, *C* but in the sort of situation in which we're caught, it's a necessity to twist around every speech and put it to the torture. Consider, then, whether I'm making sense. Is it possible not to know something earlier and understand (learn) it later?

THEAETETUS: Of course it is.

SOCRATES: And at a later time another and another.

THEAETETUS: Why of course.

SOCRATES: Then please set down for talking's sake a wax block in our souls, larger for someone and less for someone else, of purer wax for someone and more fouled for someone else, and stiffer for some and more liquid for some, and for some it's of a measured consistency. *D*

THEAETETUS: I'm setting it down.

SOCRATES: Well, then, let's say it is a gift of Memory, the mother of the Muses, and whatever we want to remember of the things we see, hear, or we ourselves think of, by submitting it to our perceptions and thoughts, we strike off into this, as if we were putting in the seals of signet-rings. And whatever gets impressed, let's say

E   that we remember and know as long as its image is in it, but whatever is wiped off or cannot get impressed, that we forget and do not know.

THEAETETUS: So be it.

SOCRATES: Then observe whether in the following sort of way whoever knows them and is examining any of the things he see or hears, might after all opine what is false.

THEAETETUS: In what sort of way exactly?

SOCRATES: In the belief that what he knows are sometimes what he knows and sometimes what he does not. Our prior agreement that this was impossible was not beautifully agreed on.

THEAETETUS: But now, how do you say it is?

192   SOCRATES: We must make a reckoning of them as follows, by determining from principle that (1) whatever one merely knows, if one gets a memorial of it in the soul, but is not perceiving it, it's impossible to believe it's something other of what one knows, if one has an impress of this too but does not perceive it; and (2) it's impossible to believe that just what one knows is whatever one does not know and does not have a seal of either; and (3) whatever one does not know, whatever else one does not know; and (4) whatever one does not know, what one knows; and (5) what one just perceives, it's impossible to believe it's some other of what one perceives; and (6) what one perceives, it's something of what one does

B   not perceive; and (7) whatever one does not perceive, it's of what one does not perceive; and (8) whatever one does not perceive, of what one perceives. And still further, (9) what one knows and perceives and has the seal of in conformity with the perception, to believe it's some other of what one knows and perceives and has the seal of that too in conformity with the perception, that's still more impossible, if possible, than the former cases. And (10) what one knows and perceives having the memorial of it correctly, it's impossible to believe it's what one knows; and (11) what one knows and perceives having it on the same terms, what one perceives; and (12) what else one does not know and perceive, what

C   one does not know and perceive; and (13) what one does not know and perceive, what one does not know; and (14) what one does not know and perceive, what one does not perceive.[71] It's in the impossibility of anyone opining what is false in these cases that all of them go beyond anything. So it's left in the following sort of cases, if there's anywhere else at all, that something of the sort must occur.

THEAETETUS: In what cases exactly? Maybe I'll get some better understanding from them, for up to now I'm not following.

SOCRATES: In those cases in which one knows, it's possible to believe them some other things of which one knows and perceives; or of what one does not know but perceives; or of what one knows and perceives, of what else one knows and perceives.   *D*

THEAETETUS: But now I'm left much further behind than before.

SOCRATES: Then hear them all over again as follows. If I know Theodorus and remember in myself the sort he is, and Theaetetus likewise, don't I sometimes see them and sometimes not, and touch them at times and sometimes not, and hear them or gain some different perception of them, and sometimes I have no perception of you all, but I remember you no less and I myself know you in myself?

THEAETETUS: Yes, of course.   *E*

SOCRATES: Well, understand, then, that's the first of the things I want to make clear, that it is possible not to perceive what one knows and it is possible to perceive.

THEAETETUS: True.

SOCRATES: And whatever one does not know, it is often possible not to perceive it at all, and it's often possible only to perceive it?

THEAETETUS: This too is possible.

SOCRATES: See then whether you are now following somewhat better.   *193*
If Socrates is familiar with Theodorus and Theaetetus, but sees neither of the two, and there is present to him no different perception about them, he would never come to opine in himself, "Theaetetus is Theodorus." Am I making any sense or not?

THEAETETUS: Yes it's true.

SOCRATES: Well, this was the first of those I was speaking of.

THEAETETUS: Yes, it was.

SOCRATES: Then the second case is when in being familiar with him (you) and unfamiliar with you (him), and on perceiving neither, I would never come to believe that the one I know is the one I don't know.

THEAETETUS: Right.

SOCRATES: And the third case is if I should be unfamiliar with either   *B*
and not be perceiving either, I would not come to believe the one I do not know to be some other of the ones I do not know. And suppose that you've heard once more in order all the rest of the previous cases, in which I shall never opine what is false about you and Theodorus, neither being familiar with nor being ignorant of both, nor being familiar with one and with one not, and about perceptions—it's on the same terms, if after all you follow.

THEAETETUS: I follow.

SOCRATES: To opine the false things, then, is left only for this kind of situation: Whenever in being familiar with you and Theodorus,

C   and having in that waxen thing the ring-seals, as it were, of both of you, I see you both from a distance and not adequately, and in assigning the proper seal of each of the two to its proper sight, I'm eager to set it in and fit it to its own trace, in order that recognition may occur. And then, of all things, I mistake them, and like those who put their shoes on backwards, I exchange them and apply the sight of each to the seal of the other. Or it's even like the experiences of sight in mirrors, when the sight exchanges its flow from right to left;[72] this is when other-opining and to

D   opine what is false result.

THEAETETUS: Yes, it does seem likely, Socrates. The experience of opinion—how amazingly you speak of it.

SOCRATES: Well, there's still further the case when, in being familiar with both, one I perceive (in addition to knowing) and one I don't, but I do not have cognition of the other in conformity with its perception—this is the way I was speaking of it before, when you couldn't understand me.

THEAETETUS: Indeed, I could not.

E   SOCRATES: Well, I meant this, if in being familiar with and perceiving the other, one has the cognition of him in conformity with his perception, one will never believe that he is some other with whom one's familiar and perceives, and of whom, too, one has one's cognition in conformity with his perception. Wasn't this agreed on?

ΤΗΕΑΕΤΕΤUS: Yes.

SOCRATES: But what is now said was surely at least left open. It's the

194   case in which we assert false opinion occurs when being familiar with both and seeing both or having some different perception of both, one does not have the pair of seals in conformity with the perception of each, but like the shooting of a poor bowman, one deviates from the mark and mistakes it—it is precisely this that has in fact been named falsehood.

THEAETETUS: Yes, it's likely enough.

SOCRATES: And so further, whenever perception of one of a pair of seals is present and one is not, and one adjusts the seal of the absent perception to the present perception, in this way thought is wholly deceived. And in a word: about whatever one does not

B   know and never perceived, it is not possible, it seems, either to be deceived (speak falsely) or for there to be false opinion, if we are now saying anything sound. But about what we know and are perceiving, it's in these very cases that opinion whirls and twists about and becomes true and false—true if it brings together its own impressions and (fresh) impresses straightforwardly and in a direct line, but false if it's crosswise and crooked.

THEAETETUS: Isn't it said beautifully, Socrates?

SOCRATES: Well, once you hear this, you'll say it all the more. Now to opine what is true (is) beautiful, and to speak falsely (be deceived) ugly. C

THEAETETUS: Of course.

SOCRATES: They assert, then, that these conditions arise from the following. Whenever the wax in someone's soul is deep, extensive, smooth, and kneaded in a measured way, the things that are proceeding through perceptions, in putting their seals into that feature of the soul which Homer, in hinting at its similarity to wax (*kêros*), said was heart (*kear*),[73] it's then that the seals for them come to be pure in the wax and with adequate depth prove to be long lasting. And people of this sort first of all learn easily and secondly have good memories, and so it's not they who interchange the seals of their perceptions, but they opine what is true. For inasmuch as their seals are plain and have plenty of room, they distribute them quickly to their own several casts,[74] and it's these casts which get called the things which are, and it's these people who get called wise. Or aren't you of this opinion? D

THEAETETUS: Yes, I am, overwhelmingly.

SOCRATES: So whenever the heart of someone is shaggy—it's that which the all-wise poet praised[75]—or whenever it's as dirty as dung and its wax is impure, or it's excessively liquid or stiff, if theirs is liquid they learn easily but prove to be forgetful, and if theirs is stiff, it's the reverse. But whoever have a shaggy, rough, and somewhat stony heart, full of either earth or dung mixed in, they obtain casts without clarity; and theirs are without clarity too who have their casts stiff, for there is no depth to them; and theirs are without clarity too who have them liquid, for they quickly become dim by being confounded. And if, besides all this, they have been made to fall in a heap together on top of one another by the narrowness of the room, if the 'soullet' of anyone is small, the casts are with still less clarity than the former. All these then prove to be the sort who opine what is false, for whenever they see, hear, or think of anything, in their incapacity to assign quickly each to each, they are too slow, and, in distributing what does not belong, they missee, mishear, and misthink most of the time. And it's these who get called fools, and they're said to be deceived about the things which are. E

195

THEAETETUS: What you say, Socrates, couldn't be more correct. B

SOCRATES: Are we to say then that, after all, false opinions are in us?

THEAETETUS: Yes, exactly.

SOCRATES: And true too?

THEAETETUS: True too.

SOCRATES: Do we believe, then, that we have by now adequately agreed upon this, that it's as certain as can be that both of this pair of opinions are?

THEAETETUS: Yes, overwhelmingly.

SOCRATES: In all probability, Theaetetus, a chatterbox of a man is truly a dreadful and unpleasant thing.

THEAETETUS: What of it? What's the point of your remark?

C SOCRATES: It's because I'm distressed at my own incapacity to learn easily and at what's truly just chattering. For what different name would anyone give it, when someone drags his speeches up and down, and by his own dullness is incapable of being convinced, and finds it hard to get free from each speech?

THEAETETUS: But why is it you who's distressed?

SOCRATES: I'm not only distressed but I'm afraid as well as to what answer I'll give if someone asks me, "Socrates, you have found false opinion, have you, and it's neither in one's perceptions relative to one another nor in one's thoughts but in the conjunction

D of perception with thought?" I shall affirm it, I suspect, and preen myself on the grounds that we've found something beautiful.

THEAETETUS: I, at least, am of the opinion, Socrates, that what has now been proved is not ugly.

SOCRATES: "Aren't you saying then," he says, "that, on the one hand, the human being we only think of but do not see, we would never come to believe him to be a horse, which, in turn, we neither see nor touch but only think of and perceive nothing else about it?" I suspect I'll say I'm saying this.

THEAETETUS: Yes, and correctly too.

E SOCRATES: "What then?" he says. "The eleven which one only thinks of and does nothing else about, would one never come to believe, on the basis of this speech, to be twelve, which in turn one only thinks of?" Come now, you answer.

THEAETETUS: Well, I'll answer that though, while seeing or touching, someone might come to believe the eleven to be twelve, but that which he has only in his thought, he would never on this condition come to opine this about it.

SOCRATES: What then? Do you believe that anyone has ever alone in himself proposed to examine five and seven—and I don't mean

196 seven and five human beings or anything of the sort, but five and seven themselves, which we say are there as memorials in the block

and in which case it is impossible to opine what is false—did any human being ever yet examine them by themselves and in speaking before himself and asking how many they are, did one of them say, and believe it, they are eleven, and someone else they're twelve, or does everyone say and believe they are twelve?

THEAETETUS: No, by Zeus. But of course there are many who say and *B* believe they're eleven. Yes, and if one examines in the case of a larger number, one is more liable to make a slip, for I suspect you're speaking of every number.

SOCRATES: Your suspicion's correct. And reflect. Does anything else then happen than the belief that the eleven in the block is the twelve itself?

THEAETETUS: It seems likely at any rate.

SOCRATES: Isn't there then a recurrence to the first speeches? Whoever experiences this believes that which he knows to be another of the things which he knows. And we said this was impossible, and it was due to this that we were making it a necessity for there to *C* be no false opinion, in order that it might not be a necessity for the same person in knowing the same things not to know them at the same time.

THEAETETUS: Most true.

SOCRATES: Then one must show that to opine what is false is anything else whatever than an interchange of thought with perception, for if it were, we would never be deceived in the thoughts by themselves. But as it is, either, you see, false opinion is not, or it's possible not to know what one knows. And which of these do you choose?

THEAETETUS: You're proposing a choice that has no way out, Socrates.

SOCRATES: Well, it's certainly probable that the speech won't allow *D* both. Still and all—one has to have the nerve for everything— what if we should try to be shameless?

THEAETETUS: How?

SOCRATES: By our willingness to say what sort of thing it is to know.

THEAETETUS: And why's this shameless?

SOCRATES: It seems that you don't realize that the entire speech has been for us from the beginning a search of knowledge on the grounds that we do not know whatever it is.

THEAETETUS: No, I realize it.

SOCRATES: And then doesn't it seem shameless if we don't know knowledge to declare what sort of thing it is to know? But as a matter of fact, Theaetetus, we've been infected for a long time now by *E* our conversing impurely, for we've said thousands of times "We recognize" and "We don't recognize," and "We know" and "We don't know," as though we somehow understand one another while still being ignorant of knowledge. And if you want, even now at the very moment we've used again "to be ignorant" and "to understand," as though it were suitable to use them if we're deprived of knowledge.

THEAETETUS: But, Socrates, in what manner will you converse if you abstain from them?

197 SOCRATES: In none, for I am who I am. But what if I were a contradictor? Suppose that sort of man were now here, he would claim that he abstains from them and he would rebuke us vehemently for what I am saying. Since we're no good, then, do you want me to have the nerve to say what sort of thing it is to know? It appears to me there would be some advantage to it.

THEAETETUS: Well, in that case, by Zeus, be nervy. And if you don't abstain from them you'll be much forgiven.

SOCRATES: Have you heard what they're now saying it is to know?

THEAETETUS: Perhaps. I don't, however, remember at the moment.

B SOCRATES: They surely say it is a having of knowledge.

THEAETETUS: True.

SOCRATES: Well, let us change it a little and say it's a possession of knowledge.

THEAETETUS: How exactly will you say this differs from that?

SOCRATES: Perhaps in none. But still listen to what the difference seems to be and join in confirming it.

THEAETETUS: If I can.

SOCRATES: Well, to have appears to me not to be the same as to possess. For example, if someone buys a cloak and becomes its owner but does not wear it, we would deny he has it but he still possesses it.

THEAETETUS: Yes, correctly.

C SOCRATES: Look then and see whether it's possible in this way to possess knowledge and not have it. But it's just as if someone should hunt down wild birds, doves or anything else, and having arranged a dovecote for them bring them up at home—we would surely say that though in some way he always has them, and precisely because he possesses them—Isn't that so?—

THEAETETUS: Yes.

SOCRATES: Still, in a different way he has none of them. But since he's got them under his thumb in his home enclosure, a capacity has
D accrued to him in regard to them, to seize and hold them whenever he wants to, once he's hunted down whichever one he wishes on any occasion, and again to let it go, and it is possible for him to do this as often as he's of that opinion.

THEAETETUS: That is so.

SOCRATES: Once more then, just as when before we were working up in souls some kind of wax mold—I don't quite know what—so now once again let's make in each soul a kind of dovecote of all sorts of birds. Some are in herds apart from the rest, some in small groups, and some are alone and fly through all of them in whatever way they happen to.

THEAETETUS: Let it have been so made. But what follows from it? *E*

SOCRATES: We have to say that this vessel when we're children is empty, and instead of the birds, we have to think knowledges (sciences). And whatever knowledge one acquires and confines in the enclosure, one has to say that he has learned or found the matter (*pragma*) of which this was the knowledge, and this is to know.

THEAETETUS: Let it be.

SOCRATES: Then the fact of hunting down once more whichever of *198* the knowledges one wants, and once one has seized it to hold it and again let go, consider what names it needs, the same as when one was first gaining the possession of them or other. You'll understand with greater clarity what I'm saying from this position. You say there's an arithmetical art?

THEAETETUS: Yes.

SOCRATES: Then suppose this to be a hunting of the knowledges of every even and odd (number).

THEAETETUS: I'm supposing it.

SOCRATES: It's precisely by this art, I suspect, that both he himself has the knowledges of the numbers under his thumb and, in trans- *B* mitting them, transmits them to someone else.

THEAETETUS: Yes.

SOCRATES: And transmitting is that which we call to teach, and receiving to learn, and having, by the fact of possessing in that dovecote, to know.

THEAETETUS: Yes, of course.

SOCRATES: Now pay close attention to that which follows from it. If one is perfectly an arithmetician, does one know anything else than all numbers? For he has knowledges of all numbers in his soul?

THEAETETUS: Why certainly.

SOCRATES: Would someone of this sort ever number anything, by *C* himself and before himself, either the numbers themselves or anything else of the things outside that have number?

THEAETETUS: Of course.

SOCRATES: But to number, shall we set it down to be anything else than the examination of how great a number there happens to be?

THEAETETUS: Just so.

SOCRATES: So it's evident that the one who we've agreed knows every number is examining as though he does not know that which he knows. You surely hear of disputes of this sort.

THEAETETUS: Yes, I do.

D   SOCRATES: Then we, in making our semblance to the possession and hunting of doves, will say that the hunting was twofold, one before the possession for the sake of possession, and one by the possessor for the sake of seizing and having in his hands what he has possessed for some time. It's in this way that for him there were knowledges for some time of the things he once learned and he knew them, and it is possible to learn to know these same things once more by taking up the knowledge of each and holding it, a knowledge he possessed for some time, but which was not ready at hand for his thought?

THEAETETUS: True.

E   SOCRATES: It was precisely this I was just now asking about, as to how one must use the names in speaking about them, whenever the arithmetician goes to number, or the skilled reader to read something, and say, "After all, in a situation of this sort he knows and yet goes once more to learn from himself what he knows?"

THEAETETUS: Well, it's strange, Socrates.

SOCRATES: Well, are we to say that it's what he does not know he'll read and number, though we've granted him to know every letter

199   and every number?

THEAETETUS: But this too makes no sense.

SOCRATES: Do you want us to say, then, that we don't care about the names, in whatever way any one enjoys dragging and tugging at 'to know' and 'to learn'? But since we've determined that the fact of possessing the knowledge is some other thing, and the fact of having it is another, we say it is impossible not to possess whatever one possesses, and so it never turns out that one does not know

B   what one knows, and yet it is possible to seize a false opinion about it? For it's possible not to have the knowledge of this, but another instead of that, whenever in hunting on some occasion some knowledge somewhere, while they're all flying about, one misses and seizes another instead of an other, it's just at that time that one comes to believe the eleven is twelve—when one seizes the knowledge of the eleven in oneself instead of the knowledge of the twelve, as if it were a ring-dove instead of a dove.[76]

THEAETETUS: That indeed makes sense.

SOCRATES: Yes, but whenever one seizes what one is trying to seize, is it then that there's no falsehood and one is opining the things which are? And is it precisely in this way that there is true and *C* false opinion, and nothing at which we were distressed before proves to be a stumbling-block? Perhaps you'll agree with me. Or what will you do?

THEAETETUS: Just so.

SOCRATES: That's because we've got rid of "They don't know what they know." For it turns out that it's no longer the case anywhere that we do not possess what we possess either when we're deceived about something or not. It's my impression, however, that a different, more dreadful experience is coming to light alongside this one.

THEAETETUS: What sort is it?

SOCRATES: It's whether the interchange of knowledges will ever prove to be false opinion.

THEAETETUS: How's that exactly?

SOCRATES: First, the fact that in having a knowledge of something, *D* one is ignorant of this very thing, not by ignorance but by one's own knowledge. Second, to opine another as this and this as the other, how isn't it a lot of nonsense, if with the presence of knowledge the soul comes to know nothing and be ignorant of everything? On the basis of this speech, nothing stands in the way of the presence of ignorance making one know something and blindness making one see, if knowledge in fact will ever make someone ignorant.

THEAETETUS: The reason is perhaps, Socrates, that we were not putting *E* the birds in beautifully when we put in only knowledges, but we should also have put in nonknowledges and have them fly about together with them in the soul. And the hunter sometimes seizes knowledge and sometimes seizes nonknowledge, and by nonknowledge he opines what is false and by knowledge what is true about the same thing.

SOCRATES: It's really not easy, Theaetetus, not to praise you. Do, however, examine once more what you said. Let it be as you say. Whoever then seizes the nonknowledge will opine, you say, what is false. Isn't that so? *200*

THEAETETUS: Yes.

SOCRATES: He surely won't be convinced at any rate that he's opining what is false.

THEAETETUS: How could he?

SOCRATES: But rather what is true, and his state will be as if he knew those things about what he has been deceived.

THEAETETUS: Why certainly.

SOCRATES: So he'll believe he has hunted and has knowledge and not nonknowledge.

THEAETETUS: Plainly.

SOCRATES: Then we went a long way around and are back once more with the first perplexity. For that skilled refuter will laugh and say, "Is it the case, your excellencies, that someone who knows both, knowledge and nonknowledge, believes that the one he knows is some other of what he knows? Or is it that in knowing neither of the pair, he opines that the one he does not know is another of what he does not know? Or one he knows and one he doesn't, and he opines the one he knows to be the one he doesn't know? Or the one he doesn't know, he's convinced it's the one he does know? Or will you tell me once more that there are in turn knowledges of the knowledges and nonknowledges, which their possessor confined in some other ridiculous dovecotes or wax molds and knows as long as he possesses them even if he does not have them ready at hand in his soul? If it's in this way, won't you all be compelled to run around to the same point thousands of times and get nowhere?" What answer shall we give in reply to this, Theaetetus?

THEAETETUS: But, by Zeus, I for one don't know what we should say.

SOCRATES: Doesn't the speech really then, my boy, rebuke us beautifully and point out that we do not correctly seek for false opinion prior to knowledge and let knowledge go? The fact is that it's impossible to come to know it before one grasps knowledge adequately as to whatever it is.

THEAETETUS: It's a necessity, Socrates, at the moment to believe it to be as you say it is.

SOCRATES: What then will one say once more from the beginning knowledge is? We'll surely not give up yet in weariness?

THEAETETUS: Not in the least, unless, that is, you are giving the order.

SOCRATES: Speak then. What could we most of all say it was and least contradict ourselves?

THEAETETUS: Just what we were trying to say before Socrates, for I at any rate don't have anything else.

SOCRATES: What sort of thing?

THEAETETUS: That true opinion is knowledge. To opine what is true surely is at any rate infallible, and everything that comes to be as a result of it becomes beautiful and good.

SOCRATES: The river-guide, Theaetetus, said, "It will show up by itself."[77] So if we go and look for it, perhaps it too might turn up at our feet and show what is sought. But if we stay here, nothing will be plain.

THEAETETUS: You're right to say so. Well, let's go and consider it.

SOCRATES: This does in fact require a brief inquiry. A whole art indicates to you that it is not knowledge.

THEAETETUS: How exactly? And what's this art?

SOCRATES: It's the art of the greatest people in point of wisdom. It's those they call public speakers and advocates.[78] They surely persuade and don't teach by their own art, but they make one opine whatever they want. Or do you believe there are any teachers so uncanny that, in cases where people were robbed of money or *B* experienced some different act of violence, they're capable of teaching adequately, with the clock running, any who were not present on these occasions the truth of what happened?

THEAETETUS: No, I don't believe it, in no way, but persuade, yes.

SOCRATES: And by "persuade," don't you mean to make opine?

THEAETETUS: Why certainly.

SOCRATES: Then whenever jurors are justly persuaded about whatever it's only possible to know if one sees it, but not in a different way, in deciding on these things at that time by hearsay, and in their *C* acceptance of a true opinion, don't they decide without knowledge, though they've been persuaded rightly if they judged well?

THEAETETUS: That's altogether so.

SOCRATES: A tip-top juror, then, my dear, if in the courts true opinion and knowledge were the same, would never opine rightly without knowledge. But as it is, it seems that each of the two is something different.

THEAETETUS: Yes, Socrates, it's what I heard someone say it was but forgot, but now I have it in mind. He said that true opinion with *D* speech was knowledge, but true opinion without speech was outside of knowledge, and of whatever there is not a speech, these things are not knowable—that's just the word he used[79]—and whatever admit of speech are knowable.[80]

SOCRATES: You're really speaking beautifully. But tell at just what point he was dividing these knowable and not knowable things. Maybe you and I have heard it along the same lines.

THEAETETUS: Well, I don't know whether I'll find it out myself; should another speak, however, I suspect I would follow.

SOCRATES: Hear, then, a dream in exchange for a dream. I dreamt *E* that I heard some people say that the first things were just like elements (letters), out of which we and everything else are composed, and they do not admit of speech; that it's only possible to give a name to each thing alone by itself, but it's impossible to address it any differently, either that (how) it is or that (how) it is not. For in that case one would be applying being or nonbeing *202* to it, and one should apply nothing to it if one will speak of it as that thing alone, since none of those must be applied at all—"it," "that," "each," "alone"[81]—and 'this' and many different ones of the same sort neither. For these expressions in running around get applied to everything, being other than the things to which they're applied. But it should be the case, if it were possible for it to be spoken of and have its own proper speech, for it to be spoken of without all these different things, but as it is, it's im-

B   possible for any one of the first things to get stated in speech. For there is nothing else for it except only to get named—for it only has a name—but just as the things that are then composed out of these things are composed by their plaiting, so too their names, once they're plaited together, become a speech. For the plaiting of names is the being of speech—that it's in exactly this way that the elements, though they are without speech and unknowable, are still perceptible, but the syllables are knowable, speakable, and opinable by true opinion. And that, in short, whenever anyone

C   gets the true opinion of anything without speech, his soul tells the truth about it but does not know, for whoever is incapable of giving and receiving an account (speech) is without knowledge of this very fact. But if he gets in addition a speech, he becomes capable in all these respects and is in a perfect condition relative to knowledge. Is it in this way that you've heard the dream or in a different way?

THEAETETUS: No, it's altogether in this way.

SOCRATES: Are you then satisfied and do you set it down for yourself in this way—true opinion with speech is knowledge?

THEAETETUS: Yes, utterly.

D   SOCRATES: Is it really so, Theaetetus, that on this day and in this way we now have grasped what many of the wise sought for a long time and grew old before finding?

THEAETETUS: I, at any rate, Socrates, am of the opinion that the present statement is said beautifully.

SOCRATES: Yes, and it's likely that so far this is just the way it is, for what would knowledge still in fact be, apart from (the) speech and correct opinion? There is, however, one of the things stated which displeases me.

THEAETETUS: What sort exactly?

SOCRATES: It's the point that seems to be most cleverly said, that the elements (are) unknowable, but the genus of the syllables (is)

E   knowable.

THEAETETUS: Isn't that right?

SOCRATES: One has to know. There are paradigms of the speech that we hold like hostages and that he was using when he said all this.

THEAETETUS: What sort exactly?

SOCRATES: The elements and syllables of letters. Or do you believe that he gave a glance anywhere else when the one who spoke said those things which we're saying?

THEAETETUS: No, but at these.

SOCRATES: Let's take them up and put them to the torture—but, rather, *203* let's do it to ourselves—was it in this way or not that we learned letters? Come. First: The syllables admit of (have) speech, but the elements are without speech?

THEAETETUS: Perhaps.

SOCRATES: Yes, of course, rather, and it appears so to me too. Should anyone, at any rate, ask for the first syllable of Socrates in just this way—"Theaetetus, speak what is SO?"—what will you answer?

THEAETETUS: That it's sigma and omega.[82]

SOCRATES: Don't you then have this as a speech of the syllable?

THEAETETUS: Yes, I do.

SOCRATES: Then come, speak in this way too the speech of the sigma. *B*

THEAETETES: But how will one say the elements of the element? The reason is, Socrates, that the sigma belongs to the voiceless. It's only a sound; it's like when the tongue hisses. And of the beta in turn and most of the elements as well there's neither voice nor sound. The saying therefore holds good that they're without speech, since the most vivid of them are the very seven that only have voice and no speech whatever.[83]

SOCRATES: Then it's this, comrade, that we've put right in the case of knowledge.

THEAETETUS: It appears that we have.

SOCRATES: But what of this? That the element is not knowable, but *C* the syllable is—have we accepted that correctly?

THEAETETUS: It's likely at least.

SOCRATES: Come then. Do we mean by the syllable both elements, or if there are more than two, all of them, or some single look (*idea*) that has come to be when they are put together?

THEAETETUS: It's my impression that we mean all of them.

SOCRATES: Look then at the pair, sigma and omega. The first syllable of my name is both. Whoever knows it, does he know them both?

THEAETETUS: Why certainly. *D*

SOCRATES: So he knows the sigma and the omega.

THEAETETUS: Yes.

SOCRATES: And what of this? Is he ignorant of each of the two, and in knowing neither knows both?

THEAETETUS: But that's dreadful, Socrates, and makes no sense (without speech).

SOCRATES: But yet it's the case that if there's a necessity to know each of the two if one will know both, there's every necessity for whoever's going to know a syllable to know first its elements. And in this way the beautiful speech of ours will have run away and be gone.

E THEAETETUS: Yes, and very suddenly too.

SOCRATES: That's because we're not guarding it beautifully. We should not have, perhaps, set down the syllable as the elements, but some single species that has come to be out of them, with its own single look (*idea*) and other than the elements.

THEAETETUS: Yes, of course. And perhaps it might rather be in this way than in that.

SOCRATES: We ought to consider it and not betray in so unmanly a fashion a great and august speech.

THEAETETUS: No, indeed we ought not.

204 SOCRATES: Let it be then as we now claim it is: the syllable comes to be one look (*idea*) out of those several elements that fit together, and it similarly holds no less in letters than in everything else.

THEAETETUS: Yes, of course.

SOCRATES: Then there must be no parts of it.

THEAETETUS: Why's that exactly?

SOCRATES: Because of whatever there are parts, it's a necessity that all the parts be the whole. Or are you saying that the whole too that has come to be out of its parts is some single species other than all its parts?

THEAETETUS: Yes, I am.

B SOCRATES: Are you then calling the all and the whole the same or each of the two other?

THEAETETUS: I don't have anything with clarity, but because you urge me to answer eagerly, I risk it and say, other.

SOCRATES: Well, your eagerness, Theaetetus, is right, and we must examine whether your answer is too.

THEAETETUS: Yes, we certainly must.

SOCRATES: The whole, then, would differ from the all, as is the present speech?

THEAETETUS: Yes.

SOCRATES: And what of this then? Is it possible that all the things and the all differ? For example, whenever we say one, two, three, four, five, six, and we say twice three or thrice two, or four and two, or three and two and one—in all these cases are we saying the same or other?

C

THEAETETUS: The same.

SOCRATES: Is it anything else than six?

THEAETETUS: None else.

SOCRATES: Haven't we then said in each of these kinds of speaking all six?

THEAETETUS: Yes.

SOCRATES: But is there no one all that we're saying in saying them all?

THEAETETUS: It's a necessity.

SOCRATES: Is it anything else than the six?

THEAETETUS: None else.

SOCRATES: So it's the same, then, that we address as the all and all of D
them in at least all those things that are out of number?

THEAETETUS: It appears so.

SOCRATES: Let's then speak as follows about them. The number of the
plethron (100 feet) and the plethron are the same. Aren't they?

THEAETETUS: Yes.

SOCRATES: And the number of the stade (600 feet) likewise?

THEAETETUS: Yes.

SOCRATES: And further, the number of the army and the army, and
similarly for all things of the sort? For all the number is all that
each of them is?

THEAETETUS: Yes.

SOCRATES: And the number of several things isn't anything else, is it, E
than parts?

THEAETETUS: None else.

SOCRATES: So however many parts it has, it would be out of parts?

THEAETETUS: It appears so.

SOCRATES: Yes, and it's been agreed upon that also all the parts are
the all, provided that all the number will be the all.

THEAETETUS: Just so.

SOCRATES: So the whole, then, is not out of parts, for otherwise it
would be an all in being all the parts.

THEAETETUS: It seems likely that it's not.

SOCRATES: But is a part which is just what it is, of anything else whatever than of the whole?

THEAETETUS: Yes, of the all.

SOCRATES: You're fighting in a manly way at least, Theaetetus. But 205
isn't the all, whenever nothing is absent, this very thing, all?

THEAETETUS: It's a necessity.

SOCRATES: But won't a whole be this same thing, from whatever nothing in any way stands apart? But from whatever there is a standing
apart, it is neither a whole nor an all, and that is the same result
for both of them at once out of the same?[84]

THEAETETUS: I'm now of the opinion that an all and a whole do not differ.

SOCRATES: Weren't we saying, then, that of whatever there are parts, the whole and all will be all the parts?

THEAETETUS: Certainly.

SOCRATES: Once more then—it's just that which I was trying to get at—if the syllable is not the elements, isn't it a necessity for it not to have the elements as its own parts, or if it is the same as them, it's a necessity that it be as knowable as they are?

THEAETETUS: Just so.

SOCRATES: Didn't we then set it down as other than them in order that this might not occur?

THEAETETUS: Yes.

SOCRATES: And what of this? If the elements are not parts of a syllable, can you speak of some different things which, though they are parts of a syllable, are not, however, its elements?

THEAETETUS: In no way, for should I concede, Socrates, that there are some proper parts of it, it's surely laughable to dismiss the elements and go to different things.

SOCRATES: Then according to the present speech, Theaetetus, a syllable must be some single look (*idea*) altogether indivisible into parts.

THEAETETUS: It seems likely.

SOCRATES: Do you remember, then, my dear, that a little while ago we welcomed the assertion, in the conviction that it was a good point, that speech is not of the first things out of which everything else is composed—inasmuch as each of them, itself by itself, was noncomposite—and it wasn't right to speak about it by applying even 'to be' to it, or 'this' either, on the grounds that they are other and spoken of as not their own but alien to them, and it was this cause precisely that made it be without speech and unknowable?

THEAETETUS: I remember.

SOCRATES: Is there really, then, anything else than this that's the cause of its being single-specied and not divisible into parts? I for one don't see anything else.

THEAETETUS: It really does appear that there isn't.

SOCRATES: Hasn't the syllable then fallen into the same species as that, if it does not have parts and is a single look (*idea*)?

THEAETETUS: That's altogether so.

SOCRATES: So if the syllable is many elements and some kind of whole, and these are its parts, then the syllables are as knowable and sayable as the elements, since all the parts came to light as the same as the whole.

THEAETETUS: Yes indeed.　　　　　　　　　　　　　　　　　　　*E*

SOCRATES: Yes, but if it's one and without parts, a syllable no less than an element is in the same way without speech and unknowable, for the same cause will make them be of the same sort.

THEAETETUS: I cannot speak differently.

SOCRATES: So let's not accept this, whoever says a syllable's knowable and speakable, but for an element it's the contrary.

THEAETETUS: Let's not, provided we're to obey the speech.

SOCRATES: And what of this in turn? Wouldn't you rather accept, on　*206*
the basis of what you yourself know about your own learning of letters, someone's saying the contrary?

THEAETETUS: What sort of thing?

SOCRATES: That you continued to do nothing else in learning than to try to recognize the elements distinctly in sight and in hearing, each one itself by itself, in order that their placement when being spoken and written might not perturb you.

THEAETETUS: What you say is most true.

SOCRATES: And in the lyre-player's studio, to have learned perfectly, was it anything else than the capacity to attend to each note, of　*B*
what sort of chord it was? It's these that everyone would agree are spoken of as the elements of music?

THEAETETUS: Nothing else.

SOCRATES: So, after all, in the case of the elements and syllables we ourselves have experience of, if one has to transfer the evidence from them to everything else, we'll say that, in point of grasping each lesson perfectly, the genus of the elements admits of a knowledge more vivid and authoritative than that of the syllable. And if anyone says a syllable is by nature knowable and an element unknowable, we'll be convinced that, willingly or unwillingly, he's being playful.

THEAETETUS: Yes, utterly.

SOCRATES: Well, my impression is that still different proofs of this　*C*
would also come to light. But let them not make us forget to look at that which lies before us—whatever is meant exactly by saying that if a speech is added to true opinion, the most complete and perfect knowledge is the result.

THEAETETUS: We must indeed look at it.

SOCRATES: Come then. Whatever does it want 'speech' to signify for us? It's my impression that it's saying some one of three things.

THEAETETUS: Which exactly?

SOCRATES: The first would be that speech is that which makes one's　*D* own thought evident through sound with words and phrases, just as if it were into a mirror or water one was striking off one's opinion into the stream through one's mouth. Or isn't it your impression that speech is of this sort?

THEAETETUS: Yes, it is. We say, at any rate, that whoever's doing it is speaking.

SOCRATES: Isn't it the case, then, that everyone, whoever's not dumb or mute at the start is capable of doing (making) this at least, regardless of whether it's more quickly or more slowly—the indication of what his opinion is about each thing? And in this way *E* as many as opine something rightly, all will evidently have it with speech, and in no case will right opinion any longer prove to be apart from knowledge?

THEAETETUS: True.

SOCRATES: Well, let's not too readily issue a condemnation, to the effect that whoever declared knowledge to be what we're now examining has made no sense at all. For perhaps the speaker was not saying this, but rather that it's the capacity, when asked what each thing *207* (is), to give the answer back to the questioner through the elements.

THEAETETUS: What are you saying, Socrates? Give an example.

SOCRATES: It's just as Hesiod in fact speaks about a wagon, "But the timbers of a wagon are one hundred."[85] I for one would not have the capacity to tell them, and I suspect that you wouldn't either, but we would be content should we be asked what a wagon is, if we could say, "Wheels, axle, carriage-body, rails, yoke."

THEAETETUS: Yes, of course.

SOCRATES: Yes, but he would perhaps believe us to be ridiculous, just as if we were asked about your name and answered syllable by *B* syllable. Because, though in this case we're opining and speaking rightly what we're speaking, we believe we're skilled in letters and know (have) and speak in a letter-skilled way the speech of Theaetetus' name. But the fact is, he'd believe, it is impossible to say anything scientifically (knowledgeably) before one goes through each through its elements from end to end with true opinion, and this surely was stated also in the previous remarks.

THEAETETUS: Yes, it was stated.

SOCRATES: Well, then, is it in this way too that he'd believe we have a right opinion about a wagon? But that whoever has the capacity *C* to explicate its being through those hundred things of it, by his addition of this, has added speech to his true opinion, and has become, instead of an opiner, artfully competent and a knower of a wagon's being, because he has gone through the whole through its elements from end to end?

THEAETETUS: Isn't it your impression that it's good, Socrates?

SOCRATES: Tell me whether it's yours, comrade, and whether you accept the procedure through elements to be speech about each thing, while the procedure which is syllable by syllable or is in terms of something greater still is not-speech (*alogia*), in order that we may go on to examine it.   *D*

THEAETETUS: Well, I very much accept it.

SOCRATES: Are you, in accepting it, convinced that anyone whatever is a knower of anything whatever, when he's of the opinion that the same thing belongs at times to the same thing and at times to another, or whenever he opines that another belongs at times to the same thing and at times an other?

THEAETETUS: No, by Zeus, I do not.

SOCRATES: Is it, then, that you don't remember that you and everyone else does this when you start to learn the letters?

THEAETETUS: Are you saying that in the case of the same syllable, we *E* believe another letter belongs at times to it and at times an other, and we put the same letter at times into the appropriate syllable and at times into a different syllable?

SOCRATES: That's what I'm saying.

THEAETETUS: Well, by Zeus, I'm not one to forget it, and I'm convinced as well that those whose condition is this do not know as yet.

SOCRATES: What then? Whenever on an occasion of this sort, someone in writing "Theaetetus" believes he must write theta and epsilon and writes it, and then, in turn, in trying to write "Theodorus," believes he must write tau and epsilon and writes it, shall we claim *208* that he knows the first syllable of your names?

THEAETETUS: But we just now agreed that whoever's condition is this does not know as yet.

SOCRATES: Does anything then stand in the way of the same person being in this condition also in regard to the second, third, and fourth syllable?

THEAETETUS: No, nothing.

SOCRATES: Won't he then, at that time, in keeping to the procedure through elements write "Theaetetus" with right opinion, whenever he writes it in succession?

THEAETETUS: That's plainly so.

SOCRATES: Though he's still without knowledge but opines what is *B* right, as we claim?

THEAETETUS: Yes.

SOCRATES: Even though he has speech with right opinion, for while he was writing, he was maintaining his way through the elements, and it's this which we agreed was speech.

THEAETETUS: True.

SOCRATES: So there is after all, comrade, right opinion with speech, which one must not yet call knowledge.

THEAETETUS: Probably.

SOCRATES: Then, it seems, we grew rich just on a dream, in our belief
C   that we had the truest speech of knowledge. Or are we not yet to issue an accusation? For perhaps one will not define it as this, but as the remaining species of the three, just one of which, we said, he will set down as speech, whoever defines knowledge to be right opinion with speech.

THEAETETUS: You recalled it rightly, for there's still one left. One was the image, as it were, of thought in sound, and one was just stated, a going to the whole through elements. But what exactly are you saying is the third?

SOCRATES: It's just what the many would say, to have some sign to say by means of which that which is asked about differs from all things.

THEAETETUS: What speech of what do you have to tell me by way of an example?

D SOCRATES: For example, if you want, in the case of the sun, I suspect this would be enough for you to accept it: "It is the most brilliant of the things that go around the earth across the sky."

THEAETETUS: Yes, of course.

SOCRATES: Take it, then, for the sake of which it has been spoken. It is exactly what we were just now saying it is: "If you take the difference of each thing by which it differs from everything else, you'll take, as some say, a speech; but as long as you touch on anything in common, the speech will be for you about those things, whichever they are, of which the commonness is."

E THEAETETUS: I understand. And it's my impression that it's beautiful to call something of the sort a speech.

SOCRATES: But whoever with right opinion takes in addition the difference from all the rest of anything whatever of the things which are will have become a knower of that of which he was previously an opiner.

THEAETETUS: Yes indeed, we say that.

SOCRATES: Now all of a sudden, Theaetetus, I don't understand anything at all, not even a little, since I've got too near to what is being said, just as if it were a shadowpainting. For as long as I stood way off from it, it appeared to me that something was being said.

THEAETETUS: How and why is that?

209 SOCRATES: I'll point it out if I can. If I for one have a right opinion

about you and take in addition the speech about you, that's exactly when I know you, but if not, I only opine.

THEAETETUS: Yes.

SOCRATES: Yes, but the interpretation of your difference was agreed to be a speech.

THEAETETUS: Just so.

SOCRATES: Then when I was only opining, whatever else I was doing, I was touching in my thought on not one of those things by which you differ from everything else.

THEAETETUS: It seems likely that you weren't.

SOCRATES: So I was thinking something of the common things, none of which you have any more than anyone else.

THEAETETUS: It's a necessity.

SOCRATES: Come then, by Zeus. However in a situation of this sort was I opining you rather than anyone else whatsoever? Set me down as thinking, "Here is Theaetetus, whoever is a human being and has a nose and eyes and mouth and so on for each of his limbs." Is it possible that this thought will make me think Theaetetus rather than Theodorus, or the most remote of the proverbial Mysians?[86]

THEAETETUS: How could it?

SOCRATES: But if I think not only the one who has a nose and eyes, but also the snub-nosed and exophthalmic, shall I any the more opine you rather than myself or all who are of this sort?

THEAETETUS: Not at all.

SOCRATES: But, I suspect, Theaetetus will not be opined in me before this snubness of yours lays down a memorial in me that stamps its difference from all the rest of the snubnesses I have seen, and in this way for all the rest of the things out of which you are—which will remind me—if in fact I meet you tomorrow and make me opine rightly about you.

THEAETETUS: Most true.

SOCRATES: So right opinion too would be about the difference of each thing.

THEAETETUS: It appears so at least.

SOCRATES: Then the fact of taking a speech in addition to right opinion would still be what? For if, on the one hand, it tells one to opine in addition in what way something differs from everything else, the injunction proves to be very ridiculous.

THEAETETUS: How?

SOCRATES: Of those things of which we have right opinion, by which they differ from everything else, it urges us to take in addition a right opinion of these things by which they differ from everything

else. And if this is the case, compared to this injunction, the pro-
E verbial twirling of a baton, a pestle, or whatever names it goes
by,[87] would be as nothing in point of nonsense. And this injunction
would more justly be called the exhortation of a blind man. For
to command us to take in addition those things which we have,
in order that we may understand (learn) what we're opining, does
resemble in a very grand manner a man who is wholly in the dark.

THEAETETUS: Then say what you just now put as if it were a question.[88]

SOCRATES: If to take a speech in addition, my boy, urges us to come
to know but not just to opine the difference, what a pleasantry
the most beautiful speech of all about knowledge would be! For
210 to come to know is surely to take knowledge, isn't it?

THEAETETUS: Yes.

SOCRATES: Then, it seems, if the speech is asked what knowledge is,
it will answer, "Right opinion with knowledge of difference," for
according to it, this would be the supplementary taking of a speech.

THEAETETUS: It seems likely.

SOCRATES: And it's really altogether naive, when we are seeking knowledge, for the speech to state it to be right opinion with knowledge,
whether of difference or anything whatever. So knowledge,
Theaetetus, would not, after all, be perception, true opinion, or
B a speech that's getting added to true opinion.

THEAETETUS: It seems unlikely.

SOCRATES: Are we then still pregnant with something, and still suffering labor-pains, my dear, about knowledge, or have we given
birth to everything?

THEAETETUS: Yes, by Zeus, and I for one have said even more on
account of you than all I used to have in myself.

SOCRATES: Doesn't our maieutic art then declare all these to have been
born as wind-eggs and unworthy of nurture?

THEAETETUS: That's altogether so.

C SOCRATES: Well, then, if you try to become pregnant, Theaetetus, with
different things after this, and you do become so, you'll be full
of better things on account of the present review. And if you're
empty, you'll be less hard on your associates and tamer, believing
in a moderate way that you don't know what you don't know. My
art is only capable of so much and no more, and I don't know
anything at all which everyone else does, all those who are and
have been great and amazing men. But my mother and I have
obtained from a god as our lot this midwifery, she of women, and
D I of the young and noble and all the beautiful. Now, however, I
have to go to the porch of the king and meet the indictment of
Meletus which he's drawn up against me. But at dawn, Theodorus,
let's come back here to meet.

Theaetetus Commentary

I. MEGARIANS
(142a1–143c7)

All Platonic dialogues are written, but only the *Theaetetus* presents most of itself as written. Its author is not Plato. The voice is the voice of Plato, but the hand is the hand of Euclides. We owe, however, its publication to Plato. A short dialogue of his own between Euclides and Terpsion makes Euclides' work known to us. Euclides seems to think, in any case, that without the kind of explanation he gives Terpsion, which Plato himself never thought necessary for his own dialogues, his writing is defective. The dialogue, then, has two authors, Plato and Euclides. The Platonic part seems superfluous. Its absence would leave us with a nonnarrated dialogue as complete in itself as *Euthyphro* or *Laws*. We would not then know Euclides' "principles of composition," nor that Theaetetus later distinguished himself in battle. But neither the change from narration to drama nor the sufferings of a mathematician can remotely bear on Socrates' penultimate question, What is knowledge? Plato thought otherwise.

The structure of the *Theaetetus* most resembles that of the *Protagoras*. There Socrates meets a comrade with whom he discusses the beauty of Alcibiades and the greater beauty of Protagoras, and on the comrade's prompting he reports the conversation he just had with Protagoras. His talk with the comrade is over after twenty-one exchanges. Here Euclides meets his friend Terpsion to whom he reports Theaetetus' dying, and on Terpsion's prompting he has a slave read to them both the conversation he has written up that Socrates once had with Theaetetus and Theodorus. His talk with Terpsion lasts for twenty-one exchanges. The *Protagoras* discusses for much of its length the problematic unity of virtue, and it ends with Socrates' suggestion that, if the good is the pleasant, what we need is a science of hedonistic measurement. The *Theaetetus* poses the problem of the unity of knowledge. For much of its length, Socrates explores with two mathematicians the Protagorean thesis that if knowledge is perception, man is the measure of all things. Protagoras determines the course of the *Theaetetus,* absent though he is and represented only by lukewarm adherents, as much as he determines the course of the *Protagoras*.

In both dialogues, Socrates is the narrator. In the *Protagoras* he reports almost directly to us; in the *Theaetetus* he reported to Euclides, who then took the trouble to eliminate Socrates as the source of his dialogue. He is less faithful to what he had heard than either the *Symposium*'s Apollodorus or the *Parmenides'* Cephalus, both of whom usually keep themselves distinct from the several voices of their informants. Euclides, in contrast, in eliminating Socrates, also eliminates himself. Confronted with the minor difficulty of separating "He (Socrates) said that he (Socrates) said" from "He (Socrates) said that he (Theaetetus or Theodorus) said," Euclides took the easy way out. He tells Terpsion that he dropped Socrates' "I said" and Theaetetus' "He agreed," or "He did not agree;" but he seems to be unaware that, for all the care he took to get his transcription exactly right, he was forced to find verbal equivalents for what might have been just a nod or shake of the head. As a Megarian, Euclides recognizes nothing but speech;[1] for all we know, Theaetetus might have reluctantly agreed to something or Theodorus fidgeted in annoyance.

The two advantages that narration has over drama—in giving us not only the sweat of Thrasymachus or the blush of Charmides, but also Socrates' understanding of what his interlocutors had in mind in saying what they did and what his own intentions were—all this vanishes in Euclides' representation. In a dialogue about knowledge, the body in its manifestations of what the soul harbors seems to be suppressed along with the silent thinking of the mind. Indeed, the dialogue's most obvious defect seems to consist in its failure to consider knowledge in its relation to learning, intention, and understanding. Socrates does distinguish between understanding what Parmenides said and what Parmenides' speech intended, but the very context in which he makes the remark prevents it from affecting the discussion. Only the explicit and utterable are admitted by Euclides or acknowledged by Theaetetus and Theodorus. The verbatim account of Euclides would thus echo the literalness of Theaetetus and Theodorus.

Euclides' manner of writing does not preclude the possibility that within its limitations ways could be found to express both bodily movements and silent intentions, but it would surely require that Euclides be as skilled as Plato. Rather than to attribute to Euclides so large a talent, we could suppose that either Socrates said nothing about any-one's expressions or intentions and refrained from all interpretation, or Socrates himself, knowing the pedantry of Euclides (Socrates chose him, after all, as the most suitable recorder of this dialogue), smuggled into the speeches all that he suspected Euclides would have otherwise omitted. We should then have in Euclides' writing virtually a writing of Socrates, his own testament, as it were, of his perplexity. In light of the question it raises, the *Theaetetus* is more comprehensively scep-tical than any other so-called sceptical dialogue. As the first of the seven dialogues that present the last days of Socrates, it lies at the opposite pole from the last of them, which in its assertion of the soul's immortality appears to be the most dogmatic. Plato has fittingly as-signed to a Megarian the apparent scepticism in Socratic philosophy, and to the Pythagoraean Phaedo its equally apparent dogmatism.

The time at which Socrates' conversation with Theaetetus and Theodorus occurred is not the time during which we must imagine ourselves to be reading the *Theaetetus*. We read it while the dying Theaetetus is being carried from Megara to Athens; it occurred just prior to Socrates' meeting with Euthyphro and his subsequent hearing of the indictment against him at the stoa of the King Archon. We are reading it not because it pertains, in Euclides' opinion, to the trial and death of Socrates, but because Euclides recalls with wonder Soc-rates' divination that Theaetetus was fated, if he lived, to become renowned. We can well wonder at Euclides' wonder. It would not have required a Socrates to make so easy a prediction. Theodorus divines as well as Socrates Theaetetus' potentiality. Euclides, however, again as a good Megarian, would have to deny the existence of potentiality,[2] and hence the confirmation of Socrates' total confidence in Theae-tetus' future could hardly seem to him to be less than a miracle. Now that Theaetetus is almost dead, he can safely bring to light, without fear of any Solonian doubt, the evidence from which Socrates inferred the future. We ourselves, however, must not connect the dialogue with the pathetic but philosophically trivial occasion of Theaetetus' dying, but with the far from trivial death of Socrates. We must turn away from the military and patriotic death of Theaetetus to the ju-dicially criminal death of Socrates. Behind the memorial to a math-ematician lurks his apparent look-alike, the philosopher.

In calling our attention to the dialogue as written, and the almost Thucydidean effort Euclides spent on translating his notes into a complete record, Plato rehearses on the level of historiography the problem with which the dialogue deals. Does the recording of what happened stand to what happened as the knowledge of what is stands to what is? Euclides presents what has happened as if it were happening now; he has suppressed the difference of time and place. Should, then, the knowledge of what is likewise present what is? But how can knowledge avoid a representation of what is? Is knowledge to eliminate its own speeches? Knowledge would then be nothing but immediate, and all reasoning would prove suspect. If, however, we are not to imitate Euclides but set the knowledge of what is apart from what is, how can this apartness consist with its title to be knowledge? We seem forced to choose between an immediacy that is unavailable and a mediacy that is uneliminable. The distortion Euclides was compelled to introduce into his writing, which thus only looks as if we are overhearing the speeches of Socrates, Theaetetus, and Theodorus, is more incorrigible but less serious than the abstraction he might have made from Socrates' account.

Euclides gives the speeches by themselves, the raw material from which we might be able to recover the several intentions and degrees of understanding of the speakers. Our discovery of their intentions and understanding would bring us to the action, the deeds, which animate the speeches, and we should then know their causes. If interpretation of the *Theaetetus* or any other Platonic dialogue precisely consists in this, can we suppose it to be the model to serve us for getting out of the dilemma with which the problem of knowledge confronts us? Can "the weakness of speeches" be circumvented through a comparable effort to discover the deeds, the beings, apart from which but of which the speeches of knowledge are? To chart the concealment and the revelation, which are inseparable from the kind of imitation Plato employs, could itself be the proper beginning for resolving the perplexity with which Socrates and Theaetetus end.

II. Looks and Likeness
(143d1–146c6)

The Euclidean part of the dialogue begins with Socrates asking Theodorus whether he has met among the Athenian young who care for geometry or some other kind of philosophy any who are likely to prove proficient. Socrates' greater love of Athenians does not fully explain why he asks such a question now. If Socrates were not old, and Meletus' indictment did not threaten him, we could suppose that Theodorus is to act as Socrates' talent scout. No one would say that Socrates, in divining the coming of the Eleatic stranger in the *Sophist*, anticipates the need to have at hand the proper interlocutor for the discussion of the sophist. Is Socrates, then, looking for his own successor—someone who will continue philosophy in Athens after him?

But Socrates already knows Plato, and the circumstances now are not like those before Plato's birth in the *Charmides,* where on Socrates' return from Potidaea (the prelude to the Peloponnesian War), he asks, in his concern for philosophy in Athens, whether anyone in his absence has come to be outstanding in wisdom, beauty, or both.

Theaetetus turns out to be among all the young men that Plato ever has Socrates converse with the most prominent within the field of philosophy. Theaetetus and Theodorus are the only "scientists"—the only theoretical men—that we meet in argument with Socrates. Both perhaps become a little less naive as a result of this one encounter, but neither turns fully to philosophy. Theodorus has already rejected it as "bare speeches," and Theaetetus merely pursued, as far as we know, the same inquiries he had already begun before he met Socrates. Socrates surely did not succeed in getting the best out of Theaetetus, for he thanks Theodorus for his acquaintance with Theaetetus only after he has listened to the stranger's conversation with him.[3] Was Socrates not competent to examine mathematicians? That he later proposes to question young Socrates implies no such disability.[4] Perhaps his relative failure with Theaetetus is indispensable for the stranger's success. The *Sophist* offers us a unique "control" for checking up on how much Theaetetus learned from Socrates. If Theaetetus had proved to be of another sort—someone for whom Socrates could have been of decisive help—would Socrates have tried to stay alive by conducting a different defense? Does Theaetetus' becoming as barren as Socrates himself determine Socrates' suicidal defense?

Theodorus praises Theaetetus at some length without once mentioning his name. This unnamed Athenian had had the discernment to associate voluntarily with Theodorus; he had chosen not to associate with Socrates, despite his interest in the questions he knew that Socrates raised. The dizziness these questions induce in him is no hindrance to his learning all he can from Theodorus. Socratic philosophy is, to say the least, not indispensable for making great discoveries in mathematics, and mathematicians themselves seem to be wholly immune to philosophy if neither Theodorus nor Theaetetus sees any difficulty in accepting the view that knowledge is perception. In the face of both Socratic and Protagorean doubts, they are serenely confident in their own competence. Science and scientists look on as neutrals at the conflicts within philosophy. Theodorus, however, cannot praise Theaetetus without defending himself against the possible charge that his appraisal is not altogether dispassionate. He is more afraid that he might be thought to be in love with Theaetetus than he is concerned with the consequences for his discipline of "bare speeches." He is certainly less afraid to offend Socrates than to be thought Theaetetus' partisan. Paederasty is far worse a charge than lack of urbanity. In the only Platonic dialogue Plato did not write, Socrates is told to his face that he is ugly. Since Theaetetus looks almost as repulsive as Socrates, Theodorus assumes either that no one could possible love Theaetetus or Socrates—Alcibiades notwithstanding—or that Theaetetus' ugliness protects him against the charge. He thinks he has adequately forestalled the accusation that he has corrupted Theaetetus.

Theaetetus has all the qualities except gracefulness that Socrates lists as prerequisites for potential philosophers.[5] He is outstanding in docility, gentleness, and manliness. He seems to be already the perfect offspring of the union between moderation and courage that the Eleatic stranger later suggests the stateman's art must effect. Socrates, however, tells Theaetetus at the end that the conversation at least has gentled him even more, so that in his moderation he does not believe he knows what he does not know. Socrates was apparently unable to enhance Theaetetus' natural gentleness without sacrificing his manliness. Theodorus, on the other hand, believes it is less difficult to combine gentleness with manliness than either or both of them with docility. The gentle are stupid, the quick-witted mad; or, since the quick-witted are impatient and prone to anger, while the more easygoing are sluggish and forgetful, Theodorus implies that the just are likely to be stupid and the smart unjust. Theodorus uses two images to convey to Socrates how remarkable Theaetetus is. The first likens him to a ballasted ship. Wind and waves are the medium through which the learner must go, and as these elements are naturally in a turbulent state, if one does not counteract them with one's own weightiness, they are apt to carry one away. The medium of knowledge, one would say, does not by itself lead to knowledge. The second image likens Theaetetus to a silently flowing stream of olive oil. The medium of knowledge would be the learner himself. Nothing outside him resists the way he slowly takes. Theodorus' two images do not exactly agree with one another. His competence in mathematics does not support him in his attempt at poetry.

Socrates seems to be rather obtuse if he cannot figure out from Theodorus' speech that the son of Euphronius is meant. How many Athenians could there be who look like a youthful Silenus? A surer way of identifying him would be for Theodorus to tell Socrates his father's name. Theodorus does not remember the name; he appeals instead to sight: Theaetetus is the one in the middle of an odd number of freshly oiled young men who are approaching them. Socrates then recognizes him. He is far from being as unique as Theodorus thinks. His father was just like him. Theodorus then gives Theaetetus' name;

he adds that Theaetetus' guardians are thought to have dissipated the large estate of his father, but Theaetetus is still marvelously liberal. Socrates is finally impressed: "How grand a nobleman you speak of." Socrates throughout shows himself as rather parochial and more concerned with superficial things like genealogy, names, and money than with Theodorus' enthusiastic analysis of Theaetetus' soul. But from the point of view of knowledge, does "son of the Athenian Euphronius" less surely identify Theaetetus than Theodorus' speech? At a distance, Theodorus could mistake Theaetetus for Socrates; Socrates could never confuse them. If we ask what is knowledge, we must ask whether, as well as how, knowledge of resemblance, knowledge of soul, knowledge of body, and knowledge of names form a unity. To answer that each is due to perception and memory does not do away with the manifest differences among them.

Socrates has Theodorus call Theaetetus over so that he can examine what kind of face he himself has. Has Socrates never looked in a mirror? Theaetetus, after all, is not as exopthalmic as he is, but because he is not looking at his own face, the love of his own will not interfere with his deciding whether he is ugly. Socrates is far too urbane, of course, to tell Theaetetus that his teacher finds him ugly. He does not initially raise the problem of knowledge because of Theodorus' praise of Theaetetus, but because Theodorus had invoked a standard (beauty) in asserting the likeness of Socrates and Theaetetus. He wants to know how Theodorus' praise and blame fit with his discernment of likeness; that is, he questions Theodorus' competence not only to assert that Theaetetus is ugly if he is not a painter but to make likenesses of Theaetetus' soul if he is not a poet.

Socrates gives a single example. If Theodorus had said that Socrates and Theaetetus had each a lyre that was likewise tuned, they would only trust him if he were skilled in music; otherwise, they would examine whether he was so skilled, and if not, they would distrust him. Theaetetus takes the arts so much for granted that he does not ask how without being an expert oneself, in which case trust in another expert would be superfluous, they could proceed to examine Theodorus' competence in music. Theodorus is now teaching Theaetetus advanced music. Socrates, in any case, distinguishes between trust and knowledge, and thereby demolishes in advance Theaetetus' later proposal that knowledge is true opinion. Socrates, furthermore, in having Theaetetus deny that Theodorus is a painter but allowing him to be a geometrician, seems to distinguish between the kind of proportional beauty a mathematician could know, of which a tuned lyre would be an example, from the beauty of the human face, to which Theodorus' mathematics gives no access. He implies that the knowledge of human beauty falls as much outside the knowledge of proportion as does the knowledge of the differences of rank among the statesman, philosopher, and sophist. Euclides calls the dying, sick, and wounded Theaetetus beautiful and good.

After having gently instructed Theaetetus that neither should mind if a nonexpert like Theodorus calls them ugly, Socrates turns to Theodorus' praise of Theaetetus' soul. Not what uninformed opinion says but only the view of experts counts. There is an extraordinary lack of parallelism between the model Socrates has set up for testing competence in the arts and the way he now proposes to handle the praise of Theaetetus' soul. It is no longer a question of resemblance but of Theaetetus' difference from almost everyone else, and Socrates does not even stop to ask whether Theodorus is an expert in souls. Theaetetus and Socrates can dismiss Theodorus' opinion about their ugliness even if they were interested in such a question, but whoever hears the praise of another in point of virtue and wisdom should at once be as eager to examine the praised as the praised should be eager to exhibit himself. They have no time to look for other experts. Either there are no other experts whom they could trust, Socrates sets himself up as the expert in souls, or they can join together in examining Theaetetus' soul without either of them being an expert. Regardless of whether Theodorus is an amateur or an expert, Socrates proposes that they test his praise themselves. He proposes that what at best could be only trust be replaced by knowledge.

Although Theaetetus agrees with Socrates in principle, he shies away from displaying himself. He fears that Theodorus spoke in jest. Socrates assures him that this is not Theodorus' way. With these few words, Socrates tells us more about Theodorus than Theodorus' highly wrought speech tells us about Theaetetus. Socrates then goes on to say that Theaetetus' pretence, as if he too must know that Theodorus is always in earnest, could only force Theodorus to swear to the sincerity of his praise. Not to be playful means not to be liable to the charge of perjury. Socrates' own playfulness, on the other hand, of which Theodorus is occasionally aware, would point to Meletus' indictment, that Socrates does not believe in the gods in which the city believes. However this may be, Theodorus finds nothing funny when Socrates soon after consults him as the expert on urbanity.

Nothing could be more abrupt than the way in which Socrates shifts from the question whether Theodorus correctly praised Theaetetus to his own small perplexity, What is knowledge? Theaetetus' self-knowledge and Socrates' knowledge of Theaetetus are presumably to be gained through an inquiry into knowledge itself. The problem of knowledge seems to come up only as a means to these ends. It is unclear whether Socrates has chosen the most direct route. It turns out, in any case, that Theaetetus' self-knowledge is paradoxically independent of his knowing what knowledge is. But what makes this shift even more surprising is that Socrates first asks that all the others present join with Theaetetus in examining the new question, and then, in the face of Theaetetus' silence, asks whether anyone else would speak first. And yet only Theaetetus could have served to discover Theaetetus' excellence. The new question, far from being connected with Theodorus' praise of Theaetetus, seems to postpone its examination indefinitely. If Euclides had preserved Socrates' narration, perhaps we would have learned that Socrates' *daimonion* checked him in midcourse and ordered him to stop talking exclusively to Theaetetus. Theaetetus does in fact remain the main interlocutor only because Socrates calls it his sacred duty to obey the wise Theodorus, and not because he has just agreed with Socrates that he should reveal himself. But whatever might explain Socrates' shifting from Theaetetus to the others, we would still have to explain the juxtaposition of the questions. The problem of the knowledge of souls somehow makes the problem of knowledge peculiarly acute, for the lack of acknowledged experts in knowledge of souls would necessarily make it impossible for Socrates and Theaetetus, no matter what they discovered about Theaetetus' soul, to decide whether it was deserving of praise or blame. Knowledge becomes a problem as soon as Theodorus speaks without authority. Even this literal-minded mathematician had to speak in riddling images when he praised a fellow mathematician's soul.

III. Mud
(146c7–147c6)

Theaetetus agrees to two propositions that seem incompatible even before he ventures his first answer. If in learning geometry one becomes wiser in geometry, and in learning astronomy wiser in astronomy, but the wise are wise by wisdom, what could this unqualified wisdom be that renders the wise wise? It cannot be the wisdom of astronomy that makes the geometer wise, to say nothing of the wise shoemaker. That Theaetetus singles out shoemaking among the arts, seems to indicate that he has heard something of Socrates' ways, and perhaps that he wishes to ingratiate himself with him. If he had not added the crafts, his answer could have been more readily generalized. Knowledge is nothing but mathematical knowledge, and therefore to know is to count and measure, or less strictly, there can be no knowledge where there is not the numerable. Since, however, Theaetetus does add the productive arts, we should have to say that for him there is no knowledge apart from the arts and sciences. Socrates' recognition of Theaetetus is not knowledge.

Socrates offers his usual objection to any manifold. Theaetetus has given a many when asked for a one, and a complex for a simple. The alternative—that which is one and simple—is not the only possible answer. Knowledge could be a one that is complex, in the way that mud is, or a simple that is a many, which would nicely characterize the set of all the mathematical sciences. Socrates wants Theaetetus to tell him neither the kinds nor the number of sciences, just as the Eleatic stranger in the *Sophist* wants the philosophers to tell him neither the kinds nor the number of beings. Socrates opposes counting to knowing, but he thereby implies that Theaetetus had tacitly asserted their equivalence. In the strict sense, one only knows in the various arts and sciences that which one counts.[6]

Socrates clarifies his question by an example. He chooses something homely and ready-at-hand. He does not ask a physicist's question, like what is water or what is earth; he asks what is mud (*pêlos*). The example reverberates for us because we recall that Parmenides once asked Socrates, when he was of about the same age as Theaetetus is now, whether he thought there was an *eidos* of water apart from all the water we see, and that on Socrates' replying that he was perplexed as to what he should say, Parmenides had pressed him with the same question about very homely and contemptible things—hair, mud, and dirt. These are, Socrates said, just what we see them to be; but he then confessed that he was troubled. Perhaps they too had the same sort of *eidê* as he was certain just, beautiful, and good had. Parmenides then remarked that Socrates' youth made him too subservient to the opinions of human beings; if philosophy really took hold of him he would no longer despise such things.[7]

The way in which morality once gripped Socrates corresponds in Theaetetus' case to the hold the established arts and sciences exert on him. All the results of science as true opinion, he will say, are beautiful and good (200e5–6). Socrates tries to be as much a liberator for Theaetetus as Parmenides once was for him. He shows Theaetetus that he has restricted knowledge to the arts and sciences, for whereas Socrates' definition of *pêlos* applies equally to mud or clay, Theaetetus' answer would have been solely in terms of *pêlos* as an ingredient in the arts of the potter, dollmaker, and brickmaker. Socrates' definition is, though prescientific, more comprehensive than the enumeration of the clays used in several arts. But the scientific answer is not as absurd as Socrates makes it out to be. It tells us that *pêlos* is that out of which pots, dolls, and bricks are made, and that if one then wants to know what is the clay of the potter, one should consult the potter, who could say exactly what constituent elements, and in what proportions, are needed to make this or that kind of pot. The scientific answer may be fragmentary, but it does give one numbers.

It is never easy with Platonic examples to discriminate between their illustrating the way in which a question is to be answered and their serving as a guide to the answer itself. If knowledge is like mud, and mud is just that out of which it is formed, then knowledge too would be nothing but its origins, and perception would be a very plausible answer. But since mud cannot be defined without specifying how its constituents are put together, knowledge in turn could only arise if its ingredients were mixed together in some way. Knowledge perhaps requires both a passive and an active element. The discovery of its material and efficient causes would then tell us what knowledge unqualifiedly is, while the various sciences would be due to the shapes we impose on its unformed bulk—the uses to which we put knowledge. The difficulty such a picture of knowledge confronts us with is that, in showing us only that without which there can be no knowledge, it sanctions our mixing its ingredients in whatever way we wish. Pure earth is not mud, nor is pure liquid, but the range of their mixture within which there is mud does not legitimately admit of any differentiation. We should be involved in a vicious circle if we appealed to what we made out of earth and liquid for our needs as the proof that we had correctly handled the mud with which we began. The transformation from prescientific knowledge (mud) to the sciences (bricks, dolls, and pots) would thus be legitimated through that which lies outside knowledge itself.

Socrates tried to convince Theaetetus of the absurdity of his answer with two very different arguments. He draws a parallel between the impossibility of understanding the name of something without knowing what the something is and that of understanding the knowledge of shoemaking without knowing what knowledge is. If "to know what something is" is taken strictly, it is certainly possible to understand the name of something, namely, that to which it refers, without knowing what it is. So Theaetetus' answer tells us to what knowledge applies and to what, by implication, it does not. If, however, "to know what it is" is taken loosely, so that it is a matter of identification, then the name of something could not be understood without such knowledge. Socrates, however, seems to compare knowledge first with the name of something, and then to turn around and compare it with the something of which the name is. But this confusion is meant to reveal the hidden redundancy in the arts themselves (e.g., the science of astronomy), by means of which they deluded Theaetetus into believing that what they jointly assume they severally show. Socrates' second argument contrasts the interminable circumlocution that a listing of all the different clays would involve with the trivial and short answer that could be given. He thereby implies that the way of enumeration in the absence of any shortcut might have to be taken. The dichotomies of the *Sophist* and *Statesman* certainly look as if epistemic roundabouts were all that was available.

IV. Surds
(147c7–148b4)

Theaetetus discerns a resemblance in what he and young Socrates had recently discussed to the question Socrates has asked them. The resemblance seems to consist in the nonenumerability of surds, despite which they found a single expression to comprehend them all, and the practically nonenumerable arts and sciences, for the division of all numbers into two cannot be comparable to the unity of knowledge. The question of knowledge would seem more nearly to correspond to asking what is number. But since, in fact, Theaetetus' now-rejected definition of knowledge already looks like Euclid's definition of number—a multitude composed of ones—the mathematical equivalent to what is knowledge is not what is number but what is one. The starting point for Theaetetus and young Socrates was Theodorus' demonstration that the square root of the three-foot line was incommensurable, and the same held for certain magnitudes up to seventeen feet. They, however, looked at the infinite multiplicity of surds, and tried to gather them into one. They first divided all numbers into two. Those numbers which could be produced by a number multiplied by itself they likened in figure to a square and called them square and equilateral numbers. So self-evident are these numbers that Theaetetus does not mention a single one. Those numbers, however, which lie between the square numbers, among which are three and five, and for which no number exists that when multiplied by itself will produce them but a greater and a lesser side always comprehends them, they likened to oblong figures and called them oblong numbers. They then said that length (*mêkos*) is the name for all lines that form as a square an equal-sided and plane number, and surds those lines which form an oblong as a square. These two kinds of lines are not commensurable in their lengths but in their squares.

It is necessary to go over again what Theaetetus and young Socrates did, for which Socrates suitably praises them, in order to see how remarkable and perplexing their procedure was. They first dropped Theodorus' talk of lines of so many feet and considered numbers by themselves, but they were compelled to turn back to geometry in order to obtain likenesses of the two kinds of numbers. Magnitude vanishes as a first-order phenomenon only to reappear as the source of images. The status, however, of the square as an image is not the same for the two kinds of numbers. The square for square numbers is an image that in no way interferes with our returning to the pure-number equivalent of the side of the square. The image for the square root of four is dispensable as far as comprehending the class of all such numbers goes. But the image of the square becomes necessary as soon as one tries to translate the negative determination of all numbers without integral square roots, in which guise they are merely other than square numbers, into a positive determination. The image of the square then acts as the standard without which their class as that of incommensurables cannot be comprehended at all. The oblong image of the number three has to be replaced by the image of a square of equal area. This second image is commensurable with the image of four as a square, but one can no longer dispense with the image and still speak of three's root. The construction which has brought it to light is inseparable from it. The root of a pure number is not a number, and yet, though it only exists in the image of an image of a pure number, it has the power to generate the pure number.

Socrates sets Theaetetus no easy task if he expects him to imitate all this in the case of knowledge. Should he say that there are two kinds of knowledge, one "rational," the other "irrational," which are not comparable with one another because of their different "roots," but a single speech can still comprehend them if one gives to each a similar image, even though only one of them needs the image in order to be understood? Socrates, at any rate, presents the knowledge he himself has in a very elaborate likeness and thus implicitly asks Theaetetus to find a definition of knowledge equally adequate for both the many sciences he has acknowledged and Socrates' singular maieutics. This twoness of knowledge turns out to dominate the three dialogues *Theaetetus, Sophist,* and *Statesman;* it was first intimated in Socrates' denying Theodorus' competence to pronounce on his own and Theaetetus' ugliness.

V. BIRTH
(148b5–151d6)

Theaetetus has now confirmed the truthfulness of Theodorus' praise, but since he cannot speak about knowledge as he had about roots, Theodorus is, though sincere, evidently a liar. Theaetetus assumes that only if he could answer any question of this type would the praise be warranted. Socrates encourages him through a likeness. Theodorus' praise was relative. He did not mean that Theaetetus had reached the peak of virtue and wisdom, but only that if compared with his contemporaries he was outstanding. Socrates' encouragement is disturbing. If the problem of knowledge will defeat Theaetetus, as it is bound to do if Theaetetus is outclassed by it, why should Socrates run Theaetetus against the strongest possible competition? It will no doubt stretch him to the utmost, but will it not just as much discourage him? Theaetetus does not seem to be in need of humiliation. Must he jump all at once from a mathematical youth to philosophic maturity? In the *Sophist,* the Eleatic stranger seems to be more successful with Theaetetus because he leads up to the problem of being in easy stages. Socrates, however, perhaps rushes Theaetetus because he is aware that he has not enough time left to go more slowly. His imminent trial forces the pace.

Theaetetus' perplexity is not new; ever since he has heard of Socrates' questions, they have resisted his own and other's efforts to answer them, but unlike Theodorus he has been unable to get rid of his concern. Theaetetus, then, is not a beginner; Socrates has caught him just before his total immersion in mathematical studies would have made him oblivious of these questions. "The reason is, my dear Theaetetus, that you're suffering labor pains, not on account of your being empty but pregnant." Theaetetus is neither pregnant without being in labor, nor in labor with a false pregnancy. "I don't know, Socrates, what, however, I've experienced I say." Theaetetus distinguishes between his immediate knowledge of his own experience, which he does not call knowledge, and his ignorance of its cause. He identifies knowledge with knowledge of causes, but as his identifying of knowledge with perception indicates, he is unaware that he has done so. Indeed, I should venture to say that Theaetetus and Theodorus are of all the interlocutors in Platonic dialogues least aware of how what they themselves say or do bears on what they are discussing.

Theaetetus' confession of ignorance can be interpreted not only as containing within it a definition of knowledge, which by its very containment illustrates how one knows when one does not know, but it also is open to another interpretation. Theaetetus' ignorance might not be about the truth or falsity of Socrates' account of the cause of his perplexity, but rather about the very meaning of Socrates' words— *ôdineis* (you are in labor), *kenos* (empty), *enkymôn* (pregnant). Socrates had spoken them without the qualification of an "as it were" or "to speak metaphorically." He had spoken as if poetry were prose; for had he so qualified them and admitted them to be elements of an image, the distinction he later draws on its basis between phantoms and truth would itself be grounded in a phantom, and knowledge of cause would be nothing more than a fiction. This is one puzzle around which much of the *Theaetetus, Sophist,* and *Statesman* turn. There is another.

Theaetetus presents himself as someone who does not know. He knows that he does not know. He thus seems to have achieved already the level of Socratic ignorance, for his modesty is such that we can readily imagine his drawing up a list of everything he does not know. But Socratic ignorance cannot be as easy as putting anything in the form "What is ———?" Socratic ignorance must consist in knowledge of the structure of such ignorance. It must be ignorance that has been fully informed by knowledge. And yet this informing cannot be due to a methodology that would predetermine what was a permissible answer; rather, the informing must be due to the recognition that something "out there" is perplexing. The Socratic question has to be encountered; it can neither be posited nor generated from a preestablished scepticism. It must be an object of wonder. The disclosure of a Socratic question as such thus hovers between a being's self-disclosure and a thinker's self-knowledge. This peculiar doubleness of a Socratic question is what allows Socrates to move from his initial question, the nature of Theaetetus' nature, to its extension, the nature of knowledge.

Theaetetus has heard that Socrates' mother was a midwife, but he has not heard that Socrates practices the same art. Instead he has heard that Socrates is most strange and makes human beings perplexed. Theaetetus, like all the nonknowers, does not know that Socrates' ability to perplex him is due to an art. He therefore did not have to take it into account when he defined knowledge. What others report about Socrates' effect and Theaetetus himself experiences has its cause in an art. The cause of the cause of Theaetetus' experience is Socrates' art. This is a secret Socrates asks Theaetetus to keep, and we are only let in on it at the moment of Theaetetus' death. The more secret part of the secret is that Socrates has the art of the go-between, which he can only reveal by informing Theaetetus that midwives, who up to this time have been as successful as Socrates in concealing it, are also marriage-brokers. Socrates is far less careful of his mother's reputation than of his own.

Since Socrates assures Theaetetus that his art and that of midwives exactly correspond, with the exception of two obvious differences, he seems to entitle us to deduce all we can from the correspondence. Midwives are women who are past the child-bearing age: Socrates was once fertile but is no longer. If, however, human nature were not too weak to obtain an art without experience, Artemis would have given midwifery to the barren: Socrates did not need experience to be the artful midwife of men's souls. Socrates has an a priori knowledge. The contradiction seems inescapable; Socrates, amazingly enough, evades it. Many, he tells Theaetetus, get so angry at him, when he removes their folly, that they are ready to bite him, for they do not believe he acts with good will, "being far from knowing that no god is ill-disposed to human beings." Socrates is a god. It would be no wonder that he urged Theaetetus to keep his secret just before he was to go on trial for impiety. Admittedly, one is inclined to shy away from such madness and fall back on Socrates' claim to be barren in wisdom, which would altogether destroy the point of his account. The barrenness of midwives is not an element in their art, but without it they could not act as justly toward their patients. Nothing of their own interferes with their care for others, but if Socrates had ever had his own offspring, he would still be their partisan, for he never could have tested them, let alone have become later the touchstone of others. He cannot be critical if he is productive, nor maintain his justice unless he is barren, and he cannot be barren unless he is a god. He could only have answered Meletus' indictment of his injustice in corrupting the young by agreeing with the indictment of his impiety. If forced to choose between Socrates' injustice and Socrates' madness, we should choose his injustice: In the *Sophist*, Socrates himself suggests that the Eleatic stranger has come to punish him.

The serious suggestion in all this apparent playfulness is that experience and knowledge are incompatible: Theaetetus had the experience of perplexity; Socrates knows its cause. Socrates seems to assume that thoughts are like crimes and unlike diseases, for whereas doctors should, in addition to learning their art, come into contact with the worst bodies, themselves suffer all the diseases, and be not very healthy by nature, judges who had consorted with wicked souls and themselves committed every kind of crime would keenly detect the crimes of others but out of a base suspicion misconstrue the character of the good.[8] And just as we prefer the judge who does not call upon his own experience in condemning the unjust, so we must choose Socrates, who solely by his art aborts the false. Experience and knowledge could only coincide if no experience produced falsehood, for one cannot oneself cure the infection of a self-generated falsehood. Self-knowledge is impossible. To say, therefore, as Theaetetus does, that knowledge is perception, is to follow Socrates' reasoning insofar as it inspires a fear of ineradicable error, but to deny Socrates his art. It seems plausible to do so, for as he proceeds, Socrates speaks as much of his guesswork as of his art.

Midwives take less pride in delivering babies than in knowing what kind of woman in intercourse with what kind of man would bear the best possible children. True midwives know what in the *Statesman* the Eleatic stranger assigns to political science and that which Socrates once posited as the art indispensable for preserving the best city: with the guardians' forgetting of the "nuptial number," the city starts its decline. Socrates does not have this presumably mathematical art, nor is his art in any way political. His art, to be truly effective, needs to be supplemented by the art of go-betweens, who can bring about the birth of the best souls by nature; in the absence of their art, Socrates can only work on what chance has brought forth. Go-betweens can only practice their art in the best city, for everywhere else it would entail the contravention of the law against adultery. It would seem, moreover, indistinguishable from unjust and artless pimping, since it would have to persuade wherever mutual desire was absent, and dissuade wherever it was incorrectly present. Socrates, then, in labeling his whole art maieutics, conceals that part of it which he elsewhere calls erotics.

At this point the resources of Socrates' image break down, for whereas the barrenness of midwives prevents them from ever considering themselves the proper mothers of the best children—Phaenarete became a midwife after the birth of Socrates—nothing prevents Socrates from considering himself the best father of wisdom. He gave out in marriage many young men, who were fertile but not pregnant, to Prodicus and other wise men, whose acceptance of money apparently condemns them to the charge of prostitution,[9] but his silence about young men whom he made pregnant seems to imply that he is not only barren but sterile as well. The birth of wisdom requires a male principle and a female and fertile soul, for falsehood is an unfertilized egg. But in the case of those who improved under his own care, Socrates speaks as if their souls were both: "They on their own from themselves found and gave birth to many beautiful things." If Socrates' questions solely induce his patients' labor pains, they either impregnate themselves or are impregnated by others, but if his questions are also the seed he plants in the soul of the young, then his art is not restricted to delivery and diagnostics. Socrates would be a father through his art of questioning. His art of questioning, however, is not wisdom, any more than is his knowledge of souls. Neither is the offspring of his soul. Socrates opposes his barren soul to his infallible art. They are as incompatible with one another as experience and knowledge. Wisdom, then, as that truth which one's own soul brings forth, is not the same as knowledge. The perplexity Socrates has now set for Theaetetus, in the course of encouraging him in his perplexity, could not be greater: the soul's experiences interfere with knowledge;

knowledge cannot become wisdom without the soul's experiences; only wisdom can tell us the truth about the arts and sciences.

If women ever gave birth to phantom children, it would be the greatest and noblest task of midwives to distinguish them from genuine children. Socrates enlarges *per impossibile* the domain of midwifery, so that he can continue to employ the language of midwifery where it has no counterpart in midwifery. He has shown that the art of the go-between and the art of the midwife are the same art, but he cannot show that an art which cannot exist belongs to maieutics in either the ordinary or true sense of the term. He therefore cannot establish on the basis of an image he has falsified the essential unity of his diagnostics and his maieutics. That Socrates can spot the pregnant and ease or intensify their birth pangs does not entail that he can tell the true from the false, unless such an art is the same as his art of discriminating between good and bad fathers and mothers. If true midwives know who should mate with whom in order to produce the best children, they must know how to tell apart good children from bad, and if they know when to abort, they must know when the fetus is unworthy of coming to term. If, then, the art of midwives completely corresponds to Socrates' art, we are forced to conclude that as bad children are children as much as good children are, so the false offspring of soul are truly as much offspring as true offspring are. Such a conclusion, however, would undercut Socrates' equation of phantoms with falsehoods. It would thereby prompt us to ask from the start how false opinion is possible. Its possibility, at any rate, is shown by the Eleatic stranger in the *Sophist* to depend on the understanding of phantoms and images.

The obstacles Socrates puts in the way of Theaetetus are not all of a "theoretical" kind; his speech lays far greater stress on his failures, of whom he names one, than on his successes. Some young men he sent away to others if he thought them virgins; all the rest, some of whom appeared at first to be stupid, improved, "whomever the god allowed," that is, some did not improve. Some of those who did improve stayed, and many, however, who did not know that Socrates and the god were the cause of their improvement—the others apparently did know—went away sooner than they should have. All of those who left too soon became stupid; many of them then carried on in an amazing way and begged to be let back in. Most of these the *daimonion* rejected; the rest improved once more. There are altogether twelve groups of young men distributed into six pairs. Four groups are outright failures, a fifth is given a second chance. The number of evidently gifted successes is very small, but Socrates nowhere says that they gave birth to the truth. They could have discovered many beautiful things that were false, and Socrates could have checked their perplexities without their having discovered the truth. Socrates would be a straightforward Protagorean if a true speech, recognized as such by Socrates, did not become Socrates' wisdom too. Socrates, then, holds out to Theaetetus the very faintest of hopes: ugly though he is, he just might have beautiful offspring.

VI. Measure
(151d7–157a7)

If philosophy begins in wonder, it must draw the distinction between opinion and knowledge, for wonder is the recognition of the disparity between our clarity about the "that" of things and the obscurity of the "why" of things. To assert that knowledge is perception is to renounce the starting point of philosophy. Socrates calls Protagoras' thesis enigmatic because he seems to be saying that each of us knows the beings, whereas in fact he means that there are no beings to be known. The truth is neither that the truth is already known to each of us nor that the truth eludes us, but rather that there is nothing there to elude us. Theaetetus' wonder, even more than his mathematics, contradicts his answer. His soul's experiences, to which he himself testifies, do not come to light in his answer. Socrates therefore can at once conclude that he took his answer from a book. Protagoras' book is the father of Theaetetus' phantom offspring.

Socrates has just said that he himself is the measure of truth and falsehood: "It's in no way sanctioned for me to make a concession to falsehood and to wipe out truth." If Socrates is a man and is such a measure by virtue of being so, then Protagoras' thesis is its legitimate generalization: "Man is the measure of all things, of the beings that (or how) they are, and of the nonbeings that (or how) they are not." Theaetetus, as Socrates interprets him, could not have more completely denied Socrates' maieutics. Maieutics is a way of saying that thinking is not in any sense a kind of making. The Protagoras, however, whom Socrates resurrects to defend himself, will hold that wisdom is nothing but a making. And so Protagoras, in both forms of his argument, has Socrates the midwife as his chief antagonist. The counterevidence to Protagoras' Truth is the maieutical conversation Socrates now has with Theaetetus. Its possibility, which is nothing but the possibility of philosophy itself, is the issue between them. Only if we confront continually the dialogue's maieutic action with its speeches, can we hope to enter into its argument.

Just prior to Socrates' account of his maieutics, Theaetetus had asserted that in confessing his ignorance he merely stated what he had experienced, and after hearing Socrates' account of his maieutics, he asserts that knowledge is perception. Socrates' account seems to have had the effect on Theaetetus of bringing about an equation between his experience of perplexity and the sign of knowledge. Socrates' account has guaranteed the genuineness of his experience, and it is very easy to move from the genuineness of the experience to its truthfulness. Socrates' account has at least had the effect of making Theaetetus forget the characterization of knowledge implicit in his first answer—that the knowable is the countable and the measurable.

Consider what has happened. A mathematician began with a mathematician's answer; then, a single counterexample was presented to him, which, no matter how peculiar, could still account for his own experience. Theaetetus abandoned the science of number for perception, but perception colored by the Socratic science of the soul's experiences. His own example of the experience of truly opining falsely is opining the ugly instead of the beautiful or the beautiful instead of the ugly (189c5–7), and in the *Sophist* he agrees with the stranger's distinction between the perception they have of moral vice and the knowledge they have of every soul's unwillingness to be ignorant (228b4, c7).

Theaetetus says that knowledge is perception. But literally he says, "As it now appears, knowledge is nothing else than perception." Socrates then yokes the terms together: "Perception, you say, (is) knowledge." He inserts between perception and knowledge Theaetetus' own assertion of their sameness. He thus brings out that their sameness depends on a bond which Theaetetus has expressed and yet concealed from himself. This express and hidden bond, which can do double duty for both "knowing" and "being," is "appearing" (*phantasia*). Since "to be" seems to be very different from "to be for me," it looks much easier to tell knowledge apart from perception than to make a distinction between "to appear" and "to appear to me." Now that appearing, however, is made to serve both for what we know (being) and our knowing (perceiving), a distinction within perception itself must collapse. "I see" and "I appear to see"—whether the latter refers to dreaming or waking makes no difference—must be the same. But to banish doubt from perception is to banish negation. How can men be the measure of nonbeings, that is, of nonappearings? When we say, "I do not sense the cold," are we saying the same as "I do not sense"? For if they are the same, nonperception is as much knowledge as perception is, and ignorance is knowledge, and if they are not the same, I should in the second case be sensing my non-sensing and therefore not be sensing my non-sensing. This difficulty, to which Socrates barely alludes, shows that Protagoras "spoke in the language of men," and a new formulation is necessary, in which the distinction between the beings and the nonbeings can yield to their union, "becomings."

Protagoras' Truth did not declare the truth; he spoke enigmatically to the human refuse heap, to which Theaetetus and Socrates belong, and told the truth in secret to his pupils. Although in deed there is nothing but appearance, there is still in speech a difference between the appearance of truth telling and truth telling. The immanifest resists every effort to get rid of it. Protagoras covered up that on which the two best poets and all the wise except Parmenides concur. Socrates tears away the veil from Protagoras' Truth only to replace it with a veiled speech of Homer: "Both Oceanus and mother Tethys, the *genesis* of gods." This says, according to Socrates, that all things are the offspring of flowing and motion, whereas it seems to say that the gods have their origin in a male and a female god, who did not themselves become. Even if one replaces "gods" with "all things" and "Oceanus" with "water," Homer would still be saying that the principle of everything is a something, permanent, comprehensive, that gives its own character to everything. The interpretation of Theaetetus needs the interpretation of Protagoras, which in turn needs the interpretation of Homer. We are now three removes from our beginning. Neither the first of the poets nor the last of the wise said what they meant; only now with Socrates can the truth be brought entirely into the light. Just after Socrates has told Theaetetus the secret of his own wisdom, he tells him the secret of the wise.

The truth is that not even one thing is; the manifest signs of this truth are of two sorts. Fire shows that motion supplies what is thought to be and becoming, while rest supplies nonbeing and perishing, and learning shows that motion is good and rest bad. We do not need the dysenteric Theaetetus, dying on his way to Athens, to know that the signs hardly suffice as signs of the second-order truths, let alone of the truth that nothing is. Socrates therefore has to go from signs, no number of which would ever add up to a proof, to an example taken from the thesis itself, which does not admit of being refuted. The example does not prove the thesis; it merely asks whether we are so convinced of our ordinary understanding that we can say confidently that this alternative is false. The thesis only needs an indirect proof: we have to disprove the thesis. Its internal consistency will be enough if it can show up our own inconsistency. Our own inconsistency lies in the way we speak when we count and measure, on the one hand, and the hallucinations of becoming, on the other. We easily abandon in our uncertainty the possibility of asserting either the sameness of another's perceptions with our own or our own sameness over time.

But we lay down for ourselves conditions for becoming, which support the way we usually speak of our perceptions, and yet contradict our protomathematical speeches. These speeches fully conform with the denial that any one thing is by itself, and cannot be squared with our account of becoming, which has surreptitiously borrowed the language of being.

The application (*prospherein*) of four dice to six, which results in our saying that six is more than four, is exactly like the Homeric-Protagorean thesis, which says that the application (*prosballein*) of the eyes to a suitable motion (*phora*) is white. White has no more a place in or outside the eyes than the ratio 3:2 has any other "place" than that between six dice and four. The obstacle, then, to our accepting the Homeric-Protagorean thesis is not as we might suppose our mathematics, but our "axioms" of becoming. To relativize our perceptions is to bring them into line with relative numbers and measures, which we find intolerable to treat in any other way. We say, however, that nothing can become greater or less either in bulk or in number, as long as it is equal to itself, for a deeply rooted illusion is always at work in us separating what is an indivisible one into two beings. The incidence of A on B, we say, can only lead to an alteration of A if A changes. But what eludes us in this "self-evident" proposition is that A and B in their coincidence are not two but one. If something were warm in itself, it would not alter in contact with another unless it itself changed, but this "itself in itself" is what the thesis denies and what Theaetetus cannot defend. When the measurer comes alongside what is to be measured, the measure obtained is not due to either the measurer or the measured in their apartness. So if "big" is the resultant reading, it does not belong to either of them but to both as one. And, likewise, if the eye and a suitable motion come together, the white seen is not due to a change in the eye or in the motion but to their union, in which the joint alteration of the eye and the motion is not a change in the eye or in the motion.

The illusion counter to this, however, would be ineradicable if it were not for our speeches about number and measure; for though Theaetetus changes in himself (increases), and thus becomes taller than Socrates, Socrates has not then changed and yet has become shorter than Theaetetus. We can save ourselves from this absurdity if we cut loose alteration from change, motion, and becoming as we understand them and allow "otherness" to be in itself. We can then say that the short Socrates solely exists as the "product" of Socrates and Theaetetus and is inseparable from that product. The short Socrates is an instantaneous other, and the instantaneous other is not what we call the result of becoming, but of what the wise call motion.

Motion must be grasped as the source of a between without place and a now without time. Only mathematics suggests a way in which this could be done, for our hallucinations of becoming are too powerful to yield to any other kind of argument.

That Theaetetus does not hide his opinion about becoming, which yet contradicts what he must agree to about number, elicits Socrates' praise. It is divine of him to have acknowledged his double standard, for he could have refused to admit the hallucinations of becoming and thus have solved at a stroke the apparent impossibility of reconciling them with either his mathematics or his thesis. Theaetetus does not suspect that his mathematics (knowledge) and his thesis (perception) are to come together in the mysteries into which Socrates is about to initiate him; all he now divines is that he could only be consistent at the expense of his soul. He could have been doctrinaire in speech with impunity if he had kept to himself his hallucinations. Without any compulsion, then, Theaetetus owns up to the contradiction which forced him to wonder.

Wonder, says Socrates, is the unique source of philosophy, and Theaetetus' wonder appears to show that Theodorus did not make a bad guess about his nature, even as he who said that Iris was Thaumas' offspring seems not to have made a bad genealogy. Iris or Rainbow, which one admires and wonders at—a set of colors without an apparent body—comes from Thaumas or "Wonder." Between one's own wonder and the source of wonder stands an apparition. The wonderful induces in the wonderer its own cause. Iris, according to Hesiod, is the daughter of Thaumas and Electra or "Shining," and Thaumas, in turn, is the son of Pontus (the brother of Oceanus and Tethys), and Electra the daughter of Oceanus and Tethys. The genealogist would then be saying, if we follow Socrates' way of interpreting Homer, that the ultimate source of everything, which is motion, is the beginning of philosophy. Theaetetus' nature has experienced a pathos grounded in the nature of things. His nature is the nature of nature. Theaetetus is motion: Theodorus had likened him to the silent flowing of olive oil.

Socrates explains, or rather points to an explanation of, Theaetetus' perplexity in terms that do not fit his former explanation of it in terms of his own art. Theaetetus' soul was pregnant, and Socrates' art had—at a distance—induced in it labor pains, which it was equally capable of easing as it brought his thoughts to birth. But now he implies that Theaetetus' wonder has its source in Theaetetus' own nature, a nature which has no need of any art to generate both an understanding of itself and perplexity before itself. Motion both perplexes and informs Theaetetus, who is motion, that there is nothing but motion. Motion like Oceanus moves in a circle. Wherever it is in its moving there is wonder and wisdom. The conjunction, therefore, of Socrates and Theaetetus is not, as Socrates implies, a togetherness in which both are two and yet each is one, but an indivisible one that simply does not allow Socrates to be the midwife and Theaetetus the mother. Socrates' detachment from his involvement is an illusion. His conjunction with Theaetetus alters each of them in such a way that whatever they agree to solely exists as the result of their conjunction and has the same truth as the assertion that six is more because it is more than four. That knowledge is not perception only holds for this being together (*synousia*) of Socrates and Theaetetus, his double. Socrates has so unfolded Theaetetus' thesis that it becomes simultaneously an examination of Theaetetus' soul, as Theodorus understands it, and of the possibility of his conversation with Theaetetus. To question Theodorus' competence is to question Theaetetus' thesis that has now confirmed Theodorus' competence and denied Socrates' art of questioning. Theodorus is guilty of perjury only if Socrates can establish the twoness of Theaetetus and himself in their union. He must show that "both" is not "one."

Theaetetus does not yet understand his own thesis; he will be very grateful if Socrates joins with him in searching out the truth hidden away in the thought of famous men. The uninitiated, however, must not overhear them; they believe nothing else is except what they can get their hands on fully. They are, according to Theaetetus, hard and repellent human beings. They have no mysteries, for they deny the invisible and the changeable, dragging everything to earth, as the Eleatic stranger says, out of heaven and the invisible, and defining body and being as the same.[10] Theaetetus applies to the partisans of earth and body the attributes of earth and body. Just after Socrates has hinted at the congruence between Theaetetus and his thesis, Theaetetus declares on his own that the same holds for those without music. They too say what they are. If Theaetetus represents "the streamers," and the Parmenideans "the arresters of the whole," what is Socrates? If he is altogether barren of wisdom, he can have nothing to say. Or does he too say what he is—nothing? The nonbeing of Socrates would seem to illustrate perfectly the Homeric-Protagorean thesis that nothing is by itself, and his conversation with Theaetetus, its complementary thesis that whatever is, is only relative to itself. Without his diagnostics, Socrates' maieutics would look as if it were in agreement with Protagorean wisdom.

Socrates splits his account of the mysteries into two parts; the first he calls the myth, the second that which the myth means. The meaning of the myth differs from the myth in one obvious respect: Socrates

drops all mention of differences in power and replaces it with differences in speed. Power must be a mythical element because it entails
a distinction within a continuum between itself and being-at-work.
But there can be no potentiality where there is no being. To read
back from a perception and a perceived, which are one, a dual power
of agent and patient, would be to distinguish agent and patient prior
to their conjunction, but "neither is there any agent before it meets
together with the patient, nor a patient before it meets together with
the agent." Eyesight is not the patient and whiteness the agent. Eyesight, a motion generated by agent and patient motions, becomes a
seeing at the moment it falls together with whiteness, another motion
generated by the same agent and patient motions that generated eyesight. The being-at-work of eyesight and whiteness does not depend
mutually on light but only on each other. Seeing occurs in total darkness.

If, however, the meaning of the myth is that there is no potentiality,
why must the myth speak in terms of power, when it would seem to
be sufficient to speak of the double motion of perceptions and their
congeners? Sights and colors are twins; they look as though they must
be identical twins, for otherwise a distinction could be made between
what each is in itself (agent or patient) and what they are together.
As identical twins, they would necessarily be commensurate with one
another, and though it would be a mistake to label one of them sight
and another color, they would still be motions whose abiding character
was optical. Neither identical twin within the range of sights and colors
could then ever jump its own class and generate a sound, and the
class of sights and colors would thus be a constituent and primitive
class of the whole.

But the whole is nothing but motion; it is not infinitely many classes
of aesthetic motions, each of which is distinct from the start. The twins,
therefore, of each aesthetic class must have nonaesthetic sources, roots,
or powers that generate them without being the same as they are.
The nonaesthetic sources split into two classes, neither of which has
any member that belongs exclusively to it, though at any moment
their aesthetic product must be due to an agent working on a patient
power. The difficulty, then, in Socrates' account can be formulated
as follows. A sight and a color must be in their conjunction identical
twins; apart from their conjunction, each must be nonidentical and
yet generated by the same principles that are different at the time of
generation and yet not permanently different. Sameness (the color
seen) must come from difference (sight and color), and this difference
in turn from another difference (agent and patient) that is always
altering.

Socrates' language suggests that he is imitating the way in which

Theaetetus and young Socrates had found a universal definition of surds. To the two classes of number, each of which comprehends infinitely many numbers, there would correspond the two classes of motion, one of which has the power to act and the other to be acted upon. Theaetetus had then made a geometric likeness of each class of numbers, square and oblong, in which numbers were translated into magnitudes (plane numbers). Socrates now does the same when he replaces power with speed, which easily lends itself to linear representation. So if the agent and the patient are considered in their linearity, then an agent acting on a patient motion (for example, four on three) will be representable as one line at right angles to the other, for Socrates says that agent and patient motions conceive their motion in the same and in contact with another (fig. 1).

Their contact will always generate a larger (faster) number (twelve), which as the product of two numbers is representable as a plane area. Let us then say that the two possible oblong figures so generated, either 4×3 or 3×4 (cf. 148a2), show the impossibility of fixing the difference between individual agent and patient motions, though in either case one number must be acting on the passive other. The two oblongs can stand for the difference between, for example, the motion from the eye and the motion from whiteness (fig. 2). We could then further suppose that the two oblongs can only come into contact with one another if they rearrange themselves into squares of equal areas, and then their simultaneous motion toward one another (at the speed twelve) will, if they are properly aligned, generate a solid representable as a cube with an irrational side of $2 \sqrt{3}$ (fig. 3).
The cube root of its volume is now the single, nonaesthetic root of

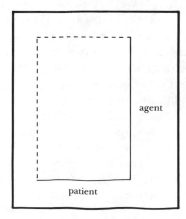

agent

patient

Figure 1

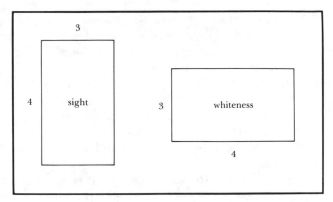

Figure 2

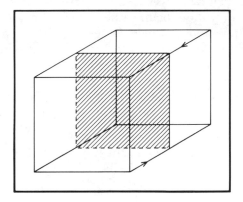

Figure 3

the identical twins, whiteness and sight, and the planes, as insubstantial as a rainbow, moving between and from the opposite faces of the cube, will be indifferently either whiteness or sight. The white seen will be a between without place. It therefore will solely be able to exist in this "solid," for its root would disappear with its dismantling, and motions (four and three) would be left that were no longer congruent coauthors of this unique perception perceived.

The significance these diagrams have lies less in their being a faithful picture—motion is to color as number is to its imaged square—than in their possibly uncovering the premises of the myth and its interpretation. Socrates had indicated that the illusions of becoming could be removed through reflection on our speeches about number and measure. The contact of six dice with four was not a becoming,

any more than the contact between two powers can lead to the becoming of a faster motion, for otherwise the faster would not remain
between them. The becoming and power of Socrates' account are not
natural but mathematical, the becoming and power which Theaetetus
spoke of in defining surds. There are no bodies for Theaetetus. Natural becoming has been replaced by mathematical metaphors, which
are nothing but the mathematician's own practice—his own construc-
tions and imagings—ascribed to his theorems.[11] Man is thus the measure of all things, for becoming is his own kind of image making, and
perception his commensuration with it.

The coincidence of the Homeric-Heraclitean thesis that all things
are moving like streams, a passive motion, with the Protagorean thesis
that man is the measure of all things, an agent motion, generates the
offspring that knowledge is perception. Between Homer of the inner
mystery and Protagoras of its outer veil there comes to be Theaetetus,
a product of both without being either. A mathematician generates a
mathematical "physiology" which comes to be between the motion of
all and the measure of man. Theaetetus' thesis duplicates in its twin
roots the origin of everything. The thesis passes the test of explaining
itself as it explains everything else. Theaetetus has read off, as it were,
from himself his own self: the union of his mathematics and his moving soul. All knowledge is, in a non-Socratic sense, self-knowledge.

VII. DREAMS
(157a7–162b7)

In summarizing these mysteries, Socrates says that we are compelled
by habit and ignorance to speak of being, but utterances according
to nature would only be in terms of change. He admits that the mysteries merely outline a program that has not yet been carried out.
The first step in such a revision of language would be to replace true
and false with pleasure and displeasure, for it seems plausible to
restrict the pleasant to my pleasure and the unpleasant to my displeasure. Theaetetus, in fact, had rejected the view that being is body
because he found its proponents hard and repellent. Accordingly,
Socrates asks Theaetetus whether he thinks the mysteries are pleasant,
and would he taste them as satisfying. To our amazement, Theaetetus
answers, "I do not know, Socrates." He had used almost the same
expression before, when Socrates had told him the cause of his perplexity. Theaetetus had then known his own experience but not its
cause; now he does not even know his own experience. Just when
Theaetetus should have become transparent to himself he becomes
opaque. Theaetetus' ignorance of his own experience does not refute

but rather strengthens his thesis, for he confesses to it out of habit and ignorance. If he could figure out Socrates' own opinion, he would know what his own taste should be. Theaetetus is a natural-born follower; it is the detrimental side of his smoothly flowing nature. He will not defend his own thesis to the death but abandon it on the slightest show of a counterargument. Theaetetus is a "pushover"; the one time he challenges Socrates he speaks against his own thesis. Theaetetus' inborn deference, then, which makes him balk at being as wise as any god, needs to be mixed somehow with a stiffening element. The dialogue's success or failure depends on whether Socrates ever manages to stop the flow of Theaetetus.

The proposed revision of language is not free of difficulties, for we speak of mishearing, misseeing, and misperceiving, as though our senses then are false, and especially so when we can connect our errors with our bodily or psychic states. The illusions of dreams, madness, and other illnesses are the accepted way of refuting the equation of being with appearing. These illusions, in which everyone agrees the distinction between to be and to appear vanishes, are the model for doing away with the distinction in all other cases. The community of the waking, healthy sane has to be assimilated to the privacy of the dreaming, sick, or mad. But the departures from the standard cannot just become in turn the standard, for then the new standard will label the old as illusions, and when we are awake, healthy, and sane, our senses will play us false. It is therefore necessary for the conflicting evidence from dreaming and waking, illness and health, madness and sanity to be resolved through a transposition of each into a language between and neutral to each.

Theaetetus himself seems to supply the clue to such a transposition. He neutralized through an image the difference betwen integral and irrational square roots. The irrationals (*aloga*) obtained a *logos* that belied their name. They are on the continuum of the straight line incommensurable with the integers, but in their squares commensurable. So if the perceptions of the dreamer do not square with those of the waking, in a suitable translation of both, each could be made to look like the other without there being any need for the translation to favor either. Theaetetus, however, does not at first recognize the way out; he is struck by the obviousness of false opinion in two cases— the madmen who believe they are gods, and the dreamers who believe they are winged and think of themselves as flying in their sleep. Theaetetus, one might say, wishes to restrict his thesis to the waking sane, for whom there is partial but not total mistaking. He draws the line at self-ignorance: what appears to someone is for someone if and only if someone is a human being and knows himself to be such. He assumes he knows what a human being is (cf. 152a8–9), and on that certain ground he proposed a complete relativism. His thesis, which in modern terms would be the subjectivity of all objectivity, seems to depend on the total objectivity of subjectivity itself.

Theaetetus had hesitated to say that the dreamer, in believing himself to be a bird, is a bird, for not even the dreamer goes in the morning to the pyramids because he dreamt he flew to Egypt;[12] but Socrates looks away from the dreamer's own belief and action to the dream itself and asks whether there would be any discernible difference between Socrates' and Theaetetus' being asleep and dreaming everything they are now thinking through (*dianoeisthai*), and their conversing (*dialegesthai*) with one another while awake. Socrates could be in Theaetetus' dream or Theaetetus in Socrates', and whatever one of them then dreams by himself would not alter if they were two and wide awake. The convertibility of a separate two, though together, into a one with an illusory other exemplifies the thesis of Theaetetus. If the resemblance Socrates and Theaetetus bear to one another concealed an identity, as would be the case if either dreamt the other, the speeches of one would be the speeches of the other, and each would be testing his own offspring. The dreaming of the individual Socrates-Theaetetus would generate a phantom offspring, as immune from the charge of falsity as it is closed to the possibility of its being true. There would then be no light into which it could be brought (157d1), but its instantaneous self-generation would allow for its instantaneous self-destruction in the ever-fleeting contact of the same with the same.

Theaetetus accepts the complete transposability of a shared conversation into a private communion, despite the consequence (but perhaps because of it) that Socrates would not then have the maieutic art and still be barren of wisdom. The equivalence of either transposition, in fact, has been inserted into the very form the dialogue itself has. Euclides had taken a narration, in which Socrates reported Theaetetus' speeches as well as his own, and put it back into direct discourse. Euclides believes that the direct discourse he has restored has not altered in its moving in and out of Socrates' narration. His indifference to the difference is the same as equating the talk you and I are having with the talk you and I have after the talk one of us dreamt has been converted into the talk you and I are having. The mutual bonding of the speakers—two agents—in the first conversation gets established in the second by one of them. One of them becomes the other's patient. But to restore the first conversation as simply speeches seems to suppress the mutual bonding of the speakers and to be indistinguishable from one's talking to oneself—a single complex of agent and patient. Thinking (*dianoeisthai*), however, is conversing (*dialegesthai*) when the soul asks itself and answers, affirms or denies. A conversation, whether open or not, would thus seem to be invariant, no matter how often quotation marks were put around it and struck out again. Is thinking, then, a kind of dreaming, and does the soul, as though it was a double agent, in asking itself a question, consistently delude itself? Perhaps the soul can be awake even in its silent self-questioning, and it does not always need the confirmation of publicity. Is there a daylight for the soul, in whose illumination thinking is possible? Without such daylight, incoherence and self-contradiction would be as much a hallucination as are, according to the thesis of Theaetetus, the hallucinations of becoming.

Theaetetus agrees that the truth cannot be time-bound. To assert just once that one is a god could be unqualifiedly true, while to assert all the rest of one's life that one is a human being would be false. The proponents of Theaetetus' thesis do not intend this; instead, they propose to preserve the truth of every instant and eliminate time. The thesis, which seems to be about motion, is a doctrine of atomicity. There is nothing but the other. Every nonidentity is an other, for each must be taken as a whole. "Socrates sick" is not a being plus an accident but an inseparable unit—a simple complex like mud—in which neither Socrates nor sickness has any priority, temporal or otherwise. Socrates does not get well while being sick or get sick while being well. He alters without changing. There is no being or becoming because everything always stands in need of another to be or to become. If numbers were beings, every number would be a ratio. Two would be twice. Being, then, is the mutual bonding together of whatever two are indispensable for each other.

That we speak of two as two and not one is the flaw in the language of habit; it is at the root of all our hallucinations of becoming. The origin of this habitual language is wholly mysterious, for the revised language seems to be parasitic on it and derivative from what it wants to deny. We are compelled to speak of two when there is only one, but this compulsion is inexplicable if there is only one. The necessity that binds two nonbeings together into being is a necessity of fact. The fact or being is contingent, but the character of every fact is necessary. Knowledge is not of the facts but of the necessary character of the facts whatever they are. The being of any being is known before any being is sensed, but every being is sensed and thereby known. Knowledge is sense at the same time that it is knowledge of the unsensed and nonexistent causes of sense. The between of Theaetetus' thesis, like the between which Theaetetus himself is, is a phantom. Theaetetus has not given birth.

The dialogue up to this point, just before Theaetetus begins to abandon his own offspring, has been carried through on the assumption that Theodorus understands Theaetetus' soul correctly. Just as the thesis of Theaetetus entails that his soul be of the sort Theodorus says it is, so his soul if it is of this sort entails the thesis he proposes. Socrates has gone the midwives one better. He has figured out, with the clue Theodorus supplied, who the parents of Theaetetus' offspring must be. The figurative poetry of Homer has mated with the literal prose of Protagoras to produce a ghostly image (*eidôlon*), which Homer called the soul that he likened to a dream. Theaetetus has to wake up. But Socrates has so vividly presented this dream, which originally had been Theaetetus' own, that Theodorus cannot but find it amazing when Socrates asks Theaetetus if he can bear to expose it. Theodorus is shocked to learn that the baby he sponsored is to be killed. He does not realize that if Theaetetus can put up with setting his thesis aside even though it is his own, which Theodorus' knowledge of Theaetetus' soul assures him he will do, the thesis is already refuted, since Theaetetus would then be affirming his authorship while denying its truth. This is the only way to kill a ghost.

Theodorus can live his own life if he is safe from the opinions of others. Protagorean scepticism guarantees his neutrality in philosophy. But Protagoras only guarantees it because his authority is godlike; if he is a human being, he can have no authority. The thesis holds for every sentient being. Men alone do not know that they know. The pig is not blind to its knowledge; men need to be enlightened. Protagoras must be either a beast or a god if he knows what no other man knows. If men do not heed Protagoras, they are ignorant; once they do, he is ignorant. Protagoras can be wise only as long as he is not an authority. He therefore cannot help Theodorus to keep his distance from philosophy. Socrates offers Theodorus a way out: Protagoras' Truth spoke in jest from the inner sanctum of his book. Theodorus refuses to take this way out; he can no more conceive of Protagoras' playfulness than of his own. He prefers that Protagoras contradict himself than that he lack seriousness, but he wants to conceal from others his acknowledgment of the self-contradiction. If he is himself not the instrument of the refutation, he has kept his friendship with Protagoras intact and not argued against his own opinion.

Theodorus is another Hippolytus. He reserves for himself the right to be insincere. He is unwittingly playful, but if no one can publicly charge him with it, he does not mind. Theodorus craves respectability. He has hitherto obtained it through the Protagorean version of the thoughtless saying "You have your opinion, I have mine." Protagoras can still be of help to Theodorus in any city in which the neutrality of the spectator is respected. Theodorus is perfectly safe from self-exposure in Athens, but Socrates asks whether he could get away with it in Sparta, where the spectators are compelled to strip themselves naked if they wish to look at the nakedness of others. If Theodorus could not persuade the Spartans to make an exception in his case, he would not stay, but he believes he can persuade the present company to leave him alone. Theodorus can always find a place congenial to his studies; unlike Socrates, he is neither bound to Athens nor in need of others. He regards himself as completely free. For Socrates to get Theodorus to examine the conditions of his freedom would entail the denial of his freedom as he understands it. But to concede him a privileged position would turn him into another god, whose wisdom is not open to question. Socrates will have to use just the right mixture of compulsion and blandishment to persuade Theodorus to give up the advantages of dreaming.

VIII. Protagoras Revised
(162b8–171e9)

Theaetetus' offspring has two parents, neither of which is exactly the same in their union as each is apart from it. Socrates therefore examines each of them separately—the Protagorean doctrine with Theodorus, the Homeric-Heraclitean doctrine again with Theodorus, and Theaetetus' with Theaetetus. He had already made the transition to Protagoras himself as other than Theaetetus' Protagoras when he spoke of his own infallibility in thought if knowledge is perception (160d1). From then on, Socrates blurs the difference between perception and opinion. This blurring, of which Theaetetus is unaware, sponsors his countering Theaetetus' physiology with lexical arguments, in which the words men use are treated as if their meanings are as plain as perceptions, and one neither had to ask, for example, whether memory was a perception, nor had to refrain from all talk of knowing as other than something lexically distinct from perceiving. Socrates himself points out the unfair advantage he takes right at the beginning. He asks Theaetetus whether he is not amazed to be suddenly as wise as any man or god, but this is to invoke the opinion that the gods are, and are wise, whereas Protagoras in Theaetetus' version should hold that not only do men not know that they know, but men believe they know what they do not know. Theaetetus, however, does not distinguish between primary hearing, through which this or that sound is known, and hearsay, through which the gods are known to be.

Protagoras, or his spokesman, gets out of the difficulty in another way. Socrates disregards Protagoras' express denial of knowing whether the gods are or are not, and since he only knows what he knows, Socrates cannot question him as if he accepted the opinion of others as his own. Protagoras demands that they refute him with demonstrative necessity, without demagogery or images. He demands a much higher standard for falsification than verification of the Protagorean measure. Protagoras did not give a proof; he only made an assertion, for what proof could he have given which would not have contradicted his measure? Before one adopts his measure as one's own, whatever man says that he is a god seems mad. Though one might persuade him that he is not a god, one could still be puzzled as to how one could prove it to him; but after one has adopted the measure, one would simply leave to everyone his beliefs, and proof of the sort Protagoras asks for would be meaningless. Socrates lets Protagoras appeal to an opinion Theaetetus and Theodorus share about mathematical proof right after Socrates has had him reject a common opinion about the gods. It is unclear why one is superior to the other: Theaetetus' definition of surds was no worse for its use of images.

The first of Socrates' lexical arguments is to ask whether in our ignorance of a foreign language or of the letters in our own, we are to deny that we hear or see if we do not know what the barbarians or the letters say or mean. Theaetetus does not observe that the difference in what the literate and illiterate know when they look at letters is not at issue, but whether there is knowledge when there is perception. Theaetetus grants that as a matter of course and distinguishes instead between primary perception, by means of which the illiterate knows the shape and color of the letters, and that which he denies is perception at all, by means of which the literate knows how to read. Theaetetus jumps beyond perception all too easily, for perception is for the literate still a means to knowledge even if it is not knowledge itself. Protagoras, moreover, could have turned Socrates' argument right around and said that the literate sees one thing and the illiterate another, and they do not differ any more than "Socrates sick" does from "Socrates healthy."

Socrates lets Theaetetus have his own way now, just as in the next two arguments he does not correct Theaetetus' errors, because he wishes to show Theodorus that Theaetetus' nature is not what Theodorus said it was. The spurious arguments for which Theaetetus falls are not demonstrative refutations of Protagoras' doctrine; they are demonstrations of Theodorus' misunderstanding of Theaetetus' soul. Theaetetus' pliability is not due to his liquid nature but to the incompatibility of his nature with his phantom offspring. The first hint of Theaetetus' true nature emerges in his hasty ascription of the knowledge of letters or a language to a nonaesthetic source. He thus misses something important: without the knowledge of a language we do not even hear its sounds distinctly. We cannot sort out the taps of Morse code unless we know what they stand for. So even if, as Theaetetus would have it, we do not perceive the meaning of a language, this knowledge still gives us access to what we do perceive. Perhaps Theaetetus' own science, mathematics, is the highest of these types of knowledge.

Theaetetus assumes that the way of demonstration itself is empty of knowledge. Since it does not assert that this or that being is, it should be applicable to any proposition. He therefore does not realize that Protagoras denies the principle of noncontradiction without which no demonstration is possible. Accordingly, Socrates can impose on Theaetetus the minimal conditions for demonstration without his meeting any objection. These minimal conditions are embedded in language. Socrates asks whether it is possible, of whatever one gets knowledge, if one still has a memory of that very thing (*auto touto*) and preserves it for oneself, not to know that very thing (*auto touto*) which one remembers when one remembers. Once one accepts this *auto touto* everything else follows, and Theaetetus, if his heart were in his thesis, should deny that a memory of something can ever be the same as its perception. That Theaetetus does not rely on his thesis shows how little his thesis is his own. But it shows something more, for when Protagoras is made to speak in its terms he must deny the very existence of memory. Protagoras would not grant that the memory someone has of what he experienced is an experience of the same sort as that which he had but is no longer experiencing. The memory would seem to be, not a memory of the experience, but of that which one had experienced, for one no longer has the experience; but the memory cannot be of the something directly unless it is a perception. If, however, the memory is the experience of an experience, the second experience must be present. But if the experience is present, there could not be a memory of it but just another experience, for which we have no name. Protagoras thus gives an example of what a thorough-going revision of language would involve: memory would vanish along with time. Protagoras cannot handle the presence of the absent, in which memory's peculiarity consists. The other, if not wholly other, must elude him (cf. 165c1, 3).

Socrates learned from Theodorus Theaetetus' name (*onoma*) and that as an orphan his guardians squandered his substance (*ousia*). Socrates now says that Protagoras' speech is an orphan, which they treat unphilosophically—they defeat it with words (*onomata*)—in the absence of guardians who are willing to defend it. He seems to imply that the substance or being of the speech Protagoras fathered has been left intact. He can draw this far-fetched analogy because being has been defined as property (cf. 172b4–5). Like property, there is no being by itself, but only if it is someone's being. And since it disappears if it is not someone's, Socrates will, for the sake of the just, impart being to what is not. He resurrects Protagoras, but the resurrected Protagoras—again according to the doctrine—is not the same Protagoras. He has been made better. Socrates does to the old Protagoras precisely that which the new Protagoras says is the mark of wisdom—to be able to change bad into good perceptions. The consequence of Socrates' justice is his wisdom. He is no longer barren. The mutual binding together of the dead Protagoras and the barren Socrates has produced a being that Socrates apparently cannot question, for he would then have to submit, not to the death of his firstborn, but to his own. The new Protagoras-Socrates intensifies the dispute between sophistry and philosophy, for with its breakup goes the last possibility of reconciling philosophy with the city.

Protagoras' speech is in four parts: (1) Socrates' verbal quibbling and how it can be answered; (2) the restatement of the thesis, still in terms of truth; (3) the explanation of the revised thesis, now in terms of the good; (4) how Socrates should justly behave. Protagoras gets out of the lexical arguments by reaffirming the most radical atomicity. He who knows is not the same as he who does not know, for there is no same which both of them know. There is no simultaneity. Protagoras, however, cannot dissolve the knower and the known into disconnected points when he maintains the possibility of wisdom. Wisdom requires that there are states or conditions (*hexeis*) which persist over time. Knowledge and wisdom are not the same. Knowledge, which Protagoras mentions only once, is of the Heraclitean flux; wisdom works within the horizon of ineradicable illusion, where the nonknowers live and the same has its place. This is best exemplified not by man's or even the pig's horizon, but by the plants', to which Protagoras attributes perceptions; when he refers to men he speaks of their opinions. The wise do not touch the illusory ground of men's opinions; they are effective only if they leave this ground alone. Protagoras speaks so carefully that it is impossible to tell whether the wise in changing opinions make the apparent and the real bad get changed into the apparent and the real good, or the apparent and the real bad get replaced by the apparent and the real good. Protagoras seems to imply that this distinction is false: the change of state can be interpreted either way indifferently. If Socrates is accused of making the weaker argument the stronger, the weaker is then weaker but only comes to appear stronger. But perhaps the weaker is and appears weaker, and then is and appears stronger. It makes no sense to ask whether it is the same argument.

In recalling Socrates' example of his drinking wine when sick and healthy, Protagoras speaks instead of eating food. The doctor changes by means of drugs the patient's opinion of a food's bitterness; he knows of its bitterness from the patient. Protagoras does not explain how the doctor would know of the patient's illness if the patient told him that the food tasted pleasant. The sophist's drugs are speeches; what, then, is the soul's food? Protagoras indicates what it is only in passing. He cites the case of cities. The just and the beautiful, or the moral, is for cities what truth is for individuals; it is whatever the city says it is. But the good is not of the same order as the moral. Each city believes the moral to be good. The sick and the healthy city believe they know what the moral is; but the sick city believes the bad is moral, the healthy city the good. The moral is the ineradicable illusion of the city; it is the way in which it sees the condition it is in. It never sees its own condition apart from the moral. The good speaker makes the city akin to his own condition; his own condition consists in the power to bring about this kinship. To be good or healthy means to be an agent-power, to be bad or sick means to be a patient-power. A city that can resist its own assimilation to another city is a healthy city, and the city in the best condition can feed on every other city.

The same holds for the soul. The soul is healthy when it assimilates other souls to itself—the teacher surrounds himself with his own duplicates—and the soul is sick when it cannot resist such absorption. Protagoras had himself proved to be quite dead. He could not change for long either Theodorus or Theaetetus into himself; but he now tempts Socrates with the hope of almost infinite power. All he must do is point out the errors of his disciples which are due to themselves and their former associations and refrain from perplexing them anew (cf. 146c5–6, 167e7). If he conceals his own doubts, he can make everyone into his own kind of philosopher, and no one will ever hate him. Philosophy means love of Socrates. At the very end of Socrates' life, Protagoras proposes a radical alteration of Socrates' stance to his art and the city. Protagoras counsels badly even in death.

Wisdom is power. He is wise who can make someone or something into his own image. The wise need the unwise or sick. The city does not become wise when it becomes healthy, for it never ceases to be patient of the wise speaker. Protagoras therefore must admit a difference between apparent and real health—a difference, admittedly, the healthy patient can never draw (this is what keeps him a patient) but without which the wise could not alter another unless he himself altered. All but the wise live in the element of the derivative. The derivative is stamped as such by the identity of being and appearing, the nonderivative by their separation and its power to cause their identity for others. To be is to be an agent-power, not to be is to be a patient-power. Nonbeing somehow is. The resurrected Protagoras still contradicts himself.

Socrates apologizes to Theodorus for the inadequacy of his aid to Protagoras. Theodorus is as innocently rude as ever; he says that Socrates is being playful in deprecating his vigorous aid. He implies that Protagoras' abuse of Socrates is fair comment and, in particular, that it is unjust to be playful. Theodorus is serious; if he engaged in the investigation, Protagoras could not complain that Socrates, in talking with a child (*paidion*), was being playful (*paizein*), for Theodorus would not let Socrates get away with it. Theodorus is so serious that he takes Socrates' pun literally, as if Socrates meant that Theodorus was qualified simply because he had a long beard, not because he was serious. His seriousness in this case is reinforced by the topic: they are to consider whether Theodorus is the measure in mathematical theorems or whether all are as competent as he is in astronomy and everything else in which he is charged with superiority. Protagoras has apparently accounted for the arts that are concerned with human goods but not for those that look to the truth. If mathematics were good for men, in the Protagorean sense, it would be like medicine; but if it is bad for them, in the same sense, like poison, Theodorus would have to prove that it is good without thereby affecting its status as being true. He would have to say why men should acquire this knowledge if it is not wisdom and lacks all power, and he would have to do this while showing that there is knowledge and his theorems are knowledge.

Theodorus' self-interest therefore not only reinforces his seriousness, it seems to compel him to abandon the dead Protagoras in order that he can maintain his self-interest. The discussion seems tainted from the start. If truth is only manifest if one keeps one's distance from it, and one can only discover the truth if it is close to one's heart (cf. 165d4), then the concern with its goodness, which one's own self-interest demands, will preclude the seeing of the truth, since disinterested concern with the truth is a contradiction. Theodorus can remain the spectator he was (cf. 177c5), but then there was no falsehood, or he can now become a participant, but then there will be no truth. He can have unfalsifiability without the good, or unverifiability with it. Theodorus' seriousness, which blinds him to the possible vanity in his competence, seems to be an indispensable but self-defeating ingredient in the examination of Protagoras' measure.

Theodorus is justifiably very annoyed with Socrates; he can find no more fitting images for Socrates than those of two mythical criminals. He had foolishly assumed that Socrates was at least as respectable as the Spartans, who leave one the choice of going away. Theodorus no longer speaks of his being a spectator, for he senses that he now must fight for his very life (cf. 165e1–4). He has hitherto lived under no necessity. Socrates has so stepped up the pressure on him that he speaks of Socrates as one of the Fates who weave a destiny he must endure. Theodorus wants to be wholly passive, stripped by Socrates, beaten to the ground, and then released. He does not believe he is another Theseus or Heracles who can defeat Socrates; he does not even wish to try. Theodorus, though nothing but serious, cannot take Socrates' challenge seriously. His dedication to geometry, to which he has fled as a refuge from the unreality of speeches, prevents him from listening to what he himself says. The extravagance of his language—Socrates is a merciless killer—covers up his indifference to the question Socrates has posed. The word that best characterizes Theodorus is *pôs*: "For some reason or other (*pôs*) we inclined rather soon away from bare speeches to geometry." He refuses to come to grips with this *pôs*. Socrates is just the reverse. He glories in Theodorus' charge of his supreme criminality. Theodorus has made a most excellent likeness of his disease (cf. 148b3). He is not healthy with the power of the wise, as Protagoras had urged him to be, nor has he ever been cured by the speeches of his opponents, so as to get the semblance of health without its reality. His disease looks like injustice because it does not allow any room for consent. His disease is his strength; it is his "awesome love (*erôs*) of naked exercise in these things." If Theodorus will not begrudge him this mutual drubbing and rubbing, he will benefit both himself and Socrates. The good comes to be from a motion (cf. 153b5–7), initiated by an incurable disease which aims at beauty. Socrates could not have put more succinctly the differences between himself and Theodorus on the one hand, and himself and Protagoras on the other.

The shift from the playful or childish form of conversation, which Socrates and Theaetetus had, to the manly contest that is about to begin, seems to be a shift from innocence to experience, in which mathematics will yield to the problem of good and evil. The two contestants, however, are very unequal in their understanding of this matter; it is therefore safer to say that Theodorus stands to the problem of good and evil as Theaetetus stood to his own experience, the cause of which he did not know. Theaetetus, to be sure, has experienced evil, but the loss of his inheritance did not bother him, since he is in spite of it still generous; but Theodorus is troubled by his experience, the cause of which he does not know. Theodorus is not pregnant with any child from which he can be delivered, but Socrates does deliver him, at least in part, from his moral indignation. Socrates asks whether his own indignation was justified in his censuring the argument that made each self-sufficient in point of understanding or prudence. Theodorus had not shared his indignation when Socrates deduced that if Protagoras was right, his own maieutics was ridiculous. But Socrates draws Theodorus' attention—he would never have noticed it himself—to the equal applicability of Protagoras' measure to his own mathematics. The mathematician and the midwife must join together in order to defend themselves from Protagoras' ridicule. It is this ridiculous alliance of the knowledge of number with the knowledge of soul that makes the discussion serious.

Socrates and Theodorus agree to examine the problem of opinion by itself, independent of both Theaetetus' equation of perception and knowledge and Protagoras' concession that in matters of better and worse some men are superior to others, and these are wise. They ask Protagoras whether everyone is convinced that he is wiser than others in some things, and others wiser than he is in other things. No one takes anyone else as wiser than himself in everything, nor does anyone believe that he himself is wiser than everyone else. Socrates replaces Protagoras' assertion that whatever each opines is true for him who opines it with a much deeper observation: all men are convinced that all men opine truly and falsely. What all men share is not the Protagorean view but a conviction about the character of human opining as such. This universal conviction is not subject to doubt; men are proof against enlightenment in this regard by any Protagorean wise man. This is not like any other opinion because men always act on it. In the greatest dangers, in which there is the greatest need and the greatest fear, men seek for saviors in the belief that others are wiser than themselves, and in the expectation that their rulers will save them, they behave toward them as if they were gods. Socrates surely overstates his case. The saviors sought for are not always those who men believe surpass themselves in knowledge. Greater strength or daring is all that is sometimes needed, and those who need it believe they themselves know how it is best to be used. Socrates' exaggeration, moreover, would imply that all men are convinced that the sole title to rule is knowledge; neither Protagoras nor the many would agree. Socrates may be pointing to his own peculiar strength, the knowledge of his own ignorance, which is neither a saving wisdom for others nor yet wisdom's lack as false opinion. Socrates' knowledge of ignorance has no place in the domain of human convictions.

Theodorus conceded that it would be unbelievable if there was someone who was not convinced of the false opinion of another. Any one can always be paired with another who is convinced of his lack of wisdom. No one, therefore, is ever thought to be wise in anything by everybody. Socrates chooses as his example Theodorus. He asks him whether thousands upon thousands (*myrioi*) on each occasion battle against his opinion with their own, convinced that he discriminates and believes falsely. One would suppose that Theodorus of all people, who does nothing but mathematics, would object to this unscientific and hyperbolic *myrioi* (cf. 196e2). Socrates, however, has touched a raw nerve: "Yes, by Zeus, Socrates, 'truly *myrioi*' (*mala myrioi*) indeed, Homer says, since they give me all the trouble that can possibly come from men." In a comical way, and with what must be the shortest and least poetical of quotations, Theodorus assures Socrates that he is not exaggerating at all. Theodorus refers to a line in the *Odyssey*, where Telemachus is telling his father, whom he has not recognized, that in the absence of Odysseus truly thousands of hostile suitors dwell in his house. Theodorus cannot bear ridicule, but he cannot help sounding ridiculous when he expresses his indignation at the ridicule he must suffer. We recall how careful he was to avoid the imputation that he praised Theaetetus because he was in love with him, and yet we also noticed that Theodorus prides himself on his freedom and that the attraction Protagoras had for him consisted in his doctrine that apparently guaranteed his right to be left alone. Socrates will soon tell him that he cannot help but appear ridiculous, and he now shows him that Protagoras' wisdom is as subject to doubt as his own. Its popular character is an illusion (cf. 161e4).

Protagoras wrote a book in which this sentence appeared: "Man is the measure of all things, of the beings that (or how) they are, and of the nonbeings that (or how) they are not." Now that Protagoras is dead, we can surely imagine that no one utters it; indeed, the sentence cannot be spoken, as it is written, by anyone, though as written it has a certain plausibility. As a written sentence it does not belong to anyone, but if it is adopted and someone utters it, the sentence alters. The sentence as written is in the indicative mood, but as soon as it is read it becomes an imperative (cf. 170d6), for it commands the reader to replace "man" with "I." "Man" is a dummy word that conceals an injunction. If the injunction is carried out, it becomes once more indicative, and the speaker can then assent to it or not. The sentence does not supply the conviction as to its truth, but the speaker's own conviction prior to his utterance determines its truth or falsity. The written sentence could be true, and yet no one might believe it, but the sentence says that whatever one believes is true. So everyone in saying the sentence is false is telling the truth and denying the truth of the truth, but it is only the sentence in the book that says that everyone's denial is true. One does not have to know that the sentence is false, one only has to suppose it to be false for it to be false. But it cannot be merely because it is one's own opinion that an opinion is true, nor merely because no one holds a certain opinion that it is false.

That the invalidation of Protagoras' sentence only follows at once when a human being reads the sentence, identifies himself as a human being, and obeys the injunction, can readily be seen if we replace human being with any other sentient being in the sentence. He might be thought a fool if someone wrote that pig or crane is the measure of all things, but the sentence would not be invalid in itself. Theaetetus drew the line at self-ignorance when Socrates mentioned dreams and madness as the ordinary counterexamples to Protagoras' doctrine. And it now is evident that the ground of his qualms were wholly in accord with the self-contradiction in his doctrine. Protagoras appealed to Theaetetus because both had forgotten themselves in taking themselves for granted.

Socrates did not examine Protagoras' measure while Protagoras was still alive but only after his death. If to be dead is to be without life or soul and thus to be like something written down, a self-contradiction would in this sense be dead, for that it is a self-contradiction becomes manifest as soon as it returns to life in its being spoken. To give it life is to destroy it. Protagoras' measure thus encapsulates the pre-Socratic failure to understand soul, for this failure is the same as their inability to account for themselves. Self-contradiction is grounded in ignorance of soul; and it would be no accident that Plato has Socrates formulate the principle of noncontradiction in the context of a discussion of soul.[13] Theodorus never speaks of Protagoras as dead; he does not use the past tense of him until he has been cured of his infatuation (178e7). The half-life Protagoras leads in Theodorus' imagination, and which Socrates has fostered by twice calling Theodorus Protagoras emerges in Socrates' picturing him as he pops out of the ground up to his neck and, after much abuse of Socrates' folly, slips below and is gone. Protagoras is likely to be wiser than themselves, Socrates tells Theodorus, because he is older. Protagoras' written sentence is the most extreme parody of the law, which necessarily asserts that it is superior to the wise man on the spot. Protagoras' measure parodies this because it insists, like the law, on its own wisdom while enjoining each of us to think of ourselves as the wise man on the spot. Protagoras' Truth straddles the timeless and the now in an impossible way. She lacks prudence.

IX. THALES
(172a1–177c5)

Socrates has now fully justified the liberty he took in revising Protagoras. He does not, however, repeat exactly what he had had Protagoras say in his own defense. For one thing, he adds to the lawful things that the city lays down for itself, about which there can be no dispute, the holy and the unholy, which Protagoras, in accordance with his exclusion of the gods from his speaking and writing, had not mentioned. For another, he interprets Protagoras' good as the useful and therefore speaks of the superiority of a city's opinion in point of truth, whereas Protagoras had divorced wisdom from truth. The parallelism Socrates draws between the recalcitrance to verifiability of the individual's opinion about hot, dry, and sweet, and the susceptibility to verification of the individual's health or illness, on the one hand, and the same recalcitrance of the city's opinion about the noble, just, and holy, and the same susceptibility of the city's advantage or disadvantage, on the other—this parallelism is more apparent than real. In the private sphere, health has a much higher rank than hot, dry, and sweet, but in the political, the advantageous as such is not asserted to be higher than the holy, the just, and the noble. Further, the individual's perception of the hot, dry, and sweet is thought to be symptomatic of his health or illness, whereas it is not as obvious that the city's opinion about the noble, just, and holy are signs of its health or illness. The city could have on its books one set of opinions and yet transgress them, but it is impossible for the individual to contravene the perceptions he has. The truth of a perception, moreover, is not the same as its correctness, for no one concludes from the wine's bitterness when he is sick that the wine is bitter. But the city never ceases to identify its own opinion as true with its correctness.

The parallelism has forced the differences between perception and opinion to be wholly blurred. The senses are thought to work independently of one another, and it seems not to be inevitable that if the individual tastes the wine as sweet he must feel it to be cool. That what the city lays down as holy should in no way determine its opinion about the just, nor its opinion about the just its opinion about the noble—this is not at all self-evident. No one pays attention to diverse perceptions of the same "hot," since everyone assumes that, since heat is a continuous magnitude, anyone who does not feel hot now can be made to feel hot later. But is the just a continuous magnitude of the same kind, and is there anything like the "luke-just"? If to pay one's taxes is luke-just, it would be because it is clearly to the advantage of everyone to do so, but if to rescue a drowning man is more just, the just would cease to be in the same sense to one's own advantage. One would therefore have to distinguish between the just which all cities lay down as just and the just about which cities disagree, but this distinction is meaningless for perceptions. There is no praise or blame attached to perceptions in themselves, but there is to opinions and the actions in accord with them.

A limited Protagoreanism must confuse perception and opinion for the following reason. Its proponents look at the city from the outside, from which vantage point it is obvious that the city holds opinions and that these opinions differ from the opinions of other cities and from its own former and future opinions. They therefore conclude that the lawful is as private to each city as perceptions are to the individual. But though a Theaetetus will not insist that as each color appears to him so it does for every or any other human being, each city will insist, to the point of war and beyond, that the just is what it says it is for every other city. Had these Protagoreans paid sufficient attention to the difference between the city's perspective and their own, they would have gone on to distinguish between the individual's perceptions as they are by nature and as they are in opinion—for which the white of one healthy man is the same as another's—and again between the noble, just, and holy as they possibly are by nature and as they are in opinion. But Protagoreans cannot do so, for they deny that there are such things by nature, a denial that no more follows of itself from the variety of political opinions than does the consensus about perception entail automatically that their doctrine is false. On the basis of their understanding of nature, they infer that the individual's perceptions as given by nature are of the same order as positings of the city. The city, they then should say, must be acting in accordance with nature in believing its own opinions to be true. But they do not draw this conclusion; rather, they project the subjectivity of the city's opinions, which they observe from the outside, and the truth of the city's opinions, upon which the city itself insists, back onto the individual's perceptions—an individual who neither observes their subjectivity nor proclaims their truth. This projection is inadvertent on their part, since they do not see where they themselves are standing. They would only sink more deeply into incoherence if they replied that the intersubjective agreement about perceptions corresponds to the agreement among fellow citizens about morality and religion. For the first is a universal agreement constant over time and place, and the second is not. It is to the credit of Socrates' Protagoras that he never mentioned nature or confused truth with wisdom.

Socrates has brought Theodorus to the point where he is trapped

in the middle of a three-sided conflict within himself: (1) the necessity
to accept the opinion of the many and abandon the measure of Protagoras, whose attraction for him was its assertion that his opinion
was no worse than that of the many; (2) his indignation at the many
for setting themselves up as his judges; (3) his subservience to the
opinion of the many, whose ridicule he fears. A modified Protagoreanism still seems possible, in which competence is neither arbitrary
nor in the control of the many. Theodorus, however, does not have
any such competence, for it has been confined to those arts which
everyone would agree are the causes of human goods. Theodorus'
competence, in terms of its lack of obvious usefulness, has much more
the status which the new doctrine of Protagoras has ascribed to the
city's opinions about the noble, just, and holy. Neither the city nor
this doctrine has any place for him. Socrates must give him a place
from which he can look down on his tormentors. The starting point,
therefore, is the kind of activity to which Socrates and Theodorus in
their different ways are devoted.

Socrates remarks that the denial of being to the just and the holy
involves them in a bigger argument than before. "Are we not at leisure,
Socrates?" Theodorus asks. With a demonic prescience (cf. 154e8),
Theodorus picks the single characteristic which marks off what he
does from the business of the city. But is Socrates at leisure? He says
in reply, "It looks as if we are." Socrates is thinking of his forthcoming
trial, at which he will not speak at leisure but will be forced to follow
the rules of the court. Theodorus is entirely oblivious of the import
of what Socrates will say, for he knows nothing of the situation Socrates
is in, who soon will not just face ridicule—Theodorus' bogey—but
capital punishment. Although they have long been friends, Theodorus has no interest in Socrates' fate, not because he does not have
some regard for Socrates, but because his fate is not his own and
belongs to the here and now to which Theodorus never pays any
attention. Theodorus could very well have been the silent auditor to
whom Socrates narrated, more than twenty years before, the talk he
had on moderation with the future tyrants Charmides and Critias (cf.
155d3–e2); for though the time of the *Charmides* narration is the day
after that talk, and the place is still Athens, Socrates' auditor has not
heard of the battle at Potidaea which heralded the start of the Peloponnesian War (153b5–6), and Socrates properly omits to tell him
what he told his acquaintances about it. What links the midwife and
the mathematician is their unpolitical character. The *daimonion*'s re-
straining of Socractes from politics is more than matched by Theodorus' indifference to the worldly.

The leisure of the philosophers consists in their being able to repeat an inquiry and flit from subject to subject. The repeatability of an inquiry—neither does the inquiry alter the being it examines nor the being impose a time limit on its discovery—has the side effect of easily becoming or looking like gossip, which is equally outside the vital concerns of both the teller and the listener. In political life, however, and particularly in the law courts, there is no possibility of our starting all over again, not only because a decision must be made now—whether it be to condemn this man or acquit that one in the face of our ultimate ignorance of what justice is, or to make war or peace on evidence which is necessarily incomplete—but because our deeds and speeches change the conditions for our next deeds and speeches. Time is always running out, and the time is never the same. The water clock of the courtroom is both that which times the length of one's speech and that which characterizes in its flowing the mutual bonding of the speaking and its occasion into a unique moment. The Homeric-Heraclitean thesis, if asserted about the nature of nature, seems an extravagant and metaphorical conceit, but it is the literal truth about political life.

Both the pettifogger as slave and the jury as his master are enslaved in the flow of things, but the pettifogger is twice enslaved, for his own life is often at stake, and he must run just to save it. The low cunning he must practice ties him to his master, and the more he is successful the more he becomes one with him. But the master, since he never has to exercise his wits, remains sunk in the belief in his own sovereignty. Theodorus is delighted by Socrates' picture. After Socrates has compelled him to speak, Socrates tells him he is not compelled to speak. Theodorus picks up the distinction between masters and slaves: he is the master, the speeches are his slaves. Although Socrates pointed to the indifference of our own mistakes to the being we examine, Theodorus stresses the patient waiting of the speeches until we resolve to complete them. The *logos* is not our judge, for there is no necessity to follow the *logos*. Theodorus wants to be the jury, whom Socrates would always flatter with pleasant speeches (cf. 177c3–5). Not in spite but because of his great distance from the city, Theodorus imitates the city.

Socrates' portrait of the tiptop philosophers begins as a portrait of Theodorus and Theaetetus. He begins with what they do not know. Their ignorance is of four kinds. They do not know the way to the marketplace, nor where the courthouse is, or any other common gathering place of the city; they neither see nor hear the so-called unwritten and written laws and decrees; not even in a dream does it occur to them to join a political club or private party; and they are as unaware of the high or low birth of anyone in the city, or of what evil befell anyone's maternal or paternal ancestor, as of the number of buckets in the sea. The philosopher's ignorance of the all-too-human things is total, for he does not even know that he does not know them. He therefore cannot inquire into the being of these things, for his thought is convinced—it does not know—of how petty and nonexistent they are. He has turned away from them out of contempt. His understanding of the beautiful and the noble determines his understanding of being. His body remains in the city, but he never asks what body is, for his thought, oriented by geometry and astronomy, never condescends to investigate what is near at hand, but flies everywhere below the earth and above the heavens, inquiring into the nature of each of the beings. Theodorus' question—"How do you mean this, Socrates?"—illustrates what Socrates has just said: Theodorus does not know what he does. The peculiarity of the *Theaetetus* is that, despite its concern with the difference between opinion and knowledge, there is no conversion in it to philosophy from non-philosophy. Theodorus is a professional, and Theaetetus an apprentice; so neither of them has any doubt that there is knowledge, or any awareness of the problem of philosophy's possibility, for after all, Theodorus already is flying.

Thales looked up at the stars and fell into a well. He stumbled into what he thought was the principle of everything, but he did not expect to find out the nature of the stars by looking at what was at his feet. And yet if the ground on which one stands is unseen, one does not know what in the ground makes it possible for one to look up. It is not every kind of ground from which one can take off. The ground must somehow be illuminated prior to one's looking up, for one does not in fact visit the stars. The Thalesian philosopher does not ask this question: if one were on a star, and looked at the earth, would one then be able to understand the ground upon which one formerly stood? One's own place is not simply interchangeable with any other place, for the sameness of the measure from Athens to Thebes and from Thebes to Athens does not entail the sameness of the motion in either direction. This is what the witticism of the Thracian servant girl seems to mean, but Socrates twists it in such a way that he too can apparently be bracketed with Theodorus.

What is before the philosopher and at his feet is not himself but his neighbor, about whom he hardly knows whether he is a human being and what he is doing. But the philosopher asks what is a human being, and what it is peculiarly fitting for human nature to do or suffer. Heaven is to earth as Socratic questioning is to gossip. But is that Socratic questioning? If one knows nothing about one's neighbor, one must take one's own nature as human nature, and one's own activity and experience as the standard. Neither geometry nor astronomy can disclose what is one's own nature, for it seems to be part of being human that one has a neighbor, and his nearness is not susceptible to measure. If the astronomer looked at himself astronomically, he should conclude that he was a bird and not a human being at all.[14] And the geometer could as well be dreaming as awake if to know human nature were the same as to know that the odd is never even (190b6–7). It is Socrates who knows the name, reputation, and wealth of Theaetetus' father and who cares more for potential philosophers in Athens than in Cyrene.[15] But Theodorus, who can only see what is close to him through the most distant prospect, must understand Theaetetus' soul imagistically, for the image is the vehicle for losing sight of what is before one.

The ridicule the philosopher encounters whenever he is compelled to speak of what concerns human beings is matched by the ridicule the pettifogger encounters whenever he is willing to discuss what justice and injustice, human happiness and misery are. The philosopher, however, must laugh hypothetically, for he can never compel the merely clever to rise up to his heights; and even if such a discussion occurred, no one would join him in his laughter, for they would not see what was ridiculous. Yet the philosopher seems compelled to laugh at himself, since his success evidently falls short of his aspirations. Theodorus is unaware of either difficulty. He believes it is possible that Socrates could persuade everyone and the consequence would be more peace and less evil among men. Socrates tells him his wish is impossible; Socrates' speech is not a proposal for legislation. The good cannot be unless there is something contrary to it. It is hard to make out what Socrates means; he cannot, at any rate, be like Theodorus, who does not know of this necessity.

Socrates could mean, it seems, only one of two things. That the good cannot come to be for men unless the bad comes to be along with it seems to be the theme of Plato's *Republic*, but here he speaks of being, not becoming. Or that since the bad haunts mortal nature of necessity, the bad ever attends the good which the philosopher obtains. But this would be a necessity of the contingent, which would not explain how Socrates can speak of the bad as a paradigm at rest in its being,[16] or how the philosopher when dead gets accepted into the region free of evils. Socrates says nothing about the immortality of the soul; he never even speaks of the philosopher's soul. Those of low cunning have a soul, the philosopher has only thought (*dianoia*). Socrates says that the punishment for injustice is misery, but since misery is to be out of sight of the divine, there is no punishment unless the unjust comes to recognize his own blindness, and such blindness is ineradicable. He therefore implies that happiness solely consists in the examination of what happiness is and all other kindred questions;[17] or, more precisely, since it necessarily consists in the examination of the bad as well as of the good, and consequently of one's neighbor and what is at one's feet, its goodness is inseparable from the badness of others. Socrates has moved from a celebration of the free Theodorus, whose inquiry into the nature of every being he calls neither wisdom nor happiness, to a celebration of political philosophy, whose ground is the despised human things and whose guide is the gods. Socrates thus looks even more ridiculous than Theodorus, for without a shred of proof or the shadow of a doubt he proclaims what god is, while saying the philosopher has trouble in finding out what man is. Socrates assigns every virtue to the philosopher except moderation.

X. Sortness
(177c6–183c4)

Socrates separates the discussion of future affects from that of present ones. The first is conducted with the revised Protagoras; the second examines the problem itself, since its Heraclitean proponents are too incoherent, according to Theodorus, to be questioned. The first discussion is reminiscent of the first book of the *Republic,* but with these differences: the just is assumed to be other than good, the good to be the beneficial, and the city to lay down all its laws with a single aim, that they be as beneficial as possible. This has one of three consequences: the just, the noble, and the holy are merely names for the beneficial; these names designate, in the present, degrees and kinds of future benefits; or, whenever the city makes a mistake, its errors are the just, the noble, and the holy. Socrates gives an example of the third possibility in the *Republic,* where he says the most beneficial marriages are sacred (458e4) and therefore marriage between brother and sister is to be permitted in certain cases. For the supposedly sacred prohibition against incest is only sacred because the city has not hit upon the good. Socrates, however, now has his own way because Theodorus is no Thrasymachus and cannot ask for whose benefit in the city does the city legislate. Theodorus is too far away from the city to see the difference between the greed of the brutish shepherd and the peevish rebelliousness of the unenlightened sheep (174d3–e1), which makes it as impossible for the city to acknowledge that it makes a mistake as a whole as for it to agree as a whole that in some instances it had hit upon the good. Would it then suffice to discredit Protagoras' thesis if the rulers would admit that sometimes they make a mistake? For Thrasymachus it would, but not for Clitophon, who is so bold as to maintain that the ruler's opinion about his own advantage is the justice of the stronger and therefore, presumably, that as long as he held this opinion (i.e., does not change the laws), he has not made a mistake.[18]

In order, then, for Socrates' argument to stand as more than *ad Theodorum,* it would be necessary that he consider whether or not the city does have a common good, but this would be to shift from opinion to knowledge and insert at this point the whole *Republic.* That is impossible, since Socrates has already summarized the culmination of the *Republic* (Books V–VII) in his previous speeches about the just, that is, the philosophic, life. Socrates had no need to go through the city to bring Theodorus to philosophy. And since he replaced the movement out of the cave with only an implicit argument about the need to start in the cave, he can ask Theodorus to look at the facts (*pragma*) as if the facts were known. Theodorus' inexperience thus makes it possible for him and Socrates to reach at once an agreement about the city which only political philosophy could establish. Theodorus has no notion of how treacherous an argument based on opinion can be.

The difference between perception and opinion becomes evident as soon as the future is introduced, for whereas there is no perception of the future, an opinion about the future does not differ qua opinion from an opinion about the present. Socrates can then show that the nonexpert's opinion about a future perception is less authoritative than the expert's; but what he does not stress is that the expert's opinion merely anticipates the nonexpert's, and the ultimate authority as to the correctness of the expert's opinion is the nonexpert's perception. The expert knows the same truth as the nonexpert for a longer time (cf. 158e1, 178e8). Art, on this basis, cannot be distinguished from knack or experience, or the spurious from the genuine art, as Socrates' example of cookery indicates. Theodorus has been led from siding with the many against Protagoras to his being shown the unbridgeable gulf between himself and the many, and then to a realliance between himself and the many. The city is the authority, not because it can figure out what is most beneficial for itself, but because it must confirm it as beneficial. The experts know the taste of the city better than the city knows it. Theaetetus had suggested this when Socrates asked him whether the taste of the doctrine satisfied him and he put off answering until he could hear what the expert Socrates would say.

The new revision of the Protagorean thesis is now stronger than ever: the wise know in advance what everyone will hold to be true.

Socrates for this reason ended his speech on the philosopher with a prediction about the afterlife, at which time, apparently, the miserable will know their own misery. Wisdom is ultimately consensus. It solely consists in knowing which turn the endless flow of things will take next. The wise are just one step ahead of the unwise, but the step never remains hidden from the unwise because it is their own step. The wise are those most honored in the cave, who predict which image is going to flash by next: Theodorus is an astronomer. The argument, therefore, against Socratic wisdom is that it can never be confirmed in this way; he cannot tell the many now what the many will later see for themselves. Socrates will suggest that had his trial lasted more than a day he could have won an acquittal, but he does not say that the Athenians would then have seen that the unexamined life is not worth living, for they have already had a lifetime to make up their minds about Socrates' way of life. Theodorus, on the other hand, can console himself; he may at any moment look ridiculous, but in the long run the last laugh will be his. The arts and sciences, no matter how abstruse, are not a standing threat to the city's opinions.

Now that all opinion has to submit to the authority of what at some time will be present opinion, Socrates must show that the grounds for asserting that present opinion is true are groundless. This, I think, he accomplishes, but the paradox of Socratic wisdom becomes all the more vivid. The many are now the authority, but the "physiology," which supports their authority, asserts what the many do not believe, that everything is in motion. They believe that some things are in motion and others at rest, and Socrates shares this belief, but he does not hold that their opinion is authoritative. So we are confronted on the one hand with a doctrine that in elevating the opinion of the many to knowledge undercuts that very elevation and, on the other, with Socrates, who in distinguishing between opinion and knowledge, and again between spurious and genuine happiness, asserts what the many will never accept—and yet he confirms in a way in which the many do not accept what the many do accept—the being of both motion and rest. It is perhaps this duality that allows Socrates to say that the greatest madness is moderation incarnate.

Theodorus claims to be familiar with the proponents of the Homeric-Heraclitean thesis. But as he goes on to describe them, he gets very angry with them, and far from their sharing in a common doctrine, he implies that they have no doctrine at all. When Socrates mildly suggests that when they are at peace and not fighting they do speak coherently and firmly to their pupils (whomever they want to make like themselves), Theodorus becomes even more indignant and denies that any of them has a single pupil. Theodorus believes they

are crazy and inspired; he finds them as unapproachable as Theaetetus had found the uninspired body-people repellent (cf. 156a1),
who do not admit that anything is but what they can get their hands
on. Theodorus' two speeches seem to imitate the incoherence he as-
cribes to the Heracliteans. The literal Theodorus resents the literalness of the Heracliteans. They are what they should be according to
the writings of Heraclitus, for this is not, as Socrates suggested, a
pretence on their part: they are unintelligible by nature and through
nature. Each of them is in the most literal sense an original: neither
the cause of others nor caused by another. Each is his own cause. This
is intolerable to the professional Theodorus, who takes as his model
for rationality the orderly transmission of knowledge from teacher to
pupil. He presents the soul-destroying and *logos*-destroying character
of the doctrine, and yet he does not conclude that this refutes the
doctrine. It would still be true with regard to being, even if one could
not live the doctrine on the level of either speech or soul.

Socrates had conducted his examination of Theaetetus on the assumption that what Theodorus had said imagistically about Theaetetus he had meant literally. This engendered a phantom offspring
in Theaetetus. But Theodorus now seems to believe that if man is not
the measure of all things, motion could still be the nature of all things,
for the Heracliteans prove by their very existence that this is the nature
of all things. Theodorus, however, has a way out of this dilemma; he
proposes that they treat the doctrine as a problem (*problêma*). A problem is the geometer's term for the setting out of a construction. They
are to attempt to construct an argument that will exhibit the behavior
of the Heracliteans, as Theodorus understands their behavior, without introducing soul. Such a construction will be intelligible while
leaving the Heracliteans as phenomenally unintelligible as they were
before. Theodorus looks upon the soul as if it were a problem in
astronomy: given the erratic motion of a planet, construct a model
that will fully describe the motion and yet will not causally explain
the motion.[19] Just as, if the planets were gods, they could do by will
what we show them as doing by design, so too the Heracliteans, each
with a god within him, will preserve their irrationality while displaying
in our model a rational order.

Theodorus is caught in a contradiction. If the souls of the Heracliteans look the way they do because we see them perspectivally (in
the perspective of war, as Socrates says), Theodorus cannot then say
that they look as they are. As an astronomical phenomenon, their
cause cannot be known, but if their cause is known, they cannot be
an astronomical phenomenon. Theodorus thus illustrates in himself
the stumbling of Thales. He looks, without knowing it, through both

ends of a telescope at once; the near becomes distant and the distant near. And so in observing from afar, as he supposes, the enthusiasm of others, he catches it himself. Theodorus' problem, then, cannot be construed on Theodorus' terms, for as Socrates points out, if the Heracliteans say what they are, the Parmenideans too would say what they are, and neither would be the nature of all things. Theodorus and Socrates got so involved with the Heracliteans that they forgot Parmenides, but now they are both trapped in the middle of the Heraclitean-Parmenidean tug-of-war. Not only are they ridiculous in the eyes of the city, they will be equally ridiculous in the eyes of philosophy if they neither take refuge with immobility nor drag themselves to safety in motion. Socrates takes it for granted that the body-people cannot rescue them.

Although the authority of the city has exposed the inadequacy of one version of Protagoras' thesis and has left Socrates as deficient in knowledge as he claims to be, it cannot be invoked again. For though the shoemaker can be neutral and laugh at both camps, on the grounds that one effectively cancels the other, neither Socrates nor Theodorus can withdraw. Even if Theodorus—his eagerness for discussion is feigned (161a7, 181b8)—gets out of the engagement as soon as he justly can and Socrates too slips out of danger in an apparently shameless way, still they both somehow recognize the authority of philosophy. In his sudden recollection of Parmenides, Socrates remembers the problem of being. The ultimate question is not what is knowledge, but what is being; it is not whether knowledge is compatible with becoming, but whether becoming is compatible with being. The exigencies of the dialogue have aligned Protagoras with the Heracliteans, but in his assertion that it is impossible to opine what is not (167a7–8), he is the representative of Parmenides as well. Protagoras will thus be demolished along with Homer and Heraclitus, only to reappear once more with the problem of false opinion. The ever-changing masks of Protagoras in the *Theaetetus* are the evidence for Socrates' last question—the sameness and the difference of sophist, statesman, and philosopher. Behind Theodorus' naive bafflement at the Heracliteans lies the problem of nonbeing.

Theodorus seems already to have admitted what Socrates is going to prove, that the Heracliteans cannot speak without contradiction; but Socrates does not admit the paradox of Theodorus, that their necessary silence is in accordance with the nature of their souls, and so they do not need any speech to show that motion is the nature of all things. Socrates, however, does take advantage of their silence; he has Theodorus agree to what in his former exposition he said they denied. He now speaks of place and of motion from place to place (cf. 153e1–2) and thus introduces two kinds of motion which cut across the former distinction of passive and active motions. Socrates is not being wholly arbitrary, for he has just implied that the denial of place properly belongs to the Parmenideans, whose "the one" is at rest in itself without place (180e4). Protagoras, it seems, in joining for the moment with Heraclitus, imported something of Parmenides, and it was his essential eclecticism that gave the doctrine all its persuasiveness. Socrates, at any rate, now shows the amazing clarity that comes with the discernment of kinds. He disregards the question of cause and effect and looks instead at what is first for us.

Motion had formerly come to light as part of a doctrine; the doctrine determined the distinctions to be made. But Socrates and Theodorus now come to an agreement about motion that is prior to any "theory" about motion. Its priority appears most strikingly in two ways. First, locomotion, in Theaetetus' physiology, only occurred in the "between" of agent and patient, and the *genesis* of *sensibilia* was this locomotion, while alteration was denied, for there was no change in the same; but neither the locomotion they did admit, nor the alteration they did not, was perceptible. Second, Theaetetus' physiology said that there was only motion and yet talked constantly of *genesis* or becoming. But as soon as one looks at locomotion, one does not see there any coming-to-be. Homer had spoken of *genesis*, the moderns of motion, but the distinction Socrates makes shows at once that they are not the same. That he never asks Theodorus whether his classification of motions is complete is the only hint he gives of the difficulty involved in becoming. Socrates therefore does not ask the Heracliteans to explain how the white comes to be out of any possible combination of locomotion and alteration; he grants them a mysterious causality and forces them to look instead at change as it shows itself to us. Socrates is very modest. His distinction resembles more the distinction between odd and even numbers than anything so high-powered as Theaetetus' classification of roots. He does not raise the question, for example, whether alteration could not be a kind of locomotion, in the sense that either something in local motion changes another into something else, or something in the same changes its place and supplants what was there. Locomotion and alteration are more certain in their difference than any hypothesis about their ultimate sameness. Socrates, however, has Theodorus agree to something that is far less certain. He asks him to include rotation in the same as a variety of locomotion. But rotation assumes a perfect body, which will not deviate locally from its axis. It assumes, in short, a mathematical construction, the existence of which could well be doubted. It is not surprising that Theodorus accepts rotation, but it does indicate how difficult this elementary dichotomy of apparent motion is. Socrates, indeed, carefully refrains from saying that any of these motions is; being only occurs in the remark "Let this be one *eidos*."

Socrates does not show that everything is not in motion; he limits himself to showing that, on the basis of total motion, knowledge could not be perception if knowledge means correct naming. The irreducible time lapse between the now of utterance and the now of perception warrants the conclusion that no possible revision of language could satisfy the requirements of the doctrine. Diagrammatically, every perception is of this sort (fig. 4).

The point of intersection of perception and quality is inexpressible, but nothing Socrates says militates against the notion that though unknowable it is always true. It would be true neither to the perceiver nor to the observer: it would be "ideally" true. Its language would be the mathematics of points, neither verifiable nor falsifiable. It order to understand what Socrates is getting at, it is necessary to ask why he replaces what he had called the perceived class (156b7) with what he now calls sortness or quality (*poiotês*), spoken of as a collective (182a9). The word "quality" or "sortness" has its source in two different models; it takes its suffix from that in hotness (*thermotês*) and whiteness (*leukotês*), and its stem from a pun on "making" and "sort" (*to poioun poion ti*). Every sort is not of something (*ti*) but solely its

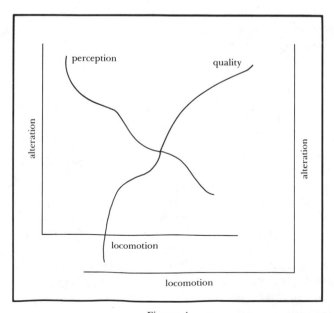

Figure 4

effect, which in turn is not perception but itself perceived, for itself perceived is the cause of it as perceived and not the cause of its becoming perceived.

Sortness is a word that belongs to the proposed revision of language. If color entirely changed, while seeing remained constant, the correct answer to the question "What do you see?" would not be a color but simply color. But since seeing does not abide either but is always changing into another sense, which includes the sensations of pleasure, pain, fear, desire, and countless others that are nameless (156b2–7), the correct answer to the question "What are you experiencing?" is not "I see" or "I am afraid," but simply "I sense." The thesis that knowledge is perception must be taken literally and, if taken literally, is irrefutable, for it does not admit of any articulation whatsoever. Knowledge is of sortness, a collection of an infinite number of names, none of which could ever be used correctly. Sortness is a universal that is never applicable, for its particularization is never perceptible. Socrates puts before us the difference between his own distinction of motion into two kinds and the spurious collection, sortness, which looks as if it separates an *aisthêsis* from an *aisthêton* but which in fact collapses them to such a point that its members vanish along with every kind of perception. We now understand why Socrates, in revealing the mysteries to Theaetetus, distinguished between the myth and its meaning. In the myth he spoke of *eidos* and *genos;* in his interpretation of it, he spoke of *hathroisma* (aggregate) and opposed it to *eidos* (157b8–c2).

XI. HELEN
(183c5–187c6)

Socrates has complied to some extent with Theodorus' demand that they treat the Heracliteans problematically, that is, without directing any question to their souls, for their thesis has turned out to be as unsayable as Protagoras'. Theodorus is relieved that he has now fulfilled his contract, and when Theaetetus reminds him that they had proposed to examine Parmenides as well—Theodorus had said, after all, that it would be unbearable not to do so—he is told not to teach his elders, young as he is, to transgress their agreements and be unjust (cf. 162d3). Theodorus is not joking. He has evidently sworn to himself to live up to his obligation but no more, not even if the compulsion is in the argument itself. Unlike Theaetetus, he prefers to be consistent at any price, for nothing must interfere with his freedom. Theodorus applies the standard of exactness found in mathematics to justice,[20] and this twin "idealism," which he takes as more real than "bare speeches," he combines with freedom. He wants to please both the truth and Protagoras, afraid to appear ridiculous and yet oblivious of his own bad manners, accepting of the authority of the city and yet wholly unaware of the city. He is a mixture of whimsicality and indignation. He meticulously draws a circle around himself and then wants to be left alone within that inviolable circle to do whatever he likes. He shuns any compulsion on himself but is not adverse to ordering Theaetetus about—"Get yourself ready to give Socrates an account of that which remains"—or treating the works of reason (speeches) as his own irrational slaves. Theodorus does not want to be the subject of comedy but of tragedy. The fate Socrates has woven for him was not an improvement but a punishment. A mathematician understands himself in the light of poetry. He whom Theodorus calls a philosopher is, according to Socrates, the one who knows how to clothe himself elegantly as a freeman should and hymns correctly the true life of gods and happy men (175d7–176a2). Of the ancient quarrel between poetry and philosophy Theodorus knows nothing.

Theodorus makes a false prediction. He thinks Socrates will do that which would give Theaetetus the most pleasure to hear—examine those who say that the whole is at rest. Socrates cannot resist, he says, the invitation to speak on anything at any time. Socrates refuses either to accommodate Theaetetus or to cover for Theodorus. But it was none other than Socrates who remembered Parmenides and put Theodorus and himself in the middle of a war without neutrals between Motion and Rest. So Theodorus was right after all: speeches do wait around like slaves for us to complete them. In the greatest dangers, Socrates had said, men acknowledge most readily the wisdom of others, and though he spoke of the war and the danger they themselves were in, it was not serious, and they do not have to play the game. The problem of being can wait. But though they are free they are not completely free: Theaetetus is pregnant. Socrates' maieutics must relieve him of his offspring. Theaetetus' soul takes precedence over being. They are to imitate political life, where the pressure of events postpones indefinitely the possibility of reaching full clarity about the foundations of political life. Theaetetus' soul is at stake (cf. 172e7). He must present himself before the infallible tribunal of Socrates' art despite his not even knowing the most important question. This is so urgent a matter that Socrates does not consult Theaetetus as to his pleasure. Socrates' subordination of being to knowledge recalls the way he had stopped speaking of philosophy (cf. 177b7–c5); for if Parmenides first asked the first question in philosophy, then to evade the question "What is philosophy?" is equivalent to the evasion of the question "What is being?" It would seem that the coming of the Eleatic stranger is a godsend.

Having liberated Theodorus from his fear of ridicule before the many, Socrates presents himself as full of fear and shame before the one Parmenides. In order to underline the disparity between Parmenides and himself, he quotes half a verse from Homer: Parmenides is "as awesome to me as uncanny." Helen spoke this line to the aged Priam. Iris, the offspring of Wonder, had arranged their meeting. They met on the walls of Troy, where the aged counselors of Priam had, on seeing Helen, said that her beauty was so awesomely like the goddesses' that the war between Achaeans and Trojans could not arouse their indignation. In reply to Priam's gentle words, Helen had burst out with the wish that death had then pleased her when she followed Priam's son to Troy. The ugliest of men, whom the gods had made barren of wisdom, compares himself to the most beautiful of women, whom the gods punished with barrenness for her crime.[21] Now that Socrates has done with Theodorus, he repudiates Theodorus' competence to judge his looks: there was not a word about the beautiful when he gave his speech in praise of Theodorus as the philosopher.

It seems absurd to say that Socrates is another Helen and the cause of the war between Rest and Motion. In describing that playful war, Socrates distinguishes between the ancients, who through their poetry concealed from the many that nothing was at rest, and the wise moderns who openly declare that everything is in motion, so that even the shoemakers could understand their wisdom and honor them. But the proponents of rest have no ancient counterparts, and though Parmenides also speaks poetically, he apparently has no followers who try to make the many understand their wisdom, let alone honor them.[22] Socrates, however, who will soon be put on trial, seems to have been even worse than Homer's proselytizers. He has surely not tried to impress the shoemaker with his wisdom, for he has none, but he has done nothing else but talk about shoemakers, and he has already admitted to Theaetetus that his practice has caused much hatred. Socrates' Protagoras had urged him to stop inciting enmity for philosophy and start converting, but Socrates defended himself to Theodorus on the grounds that evil was necessarily coterminous with good. He had further indicated that the many can never accept Protagoras' wisdom, nor do they have to concern themselves with the conflict between Motion and Rest.

Socrates has become the greatest threat to philosophy ever since he brought her down to earth and began to consider things like hair, mud, and dirt. Parmenides, indeed, had told him to do so, though he could now very well wonder whether he had understood Parmenides correctly. Socrates here hesitates to justify himself before the tribunal of philosophy. He chooses instead a middle course between the problem of being on the one hand, which is never urgent, and the issue of philosophy's relation to the city on the other, which he himself has brought to a head and which now involves his own life. The compromise between a matter of the greatest urgency and a matter of the greatest importance is Theaetetus' soul, on whose behalf he continues to do what he has always done. It is in this context that Socrates let us infer that he is beautiful.

Socrates' conversation with Theodorus has purified Theaetetus' original answer; that knowledge is perception now stands by itself as Theaetetus' own opinion, without either Homer or Protagoras as its parent. If, Socrates asks, Theaetetus were asked by what or with what a human being sees the white and black, and by what or with what he hears the high and low, he would presumably say by or with eyes and ears. Socrates does not let Theaetetus say by or with sight or hearing.[23] He compels him to say that it is more correct to speak of the eyes and the ears as those through which we see and hear than of the eyes and ears in the instrumental dative without any preposition, but only after Theaetetus has agreed to this does Socrates explain its greater correctness. In poetry, to be sure, the preposition *dia* with the eyes or ears is common, but we do not look on poetry as the model of exactness. Throughout Plato the dative is used alone, even in passages where exactness would seem to be in order.[24] The instrumental dative is neutral with regard to the question of soul or no soul, but the prepositional phrase requires something like soul to complete it. Socrates uses brute force on Theaetetus in order to introduce soul. The dative *ommasi* (with or by the eyes) runs together eye and sight; it is the more correct answer if the eye strictly understood is the seeing eye. But the phrase *dia ommatôn* (through the eyes) entails a distinction between the nonseeing and seeing eye, and once the eye has thus become equivocal, it becomes terrible for the senses to be lodged in us as if we were wooden horses. The more precise answer shows the necessity that the manifold of perceptions jointly pertain or extend to a single whole or class (*idea*). The less precise answer, on the other hand, because it treats the sense organs only in their being-at-work, lets us be content with what seems to be a limited number of beings-at-work. But as soon as we consider touch, we would have to allow it to be infinite in number—each hand, each finger, each patch of skin—and we would perhaps be driven to suppose that the body as a whole in its being-at-work was that with which (or by which) we touch. The body as a perceiving whole raises the question of the cause of its being such a whole, and once again something like soul would have to be invoked. Socrates avoids this more roundabout argument through the nonce distinction he has imposed on Theaetetus. The way in which the manifold of perceptions pertains to a single whole is not simply as their container, but as a cause of the manifold being what it is. The *idea* is that which gives to its members their class character.

No sooner has Socrates extracted from Theaetetus what he wants than he lets him go again. He will no longer meddle in his answers but will let Theaetetus speak for himself. Theaetetus thus becomes free again, but at a price: the argument loses its newly won precision. Socrates asks Theaetetus whether the instruments of perception belong to the body or to something else, and whereas Socrates had suggested that these instruments could be referred to the body, Theaetetus says that they belong exclusively to the body. If they are instruments, they could only be the soul's, and only in their idleness could they be the body's. Socrates then speaks, without explanation, of the power through which we perceive and has Theaetetus' willing assent that one power cannot do the job of another. He implies that all the powers of perception belong to the body (185e7), and that as instruments are to their user, so the five powers are to a single *idea*. Perhaps, however, the powers are like the fingers of the hand, and the hand as a whole is the single *idea*. The mention of soul, indifferent though Socrates declares the name for the *idea* to be, predisposes Theaetetus toward a separation of *idea* from body. He imagines the body to be a wooden horse pierced like a sieve, inside of which an Odysseus sits in control of an unruly host of sensations. Theaetetus rejected the body-people out of hand.

Socrates offers four statements, the first three of which would seem to be always true, and the last suggests wherein error could arise. Theaetetus, in any case, assents to the first three and hesitates over the last. Theaetetus thinks about both sound and color that (1) both of the pair are; (2) each of the two (is) other than each of the two, but the same as itself; (3) both of the pair (are) two, and each of the two one. As Socrates presents it, "two" and "one" are somehow derivative from "both" and "each," "same" and "other," and of these in turn "both" is prior to the rest. The being of sound and color first gets thought with the coupling of them in thought, and it is as a thought couple that what they share gets thought through. The community they are given in thought as a couple precedes the thinking of what is common to them: being, otherness, sameness. It therefore does not follow that without qualification each is the same as itself and other than the other, for Socrates asks whether Theaetetus could not go on to examine whether they are like or unlike one another. Unlike being, sameness, and otherness, the like and the unlike are not "known" instantly, and since nothing forbids one's examination to conclude that color and sound are wholly alike except in the way we perceive them, the three statements are not so much instant knowledge as they are conditions for our thinking. The first part of the dialogue raised the question whether knowledge and perception were the same or other, but as long as they were taken for the same, thought was completely paralyzed, for there was no room for thought in such an equation. It could not think without already knowing, and yet it only had to think for the equation to vanish.

However, Socrates now has led Theaetetus back to what was latent in his very first answer, that there is no knowledge where there is not number. Theaetetus counts color and sound; he cannot count them unless he thinks of their common being. Their common being makes them countable, but does it also make each of them what it is? Does the common being of sound and color stand to sound and color each by itself, as the single *idea* stands to the manifold of perceptions? Soul would then be the common being of all perceptions (like Aristotle's aesthetic soul), and to speak of it as by itself would be as if one spoke of the two of sound and color as simply two. Soul by itself would then be to the soul of perception as two is to two perceived things. Theaetetus, at least, assumes that the soul, which, he says, examines what is common, is the same *idea* by means of which we perceive through the instrumental powers of the body. That which is the common ground of perception is that which examines the common ground of everything perceived, and this common ground is not body, magnitude, motion, or rest, but being. Being is wholly unmysterious to Theaetetus.

If it were possible to find out whether sound and color were both salty, Theaetetus would say that the power through the tongue would be the means to determine it. Socrates asks in this indirect way how one can say of both a sound and a color that they are both intense, or both pleasant or unpleasant, and most of all, how one knows that one cannot taste a color or a sound. The things common to the senses, along with the discrimination among the senses, elude Theaetetus. The phrase "the power through the tongue" is his own; it is his way of combining "through an instrument," "through a power," and "through a sensing." Power could now be the soul's, which would use the tongue as its instrument for this particular job, and the soul would be, as an *idea*, a power. If Theaetetus had listened to his own answer, he would have realized its beauty (185c4), for it not only shows that the tongue cannot by itself discriminate between two tastes, but also that it contains the answer to Socrates' next question. Socrates accepts Theaetetus' "power." The question he asks is, The power through what, that is, the soul through what, makes plain to us that which is common? The answer is, through speeches (*dia logôn*), whose corporeal instruments are the tongue and the ear.[25] Theaetetus, however, hears Socrates' question in terms of Socrates' original formulation and not in terms of his own: Through which of the instruments of the body do we perceive by means of the soul the common?

It appears to Theaetetus that the soul has no proper instrument for the common, but it by itself is its own instrument. And it appears thus to Theaetetus, Socrates says, because he is beautiful. Theaetetus' beauty is a cause; its effect is to open up to him something that would otherwise require a long argument. Beauty is insight; it is the shortcut through an argument. It therefore bypasses the "weakness of speeches" and runs the risk of oversimplification.[26] The beauty of Theaetetus consists as much in his ignoring speeches as the soul's instruments as his hitting upon soul in itself. It is inseparable from Theaetetus' benefaction to Socrates, who does not have to supply a long argument. Socrates, who has cast himself in the role of Helen, tells his look-alike Theaetetus that he is not ugly. Socrates was beautiful because he avoided the problem of being in order to help Theaetetus; Theaetetus is beautiful because he gets hold of the soul by itself without the help of speeches. But their joint evasion has brought them back to being, which more than anything else is common to everything. Parmenides, without Theaetetus' awareness, has slipped into the argument. His beauty seems to have made a confrontation with Parmenides unavoidable. This confrontation takes the form of Theaetetus' own experience of false opinion—that knowledge is not perception—against the Parmenidean contention that false opinion is impossible. That Theaetetus cannot defend his experience against these arguments shows up the weakness in his beauty.

The difficulty to which Theaetetus' insight is exposed immediately becomes plain in the concluding part of the argument. He tells Socrates that in his opinion being is one of the things which the soul alone by itself aims at or desires (*eporegetai*). This is the most extraordinary remark that Theaetetus ever makes. Nothing has prepared us for it, for we should have expected him to say that being is one of the things which the soul by itself examines. It seems as if Theaetetus' newfound beauty has affected his understanding of being, or, better perhaps, that his understanding of being comes to light in his newfound beauty. He says, at any rate, that especially in the case of the beautiful and the ugly, the bad and the good, the soul by itself examines being, "calculating in itself the past and the present things (goods, etc.) relative to the future." Theaetetus remembers the argument in which Socrates got Theodorus to agree that not everyone was equally competent about the future. The gathering point of being and benefit is the future. Being primarily consists in the being of temporal relations, and the science of being is a kind of divination. There is no being in perceptual experiences through the body because there is no experience in them of the future. Theaetetus seems to discern the soul's independence from the body as most evident in its hopes, fears, and desires.

The relationship, then, of these experiences of the soul to perceptual experiences through the body would be being, and the science of their relationship would be that science which comprehends the manifold of arts and sciences into one class. The unity of knowledge is warranted by the unity of soul. Theaetetus' beauty, which Socrates has sparked into shining out by reminding him of his mathematics, has led him away from his own body. Body has disappeared altogether into the experiences we have through it. If truth is ungraspable by means of perception, no perception is true or false, and truth is obtained by reflection on what has neither truth nor being. Theaetetus has fallen back into Protagoreanism. When asked to supply that name which the soul has whenever it alone by itself deals with the beings, of which there has been no mention, Theaetetus does not say "to figure out" (*syllogizesthai*), "to calculate" (*analogizesthai*), or "to think through" (*dianoeisthai*), but "to opine" (*doxazein*), the key word of Socrates' Protagoras (cf. 170b8–9). Theaetetus in his beauty has forgotten *logos* along with body and that ordinary human beings, according to Socrates, believe wisdom to be true thought (*dianoia*).

XII. PARMENIDES
(187c7–190c4)

For the rest of the dialogue, the recurring example of knowledge is knowledge of Theaetetus, Socrates, and Theodorus, any two of them, but especially of Theaetetus and Socrates. The dialogue thus becomes reflexive and turned back on itself—a conversion to their own doing and being. This conversion is initiated by Socrates, who exhibits to Theaetetus his barrenness of wisdom. What we now witness is no longer Socrates' practice of maieutics on Theaetetus, but Socrates' giving birth *per impossibile*. The proper element of this impossibility is false opinion. Socrates is recalled to himself by Theaetetus' reminder of what he had said about leisure, but since Socrates in fact is pressed for time, it would seem that, if it is now opportune to examine false opinion, his forthcoming trial must bear on the question. At the trial, he asserts that he knows that he knows nothing, which, if translated according to Theaetetus' definition, would apparently run "Socrates has the true opinion that he has no true opinion about anything." Socrates therefore would truly opine that he opines falsely. Even if we exclude Socrates' true opinion from everything he opines falsely, it is absurd for Socrates to hold onto opinions he truly opines to be false (cf. 189e7). If, however, "to know nothing" means "not to have any opinion," Socrates would truly opine that he has no opinion about anything. But this is no less absurd, for Socrates has many opinions, all of which he must hold to be true, and one of which is that the soul deals with some things alone by itself.

Theaetetus, in reminding Socrates of the city, has compelled him to reflect on the meaning of his own ignorance. Socrates' ignorance stands naked before the all-wise philosophers, all of whom, despite their "ontological" disagreements, agree with each other on the impossibility of false opinion. The shift from Theaetetus' second offspring to the problem of Socratic ignorance resembles the shift from Theaetetus' soul to the problem of knowledge, which Socrates had as abruptly introduced at the beginning of the dialogue. But just as the problem of knowledge turned out to be at the root of the question of Theaetetus' soul and Theodorus' competence, so now Theaetetus' offspring points directly to the problem of Socrates' competence. The city and the philosophers together apply the same kind of compulsion to Socrates as Socrates had just applied to Theaetetus. Theaetetus then emerged as beautiful. Will Socrates fare as well?

The *Theaetetus* as a whole thus examines two Socratic characteristics, his midwifery and his knowledge of ignorance, and for the most part each is treated separately. The first is under the surface of the Heraclitean-Protagorean section, insofar as Heraclitus and Protagoras seem to supply the epistemological and physiological basis for the uniqueness of Socrates' art. The second dominates in a more explicit way Socrates' discussion with Theaetetus, once Theodorus has abandoned both Heraclitus and Protagoras, for the question of identity, in terms of which the problem of false opinion is posed, amounts to various attempts to distinguish Socrates from everyone else. In the *Sophist,* it is their apparent failure to discover the *logos* of Socrates that makes Theaetetus and Theodorus ask the stranger almost the same question Socrates asked: How is the philosopher to be told apart from the sophist?

If knowledge were true opinion, Theaetetus would now know (have the true opinion) that this was the case. But if Socrates and Theaetetus will discover that Theaetetus had a true opinion, his true opinion would then have lacked the proof that true opinion was knowledge.

Knowledge as true opinion is indistinguishable from an inspired guess. Theaetetus does not realize that the distinction between true and false opinion cannot be made on the basis of true opinion, for if both are by nature (187e7), that is, prior to any calculation, both are as experiences equal, and neither can do any more than deny the truth of the other. A true opinion affords no access through itself to the validation of its truth. It has precisely the same status as an individual's perception had in Theaetetus' physiology; the soul, simply because it acts by itself when it opines, does not at once become superior to its joint action with the body in perception, for it opines either truly or falsely. To work out a way, then, to tell true opinion from false is already to be beyond true opinion, but Socrates and Theaetetus cannot make this step before they backtrack and examine the true and the false in perception.

Perception had first been tied into a doctrine of motion, but now that they are to consider knowing apart from learning and forgetting, motion must be discarded. The very mention of Parmenides has had its effect. No "physiology" accompanies the three successive arguments Socrates employs to account for false opinion; as arguments, they prove to be so powerful as to destroy its very possibility. But Socrates begins to make some progress when he resorts to images. The two images—of wax and of birds—impart imaginary motion and body into the presentation of soul. Motion and body are more real in these images than they were in Theaetetus' physiology, where body and motion only existed (if at all) as the geometrical imaging of number. A physiology of soul in images seems less illusory than a physiology of illusion. Socrates and Theaetetus end up once more in need of the Eleatic stranger.

In the first argument, Socrates not only speaks of knowledge and ignorance but also of belief (*oiesthai*) and conviction (*hêgeisthai*) and thus implicitly marks off the real state of the knower or nonknower from his own awareness of his state. Such a separation seems not to have any effect on the first two cases, but in the third, in which Theaetetus thinks it monstrous, it is not so obvious that false opinion is impossible. "Surely no one believes," Socrates says, "that what he knows is what he does not know, nor, in turn, what he does not know, what he knows." A businessman knows how to make money; he believes that this knowledge is knowledge of how to manage a city. Closer to home, Theodorus knows mathematics, astronomy, and music; he believes that this knowledge is knowledge of soul. Theaetetus' exclamation of horror at such vanity—how could anyone be so dishonest with himself?—testifies to his innocence and shows the danger of argument if one does not know the way to the marketplace. Theaetetus knows nothing of the spurious extension of itself into which each art and science necessarily lapses if it is not guided by an awareness, which it itself cannot supply, of itself as a part of knowledge. So if one now reconsiders the second case, it too becomes far less certain. "Can anyone be convinced," Socrates asks, "that what he does not know is something else he does not know, and knowing neither Theaetetus nor Socrates to get it into his head that Socrates is Theaetetus or Theaetetus Socrates?" Although Anytus knows neither the sophists, as he himself admits,[27] nor Socrates, as we should say, he certainly believes that Socrates is a sophist. Theaetetus' sincerity, which prevented him from playing the part of Hippolytus, totally blinds him to its possible lack in others. If, however, knowledge is replaced throughout by true opinion, and ignorance by no opinion, then false opinion is impossible, and Theaetetus' definition collapses, for true opinion must vanish along with false opinion. Theaetetus and Socrates have each a stake in establishing false opinion, one in order to maintain his definition, the other in order to distinguish true opinion from knowledge.

The second argument reveals the difference between perceiving and thinking, for the parallel Socrates draws between seeing and opining shows that "nothing" has its proper home in perception. To see nothing in the absence of light is an everyday experience, but the minimal conditon for thinking, inasmuch as it is an activity of the soul by itself, is thinking "at least one." Since being rides in on the coattails of one, thinking must involve the thinking of being. Is the "at least one" of thinking an a priori object of thinking? And if it is, does thinking bring it to light, or is the light which makes possible its being thought prior to thinking? And, finally, if thinking does not furnish its own illumination, does the illumination necessarily cast light on some particular one, as Parmenides seems to believe, or does it merely guarantee the possibility of thinking anything, while the something thought comes in from elsewhere? Furthermore, to look and not to see anything, or to listen for something and not to hear it or anything else, is an equally ordinary experience; it seems impossible to conceive of any kind of thinking that could be an attempt to think and yet think nothing. Thinking is either off or on, in contact or not.[28] One cannot first be thinking and then turn one's thought, as one directs one's gaze, to something. Thinking is a being-at-work without potentiality. Socrates, therefore, has justified through a proof of the impossibility of thinking nothing his seemingly arbitrary assertion that the soul alone by itself deals with the beings.

The third argument proceeds on the basis of the preceding two arguments, and hence completes the number of possibilities for false opinion. It borrows from the first argument "the other" and from the second "being" and considers false opinion as the exchange of one being for another. Two beings would seem to be the minimal condition for false opinion. Is it also the minimal condition for true opinion? Thinking was first presented by Socrates as the thinking of a both; Socrates is now implying that there might be two kinds of thinking, for one of which "two," and for the other "one," would be its minimal condition. However this may be, Socrates' description here of false opinion seems to fit better what occurs when one misunderstands an intention, an example of which is found in the *Republic* (523a10–524c2).

Some things, Socrates tells Glaucon, do not invite the understanding (*noêsis*) to reflection, on the grounds that perception has adequately discriminated among them, whereas other things urgently require reflection, since perception is not acting soundly. "It is plain," Glaucon said, "that you mean things that appear from afar and shadow-paintings." "You have scarcely hit upon what I mean," Socrates said. Glaucon gives examples where perception invites perception to further investigation; he is literally thinking of something else and therefore has a false opinion of what Socrates means. But though he is not in himself opining falsely, still, since he was intending to hit on Socrates' meaning, he has hit on something else than what he wanted. What he wanted, Socrates has given in a speech, and Glaucon believed he had found the being that fitted the speech. It is not, then, the exchange of one being for another that brings about false opinion, but the connecting of a being with a speech to which it does not belong. Diagrammatically, the situation is as follows:

Speech₁ (things not inviting reflection)	Being₁ (the region of trust)
Speech₂ (things inviting reflection)	Being₂ (the contrarieties of beings)
Speech₃ (things not inviting further perception)	Being₃ (the phenomena seen close at hand)
Speech₄ (things inviting further perception)	Being₄ (the phenomena seen from afar)

Glaucon mistakes being$_3$ for being$_1$, for he mistakes speech$_3$ for speech$_1$, and being$_4$ for being$_2$, since he takes speech$_4$ as speech$_2$. The minimal condition for this kind of false opining is two beings and one speech, where given the speech, one finds the wrong being of the speech, and in this sense exchanges one being for another. We therefore see how fateful it is for Theaetetus that he overlooked speeches as the soul's instruments.

Theaetetus illustrates the interchange of beings in false opinion with an example of opposites. "Whenever anyone opines what is ugly as what is beautiful, or what is beautiful as what is ugly, then truly he opines falsely." He seems to be thinking of Theodorus, who took him to be ugly, as he has now learned from Socrates, instead of as beautiful, but since without speech the universal and the particular are indistinguishable, Theaetetus misses the fact that to opine is to opine something about something, and on the nonpredicative level mistaking is impossible. Theaetetus, therefore, misunderstands precisely in the way he thinks is impossible. He takes the two of predication for the one of nonpredication and thus persists in treating thinking as if it were perceiving. Socrates pokes fun at Theaetetus' "truly" and complains that Theaetetus does not hold him in the same awe and fear as Socrates holds Parmenides. Theaetetus' "truly" validates his opinion that if someone exchanged the beautiful for the ugly he would be opining falsely. Socrates playfully asks whether this "truly" is compatible with knowledge as true opinion (cf. 189d7). I know or truly opine, Theaetetus says, that Theodorus opines falsely; but that Theodorus opines falsely is the consequence of a definition, and Theaetetus' true opinion is not open to correction but is necessarily true, whereas in true opinion there can be no "knowledge" of necessity. "Theodorus truly opines falsely" means that he takes the beautiful for the ugly without knowing it. One cannot replace the inadvertence expressed in "without knowing it" with "without opining truly." Theaetetus, moreover, fails to observe that to opine the beautiful could be a false opinion without any exchange of the beautiful for the ugly, for someone would, if he believed he had a golden soul, nobly opine falsely. Only if the true were the beautiful, and the false ugly, would it necessarily follow that such opining of the beautiful would involve an exchange with the ugly. Theaetetus takes it for granted that the true is the beautiful (194c1–2; cf. 195d2–5, 200e5–6). He seems to be a duplicate of Socrates when young.

Socrates tries to get Theaetetus to recognize his own speaking and conversing. On account of Theaetetus' self-forgetting, Socrates can only do this if he translates the speaking of Theaetetus to Socrates into his soul's silent conversation with itself. Theaetetus stands before his own speaking as if it were a foreign tongue. If to opine (*doxazein*) and to think (*dianoeisthai*) are the soul's silent versions of to speak (*legein*) and to converse (*dialegesthai*), then one can genuinely opine if and only if one has gone through the thinking that has resulted in a conclusion (*logos*). (To share a *logos* (*homologein*) does not count as the sharing of an opinion unless the reasoning is also shared.) Socrates here interprets the relation of the images of pregnancy and giving birth as that of silent thinking and silent speaking, and maieutics as nothing other than dialectics. This interpretation, however, does away with both Socrates' barrenness and the infallibility of his art. He now does not know, and the soul only phantomlike appears (*indalletai*) in its thinking to be conversing.[29]

The identity Socrates claims between a spoken and a silent questioning and answering equates the self-identity of the soul with two different speakers. But even within the soul there is a difficulty. If the soul asks and then answers itself, the soul must deceive itself in its either denying or assenting to what it already has figured out. The condition for all thinking would be to take the same for the other, and what Theaetetus has just said to be false opinion would be thinking. The impossibility of positing something (*heteron ti*) as another (*heteron*) in one's own thought, would thus be due to the spurious otherness in thinking itself. Mistaking could not occur within a soul which already is both the knower as answerer and the nonknower as questioner (cf. 145e9, 187d2). Meno's paradox flourishes anew, and neither the image of wax nor that of birds can adequately resolve it.

Socrates now points out to Theaetetus that the consequence for his definition of false opinion is somewhat the same as what they formerly concluded from the equation of knowledge and perception. In terms of what one might opine falsely, dreaming cannot be distinguished from waking, sickness from health, or madness from sanity. But there is a difference. With perceiving, one's perceptions varied according to one's condition, but with opining, though the assertions themselves are just as private (to oneself), they are all invariant and held in common, regardless of anyone's condition. It looks at first as if their invariance were that of empty "concepts"—the odd is odd, the ox is an ox, and the two is two—while the noninvariance of perceptions showed richness of content but they were wholly nonconceptual. The problem is then to put together the invariance of empty concepts with the invariance of content-rich experience. This, however, is not the case, for odd, even, ox, horse, two, and one are beings and not concepts. Socrates means something else, and Theaetetus has not been listening closely enough. It is perfectly possible to utter the sentence, "Odd is even," but it is not possible to speak it, if to speak means to draw the conclusion of one's own thinking. The sayable is not the opinable, for speech as it is ordinarily understood is not thought. Speech, properly understood, is always a conclusion and never a premise. A proof, known to the ancients, shows that, if the hypotenuse of an isosceles right triangle is commensurate with its side, the odd would be even. Someone could surely have the opinion, in the non-Socratic sense, that they are commensurable, but he could not have that opinion, in the Socratic sense, for the reasoning which must accompany it as an opinion would cancel it. Socrates' conversation with Theaetetus now illuminates the same point. They prove that to have the opinion, in the strict sense (190e1), that false opinion is heterodoxy or opining the other, is to speak nothing, and therefore it is to opine nothing, which the second argument has shown to be impossible. The dialogue itself is the proof of the definition's alogical character, from which it cannot be separated if its irrationality is to be grasped. Socrates has now vindicated Parmenides. His vindication is twofold. Whether the being which is thought is just what it is and nothing else, or an opinion is genuine only if it is backed up by a proof—in either case mistaking is impossible. Neither Truth nor Opinion admits of falsehood.

XIII. Wax
(190e5–196c3)

Theaetetus has not understood what he has just experienced; he has fallen back into the same condition he was in before Socrates explained to him the cause of his perplexity in the face of Socratic questions. He does not even know the very strange consequences if false opinion will not come to light—that the false opinion they had about false opinion would, despite their proof, cease to be false. Socrates refuses to enlighten him. He is very hard on Theaetetus. His inoculation of Theaetetus against sophistry and the ordinary understanding of Parmenides has not "taken." It can only "take" if Theaetetus rehearses by himself what he has experienced. No one can conduct this internal dialogue for him. Theaetetus would literally have to become Socrates in order for the argument to become manifest to him, for the *logos* remains invisible as long as the speaking is embedded in sounds spoken to another. As the phantom image (*eidôlon*) of thought, it resists every effort to make it transparent in itself (cf. 206d1–6). Speaking out loud has the same apparent reasonableness as the sentence Protagoras wrote in his book, which only collapsed when the reader obeyed its concealed injunction. Euclides, therefore, acted correctly without knowing it when he put Socrates' narration into direct discourse. Theaetetus is in the position of someone who looks at a mathematical proof in a textbook and confesses that he does not "see" it. No one can "see" it for him. Theaetetus is wholly enslaved to the *logos;* he cannot get free of it if he turns away from it as Theodorus did, but only if he understands what the *logos* is. Understanding resists *logos* even though it is a *logos*. If, for example, Socrates' "I have nothing wise" is said ironically, it can be translated as: "Socrates knows nothing which Theaetetus would accept as wisdom." This ipso facto cannot be explained to Theaetetus. But in the meantime, in the face of Theaetetus' incomprehension of the bare *logos,* it is necessary to examine the corporeal counterpart of speech as the image of thought-memory.

Socrates proposes a wax block in our souls for the sake of argument. The wax block is an image which contains images; it is not an image in the way in which the images it receives are images. The original, whether it be a perception or a thought, is not to its image in the wax as the unknown something in the soul is to the wax which is its image. Socrates begins by exchanging one being he does not know for another. The mnemonic image is the product of its original; it cannot do what the original can do. But the wax block is not a product of the unknown, for it is set up to do what the unknown does. The wax is not there merely as a receiver of everything; if it is to count as a source of knowledge, we must be able to submit it to whatever we want recorded, for otherwise retrieval would be hampered if not blocked altogether, and everything we perceived we would know.

The wax has a finite capacity, both as to the number of images it can receive and the degree of subtlety its impressions can have. It requires, moreover, that perceptions and thoughts be interpreted in a certain way, "like the seals or signs on rings." These signs cannot be what the beings themselves are; they are stand-ins for the beings. As stand-ins they can be either arbitrary—like a letter for a sound— or natural signs of the beings, and if they are natural, does their reversal in the wax reproduce something of the originals which they themselves do not have? We do not know, moreover, whether the perceptual or intellectual signs are spoiled by the wax, so that only the first impression can be good, while afterwards every repeated application of the seal blurs the original clarity. Socrates seems to assume that each perception, once it has made its impress, is completely wiped out, just as he had urged Theaetetus, in the case of his thoughts, to wipe out all that had gone before. In the memory, the difference between thoughts and perceptions fades, for now every term like "blunt" or "sharp," with which knowledge, if it were perception, would have to be qualified, admits of a possible meaning.

Now all of these, at which Socrates barely hints, are deductions from the wax block as image; they are inseparable from almost any image that prior to its serving as an image exists in its own right. It is therefore always difficult to "read" any but the simplest image, for one can easily mistake that which only belongs to the stuff of the image and without which the image would cease to be an image and become the thing itself. Of the two images Socrates employs, the wax block, because it seems to be so close to what the soul must do in remembering, is more liable to mislead us than the birds, whose outlandishness and recalcitrance to a one-to-one correspondence make them perhaps more revealing if less easy to read.

Not even Plato's Parmenides, who offers to the young Socrates his way of hypothesis as a way out of the impasse created by the necessity for and the impossibility of the "ideas," can altogether abstain from images and examples. Parmenides' own stance, before he embarks on the illustration of his hypothetical way, requires for its understanding an allusion to a poem of Ibycus that contains an elaborate metaphor. The eighth hypothesis becomes intelligible only when Parmenides cites shadow-paintings and dreams;[30] at which point we cannot but suppose that, had Parmenides been willing to be less austere in the other hypotheses, we should have had much less trouble in following him. What seems casual and adventitious in Parmenides' speech becomes in Plato's Socrates a matter of policy. Examples and images everywhere abound, and whenever Socrates does not bother to connect his own thinking with what his interlocutor understands, the interlocutor has to stop him and ask him for an illustration. One of the longest passages Plato gives of Socrates' sustained thinking is now before us. Socrates lists fourteen cases in which mistaking is impossible and then three in which it is possible. Within the limits of the argument, this is as sound as it is an exhaustive enumeration. Quick as Theaetetus is, he does not follow until Socrates gives an example. Here, Plato seems to be saying, is the way in which Socrates silently spoke to himself: completeness and necessity were the criteria to which he always tried to measure up.

For his not understanding what a *logos* is, Socrates almost punishes Theaetetus with a *logos* he cannot understand. Socrates' account raises several questions. Knowledge as recognition would seem to consist in the ability to report on the congruence between a past impression and a present perception; at best, this can only be true opinion, for one can always be deceived. In order to check on congruence, one would have to compare the impression with the seal. If the seal were replaced in the impression, the impression would become adjusted to the seal; there would always be congruence, and one could not say that here is Socrates, but he looks older. The seal must be "projected" on the impression, or the impression on the seal. The wax block would seem to need both depth for memory and a reflecting surface for projection. If, moreover, the impression is poor, over which one has little or no control, the impression is not congruent with the seal even at the moment of impression; but at that moment, the speech label is put down correctly, and when the seal is withdrawn, the label remains attached to the impression, which is of nothing that one has perceived. If, for example, a seal with three vertices left an impression of four vertices but with the label "triangle," there would be knowledge in some sense. As long as nothing but this seal recurred, there would be recognition, even though the impression itself if read would say "rectangle." Socrates thus fails to consider possible mismatchings of impressions, where "three" is linked with "four" in the wax but is labeled "three," so that "three" is unknown when there is no perception and known when there is. Theaetetus' addition of *logos* to true opinion might be a way of avoiding such errors. There are also possible misreadings of seals—those cases in which what is perceived stands on two levels at once, as, for example, in Theaetetus' distinction between letters in their shape and color and as representations of words. Perhaps all perceptions are double in this way, and knowledge is that which transforms a perception as a possible sign into an actual sign of a being.

The wax block makes one think of all the senses in terms of touch. But if a color becomes in the wax a kind of surface, it would seem that, in the absence of the perception, it would be known in its corrugations and not as a color. We should perhaps suppose that a sound recorded in the wax block would not preserve the sound as sound but a simulacrum of that which made the sound. Though present, it would not then even be known until one "played" the simulacrum with a mental needle, and recognition would only arise if the sound when reheard played the simulacrum without damaging its grooves. We are more likely to remember a speech than the sound of a speech, and we might surmise that something similar happens with sight. We see MAN and read it even if it is now shaped in a way we never saw before.

The reversal, then, of the seal in the block would mean that the present perception undergoes there two transformations. First the wax block simulates at least one cause of every kind of perception without being any one of them; second, it separates the "intention" of the perception from the perception to the same extent that Socrates had distinguished between his understanding what Parmenides said and his following what Parmenides intended. Error, therefore, could arise either on the level of intention, to which Theaetetus now points in his not following Socrates' enumeration (cf. 184a3, 192d2), or on the level of matching impressions in the wax. Socrates speaks exclusively of mismatching and ignores misunderstanding, for misunderstanding, as we have said, cannot be explained.

Socrates has now listed seven possible states of the soul: (1) Knowledge, (2) Ignorance, (3) Perception, (4) No Perception, (5) Knowledge and Perception as True Opinion, (6) Neither Knowledge nor Perception, (7) Mismatching as False Opinion. Since to know is not to mistake something for something else, to know is to identify. Socrates seems to indicate what knowledge as identification involves when he speaks of the poor bowman who hits the wrong target. First of all, there is the distance, whether of time or place, between the would-be knower as bowman and the target as that which is to be known. Next there is the soul as the sight which looks at what is to be known, identifies it as such, and itself will do the knowing. Third, the pair of hands is the power that is to initiate the bringing of the arrow into contact with the target; the hands correspond to thinking, which the soul guides while it itself manages the bow, which are the speeches, and the arrow, which brings what is to know into contact with what is to be known, is knowledge. Knowledge is the bond between soul and being, and truth is the light in which the soul sees that the bond is a bond. This kind of knowledge, however, could not occur unless the target or being had first been singled out, prior to its identification, as something to be known. The being must already have been set up before us. Who or what does this? If the beings were already in place for us, knowledge would necessarily fall to our lot, provided that the soul were at all capable of knowing. The beings, then, must not be in their proper places, and we must sort them out. Error is always possible because we must constantly sort, for we cannot fundamentally alter the confusion in which things are. This sorting-out is what the Eleatic stranger calls dialectical knowledge, in the *Sophist* and the *Statesman,* but Theaetetus, despite his sorting of numbers into two kinds (though he did not call them kinds), does not recognize the necessity for such sorting, for the numbers do not lie in confusion but in order. Had Theaetetus imitated in his answer to the question of knowledge what was latent in the very first step of his division of numbers, he would have hit upon the truth. He missed the mark because the numbers had for him complete clarity and distinctiveness. His knowledge interfered with his recognizing what knowledge is.

Instead of having straightforwardly said what false opinion is, Socrates enumerated all the possible cases of both false and true opinion. If his enumeration is complete, his subsequent assertion of what false opinion is should hold regardless of whether the "physiology" implicit in his image of the wax block were true or not. The image should now be dispensable. Socrates, however, does a very strange thing. After Theaetetus has asked, "Isn't it beautifully spoken, Socrates?" (cf. 195d4), Socrates tells him that when he listens further he will say it is still more beautifully spoken. On the basis of Theaetetus' agreement that to opine the truth is beautiful and to lie or be deceived is ugly, Socrates proceeds to replace the wax as an image with the wax as the literal truth (194e1). The beauty of true opinion requires the beauty of its instrument, just as the ugliness of lying requires a comparably ugly soul. The wax in the soul is that which Homer allusively called the heart. Heart in Homer is a metaphor for wax. However, Homer did not understand his own riddle, for otherwise he would not have praised the shaggy heart, which again is not a metaphor for fierceness, but is literally the condition of the forgetful, whose impressions (*ekmageia*) are indistinct. The word *ekmageion* had formerly denoted the block of wax as an image; it now reappears as the impressions in the heart. Socrates seems to be indulging in a gratuitous beautification of Homer, who had, at any rate, a much higher opinion of lying.

The consequence of this beautification is that Socrates' proof of possible kinds of true and false opinion turns into an assertion of the necessity of the beautiful and ugly, for false opinion is now a necessity for some kinds of souls. Indeed, one could take Theaetetus' vehement assent to the question whether false opinions are "in us" as meaning that no human soul is altogether beautiful (cf. 195b1). Socrates had told Theodorus that the bad could not be banished, for there necessarily must be something contrary to the good. It now appears that the same is true of the beautiful: false opinion is indispensable for knowledge. Socrates and Theaetetus have just found something beautiful—a true opinion, which is beautiful, about false opinion, which is ugly.

Socrates' beautification of himself (*kallôpizomenos*) is, however, spurious. He really is ugly. Socrates presents himself as being as terrible as Parmenides, but disagreeable and not at all an object of respect. He is disagreeable because in his sluggishness he cannot leave any argument alone. He learns slowly, which means, according to his own account, that his heart is hard and probably shaggy. Perhaps, then, the all-wise Homer praised such a heart correctly, but only if the beautiful wax is not good. My ugliness, Socrates seems to be saying, is that of an old woman, and signifies the art I practice. The concern of my art with the ugly—hair, mud, and dirt—is due to the affinity between the ugly and my soul. But we should not forget that Socrates by this same art revealed that Theaetetus was beautiful, and beautiful precisely because he forgot speeches (cf. 157c7, 167b7). Dialectics, then, seems to be the art of properly making use of the ugly and the beautiful.

The question which demolishes the beautiful discovery of Socrates and Theaetetus is a question about questioning. Since the literalization of the wax block has led to its assuming the character of the whole soul insofar as it is cognitive, the soul can no longer think or ask itself questions. The beautiful wax, which is necessary in order to guarantee perfect recognition, precludes thereby the possibility of putting two and two together. The wax stands in the way, not only of our ever making a mistake, but also of our combining anything with anything else. The "and" between five and seven has no place in the impressions of the wax. Plato's Parmenides leads the young Aristoteles to overlook "and" in the second hypothesis.[31]

> PARMENIDES: Is it possible to say "being"?
> ARISTOTELES: It is possible.
> PARMENIDES: And again to say "one"?
> ARISTOTELES: This too.
> PARMENIDES: Isn't then each of the pair said?
> ARISTOTELES: Yes.
> PARMENIDES: And whenever I say "being and (*te kai*) one," aren't both said?
> ARISTOTELES: Certainly.

The command to say both "being" and "one" can be obeyed either by saying "being and one" or by saying "being, one." The both that characterizes one's own performance as a speaker is transferred in the first case to that of which one speaks. To say both is to say "both." The both of the counting (speaking) is applied to the counted, for otherwise there would be no counting. "Five, seven" is not "five and seven." If five and seven were two consonants, and someone was asked to utter both of them, he could not comply with the request unless he inserted a vowel between them. They will not "add up" otherwise. He could, to be sure, give their word equivalents, but this would be as if one answered "five and seven" when asked what $5 + 7$ are. If, however, we imagine *per impossibile* that thought can move the impression of five and seven around, and the impressions of the four numbers are like those in figure 5, then, of course, the comparison of the newly combined twelve with the old eleven and twelve could easily lead to mistaking it for eleven. The wax block would then be working both as memory and the equivalent of perception. Socrates had excluded this originally because the wax had at first a very modest role; only when he had let the wax (now the heart) usurp every cognitive function, in order that true opinion could be wholly beautiful, did it collapse.

The manifold of numbers does look like the manifold of perceived things, but the separate stamps of Theaetetus and Theodorus are not at all like those of five and seven. Theaetetus and Theodorus together are two human beings; five and seven together are not two numbers but twelve. Theaetetus acknowledges the difference when he says that

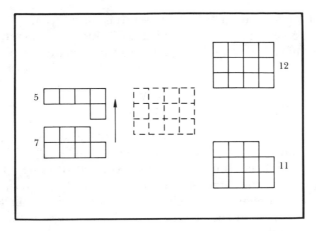

Figure 5

mistaking becomes more common among very large numbers. Again he does not hear what he himself says, for no one has a stamp in his heart of $12^{69} - 1$, even though one might readily make a mistake about it in some calculation.

Theodorus is wholly mistaken about Theaetetus' soul; it is not moderation itself, but in the most exalted state a soul can be in. His soul's exaltation is so dazzling that Theaetetus himself does not know the state he is in but, as he says, sometimes spins around in darkness when he looks at questions of relation. Had Theaetetus understood himself, he would have said that knowledge is intellection (*noêsis*), the contact of the soul with the beings without mediation or the need for thinking. Knowledge is not knowledge of causes but of beings in themselves.[32] His actual answer intends the same, for not only does perception, especially as Socrates interprets it, have the character of intellection, but the word *aisthêsis* in the sense of awareness even could serve for *noêsis*.[33] Nothing, indeed, would have changed if Theaetetus had said that knowledge is intellection. The disappearance of the distinction between what is perceived and what perceives would have recurred on the highest level, and the thesis would have proved to be as inherently contradictory.

Socrates seems to have discerned at once what Theaetetus was— someone on an almost permanent "high" as we say—and he has tried to verify the guess and at the same time bring Theaetetus down to earth. Socrates saw in Theaetetus a look-alike of his younger self, who heard and talked with Parmenides, but with differences. Theaetetus has not yet come to the "ideas," nor has he reflected on the problem of cause. He has altogether bypassed the body, and is more a potential convert of Parmenides than of Socrates. It is therefore not surprising that in the *Sophist* an ex-Parmenidean, the Eleatic stranger, will be able to do more with and for Theaetetus than Socrates can.

XIV. BIRDS
(196c4–201c7)

Socrates offers Theaetetus the alternative of either denying his experience of false opinion and obeying the argument that knowledge and ignorance of the same thing cannot consist with one another at the same time in the same person, or affirming his experience and denying the argument. Theaetetus says it is no choice at all. Socrates proposes that they act shamelessly and say what sort of thing it is to know. Theaetetus does not know why it is shameless. He has assumed from the start that knowledge is available and that Socrates really knows what it is; he is further unaware of the priority of the question of what something is to that of its quality. Socrates tells him that he seems not to have realized that their very question implied that they knew from the start what it meant to be ignorant, and that they understood one another while saying "we recognize" and "we do not recognize," and "we know" and "we do not know." Their conversation has long been infected with impurity (cf. 194e6); the beautiful heart of wax is worthless as long as they must speak with one another as if they know what not to know what knowledge is means. Socrates here gives casually the strongest argument against the equation of knowledge and perception, for if perception did not both reveal and conceal at the same time, we should never ask questions. Things could not be riddling if we were wholly in the dark, but the fact that we all are very much in the dark, Theaetetus has interpreted as his own occasional spells of vertigo. Socrates says that they must now be shameless and advance in the face of their own ignorance; as good-for-nothings they can get away with it, for that is how such people are expected to behave. They cannot avoid being the subject of comedy.

The distinction between possession and use or having was already implied in the image of the wax block, for there was knowing apart from perception and knowing with perception; and to label the impression by itself knowledge as a possession (prior to its being either recalled in thought or called on to identify a present perception) would seem to be far simpler than for Socrates to indulge in a fancy as grotesque as his birds. Socrates must be after bigger game. How easily he could have adapted the wax block for his ostensible purpose is shown in the conversation Theaetetus and he have.

SOCRATES: Have you heard what they're now saying it is to know?
THEAETETUS: Perhaps. I don't, however, remember at the
    moment.
SOCRATES: They surely say it's a having of knowledge?
THEAETETUS: True.

Theaetetus has an impression he is not using; before he uses it he cannot be certain that he even has it. When he does remember, he is using it, and finds that it conforms with what Socrates says. The small correction Socrates now suggests in the way people speak of knowing is reminiscent of the distinction he forced on Theaetetus between the preposition "through" and the instrumental dative for the eyes and ears, where the prepositional phrase entailed a difference between possession and use, while the dative only acknowledged use. That distinction had enormous consequences; this one looks as if it only peters out in a return to the original perplexity. It is striking, however, that the same inexactitude of terms which then crept in under the cover of compulsory exactness is repeated here.

To buy a cloak and not wear it is like possessing knowledge and not using it. To be without knowledge is to be naked. A bought but unworn cloak would correspond to barbells bought but not used; it would seem not to be like knowledge, which cannot be yours to the exclusion of everyone else's: strictly speaking, a cloak one buys and never wears more resembles a book one buys and never reads—the dialogue Terpsion is hearing now that Euclides has long kept in his drawer. This parallel indeed is not exact. That Euclides wrote it down does not mean he understood it. Socrates, moreover, complicates his presentation by likening knowledge or sciences to wild birds, for whom one has built a cage at home in which one feeds them after their capture. Socrates thus implies that (1) all sciences must be hunted before they can be possessed; (2) when captured, the sciences do not become completely domesticated, that is, clipped of their wings and staked somewhere in the cage; (3) the sciences are alive; (4) they do not naturally move in the element in which we live; (5) their capture requires secrecy and guile, for they are elusive and unwilling to be captured; (6) there is possibly something unnatural about our possession of them, that is, we are not of the same kind as the sciences, for we never fully assimilate them; (7) if the hunter hunts by knowledge, this knowledge cannot be a bird, unless there is among the birds an informer or traitor of the birds, the only bird that is by nature tame; and (8) it is not necessary to hunt the sciences oneself, for one can buy them from a science hunter. Some of these immediate implications Socrates makes use of, others he reinterprets. Although the image is as complex as the wax block, it differs from the wax block in two important respects. First, it can never be so abused as to be understood physiologically; it remains distinct as an image from that of which it is an image, for unlike the wax block all the cages are the same and not a lucky or unlucky gift of a goddess. And second, whereas the wax block implied that knowing was a kind of image making over which we have no control, the birds imply that this is not the case; they are essentially outside the cage of our soul what they are inside it.

In his first application of the image, Socrates introduces another kind of hunting, that which one does when one wants to use a particular science one has. It surely is not the same science one might have used in capturing it originally—there is no need at any rate for the same subtlety—but if it is a science (mnemonics), it is closer at hand than any other science. In his second application, Socrates introduces the notion that the cage in the soul—it is not the whole soul—has all kinds of birds. This cage is not made by us, for it exists when we are children and is then empty. The cage does not contain knowledge of perceived individuals (cf. 186b11–c2); it is a cage peculiar to man as man. Socrates, therefore, can only be speaking of men who have many different kinds of knowledge, for the shoemaker, however vast his experience, has only one bird. Not even Theodorus, but only a polymath like Hippias, would be a suitable candidate for such a description. For even if the arithmetician has a different bird for each number he knows, all his birds would have to flock together. Some birds flock together in herds apart from the others, some are in small groups, while others are one of a kind and fly through all the birds at random. Sciences come in kinds; one never acquires the kind itself but only an individual member of the kind. Two individuals can thus have the same science but not necessarily the same degree of proficiency in that science. But if there are no perfect birds, no science is complete; so perhaps Socrates means that in feeding the birds we make them more complete than they were at the time of capture. Sciences in their wild state are poor specimens.

Their quasi domestication suggests a political setting for the sciences (cf. 174e1–2, 197e4). We could then picture the inhabitants of a city, insofar as each is understood solely as a knower, as the various birds. Those which congregate in flocks would be the artisans, who in taking care of our various needs belong together (e.g., tailor, cleaner, shoemaker, hatter, etc.); those in small groups but not flocks, who are not said to stay apart from the others, would be the judge, the orator, the priest, the poet, and the general; and the isolated birds would be the mathematician, the physiologist, and the dialectician. All the arts keep to themselves "naturally," but not philosophic wisdom. There is no necessity for it to join any group, and it never stays anywhere for long: each art points to wisdom but not for everyone who has the art.[34] In terms of the *Republic* and the *Statesman,* this interpretation of the image makes some sense, but Socrates says the cage is in each soul, and unless the soul is an image of the city, the interpretation breaks down.

Knowledge itself no more exists than bird itself does; knowledge is always knowledge of a thing (*pragma*). The thing which each knowledge knows shows up in the knowledge as the kind of knowledge it is, and the kind of knowledge is the species of the bird. One would thus be inclined to say that arithmetic as a whole is "dove," and the knowledge of each odd and even number is a particular dove. But Socrates speaks of eleven as a ring-dove and twelve as a dove, and even if he had not said so, the knowledge of twelve could never then be shared with anyone. If, on the other hand, knowledge of each number is a species, there would be an infinite number of species, and arithmetic would be an essentially incomplete science. Theaetetus accepts without question that the arithmetician knows all numbers perfectly, and obviously he can say at once about any number whether it is odd or even, and that it is different from any other number. However, if knowledge of twelve means knowledge of all its factors, whether by addition or multiplication, not only could he never mistake seven and five for eleven, but he would have the same knowledge of every number, no matter how large, and that seems to be beyond the capacity of even a Ramanujan. We could then say that Socrates is presenting knowledge, which is always of kinds, as true opinion, which can never be of kinds, and the difference between them is in this way revealed. True opinion is always of individuals; it can never supply the connection between one individual and another, both of which it truly opines.

Socrates, however, does seem to be pointing to a genuine difficulty if knowledge is knowledge of kinds. He replaces our ordinary picture of a science, in which the science ranges over an indeterminate number of individuals, with the apparently more exact picture of any science being as distributive as what is known (cf. 207d3–7).[35] Arithmetic is not meaningfully the science of number, for there is no number which is not either odd or even, and therefore no knowledge which is not knowledge of some odd or even number. Socrates would thus be casting doubt on Theaetetus' dichotomy of all numbers into those with either rational or irrational square roots and instead be praising Theodorus for having proved the irrationality of each magnitude up to seventeen separately. Theaetetus' procedure tells us the character of every irrational square root, but it does not show that 288 is not the square of some integer. We should then be back at the original question as to how one could comprehend all the arts and sciences in a single kind. Such a comprehension now looks as if it could not be knowledge, while a complete enumeration of the sciences is impossible. We have not yet unriddled Socrates' birds.

There is something spurious even about asking how someone can mistake seven plus five for eleven. It is simply due, as we say, to the inattention of the adder, who perhaps also does not know that the sum of any two odd numbers is even. One can, moreover, ask for the sum of two numbers which no one could mistake. How much is 100 and 2? One hundred and two. A language could be devised, it seems, in which the difference between the question and the answer was only that of stress. In Homer, after all, twelve is two and ten (*dyo kai deka*) spoken as one word (*dyokaideka, dyôdeka*, or *dôdeka*). If Socrates wanted to explain error in terms of inattentiveness, his image of the wax block would be far more suitable, for he could have said that the indistinctness of an impression has inattention as its equivalent in the act of looking at an impression. Errors as an occasional event seem incapable of illustration. Lichtenberg's paradox is well-known: illustrate a misprint. To take a ring-dove for a dove illustrates the fact of the mistake but not the mistaking itself, since in our having the ring-dove in hand, one is knowing eleven. If our left hand held the bird of five and the bird of seven, the fact that our right hand held the bird of eleven would not entail that we mistook them. The link between the two hands is not itself a bird.

Socrates' silence about seven and five throughout the bird section shows that arithmetic cannot be the kind of knowledge he has in mind. If the question is how much do seven and five make, they are two facts (*pragmata*), and one would, in hunting for the knowledge of their sum, not have it at home in the cage. If one did have it there, one could have forgotten it (i.e., not attempted to use it), or have done the sum again to check it against the knowledge already possessed. Socrates, moreover, calls Theaetetus' attention to the unsuitability of his image when he has him agree that arithmetic is transmittable. The pupil does not receive the teacher's birds. Does the teacher breed his birds? Does the bird of twelve suddenly materialize inside the pupil's dovecote when he has understood the lesson? The absurdities seem endless.

The distinction between the use and the possession of knowledge has the consequence that one's own knowledge makes one ignorant, so that possibly one's own ignorance could make one know. To be ignorant by knowledge is to know that one knows nothing; to know by ignorance is to know that the unexamined life is not worth living. Neither is false opinion; together they describe Socratic philosophy. If the bird cage is the philosopher's, and especially Socrates', then to say that a science or an art is a living bird means that Socrates always considers each science and art in light of the human soul that possesses it. He never puts anything into his soul in which the soul itself is omitted. The image for the way in which competence about something and the soul show up in any knowledge is a bird, for competence becomes elusive as soon as the question of the soul is raised.

Theodorus was a bird, according to Socrates, who flew above the heavens and below the earth, and if Theaetetus can deliver a wind-egg, he too must be a bird. Socrates has shown that both are the dreamers who, Theaetetus said, believe themselves winged and think they are flying. Theaetetus had the insight that being and benefit were the subject of dialectics, for their conjunction is to be found in soul. Socrates' image of the bird cage, therefore, looked like the city. Only in the city with its urgent questions does the good intrude on competence, and though political urgency cannot perforce reveal that the good and competence are themselves problematic, to be oblivious of the city is tantamount to not even seeing as much as the city does. Theodorus' alliance with Protagoras is meant to show us that. Theaetetus, however, is far more innocent. He has forgotten that he is a human being. He is Euthyphro's nobler twin: he urges the Eleatic stranger to kill his father Parmenides.[36] Socrates juxtaposes the wax and the birds in order to put Theaetetus and himself side by side. Theaetetus' competence, on reflection, becomes knowledge of beautiful fictions; Socrates' competence is just this knowledge of Theaetetus. Knowledge of soul is not knowledge simply; but without knowledge of soul's delusions, each and every knowledge, as the breeding ground of soul's delusions, would be unapproachable. Competence would be an inviolable sanctuary for the expert were it not for knowledge of soul.

A moment's reflection would show that nonknowledge cannot be, as Theaetetus proposes, a bird which flies together with the bird of knowledge in the soul. Who would ever have gone out to hunt for ignorance? If, however, Theaetetus had said that knowledge and nonknowledge looked as if they were one and the same bird outside the cage, and in hunting knowledge, ignorance took its place, he would have hit upon the truth. Nonknowledge is such a good mimic of knowledge that it induces in its possessor the belief that it is knowledge. Nonknowledge is a decoy, but it could not be a decoy unless it had borrowed some of the plumage of knowledge and therefore in a sense is knowledge.

Theaetetus will not acknowledge that unadulterated knowledge is not in front of us (201a1). False opinion would not be in the soul if it were not first outside the soul. Since Theaetetus believes that being never appears as anything other than itself, he is driven to believe that being and appearance are the same. Clarity thus becomes darkness, and sight blindness. Theaetetus is a somnambulistic hunter of knowledge. Anything he puts in the cage must be knowledge because the cage is, after all, the cage of knowledge. Socrates had given hunting a fourfold character: (1) the hunting of the knowledge; (2) its capture and possession; (3) the secondary hunting of the knowledge once possessed; (4) its use. Theaetetus entirely ignored the first step. The fact (*pragma*) one seeks to know is for him entirely unproblematic (cf. 194c6, d6). False opinion, therefore, becomes something "mental," an aberration in the soul as trivial and as mysterious as is the mistaking of eleven for twelve. It is false opinion as the semblance of knowledge that is the true perplexity. Theaetetus needs the Eleatic stranger in order to learn what his semblances of knowledge are, and how they are possible. Socrates can only give him the experience of them.

Socrates assumes that Theaetetus' definition of knowledge as true opinion is done with. If they have not found out what false opinion is, they did not find out what true opinion is either. If they had accounted for false opinion, they would have accounted for true opinion as well, but such an account would have replaced their true opinion with knowledge. Theaetetus, however, does not understand that, even if his definition is true, he is now in the position of a just jury who have been persuaded and not taught. If they remain where they are, Socrates says, nothing is evident. In order to establish that true opinion is knowledge, it would be necessary, according to Theaetetus' own criterion, to enumerate every case of it and show that none of its consequences is ever ugly and bad, but a single counterexample suffices to refute it.

Socrates' counterexample is taken from the city, about which Theaetetus knows nothing. Theaetetus is obviously thinking of mathematics: if someone's answers were always correct, his true opinion would be indistinguishable from knowledge. The teacher gives the pupil problems in order to find out whether he only knows by rote, but no test can be devised that the soul of beautiful wax cannot pass perfectly. But Theaetetus would be hard put to affirm that someone who copied his own test paper, or said whatever he said, really knew the answers. Such dishonesty does not occur to him. He is not Hippolytus. In his innocence, he overlooks mimicry and persuasion, the two elements in which every city lives. Theaetetus is too distant from the city either to see these elements in others or to think of their applicability to himself. He solely becomes wise by wisdom; he learns everything he knows (145c7–d12). The cogency, however, of Socrates' example would seem to be diminished by its appeal to the difference between hearsay and an eyewitness report, for the senses have presumably been disallowed as sources of the truth. Socrates is thinking of his forthcoming trial and Plato of his dialogues. Just as Socrates will not have taught even those who will acquit him that the unexamined life is not worth living, so Plato will have us decide, without any first-hand evidence of either Socrates or philosophy, on Socrates' innocence. The section on false opinion both begins and ends with an allusion to Socrates' trial.

XV. LETTERS
(201c8–206b12)

No sooner has Socrates said that knowledge and true opinion must be different, than Theaetetus, without stopping to acknowledge Socrates' proof, suddenly recalls what he once heard someone say: Knowledge is true opinion with speech (*logos*). Since, however, Socrates' proof consisted of an example in which speech as hearsay was true opinion as opposed to knowledge through eyesight, Theaetetus must mean by speech something else. Theaetetus seems to have finally caught up with Socrates, for Socrates had defined opining (*doxazein*) as a silent speech backed up by reasoning (*dianoeisthai*). Theaetetus therefore would mean by *logos* proof. To have knowledge is to have the proof of a true speech.[37] Theaetetus has just experienced this; he has heard from Socrates a proof of why true opinion cannot be knowledge. This is now known. But Theaetetus knows neither the Socratic source of his definition nor his own experience. He does not know why he just recalled the definition. The seal of his present experience seems to have fitted so perfectly an impressed memory that it has been obliterated in the matching. He is in fact mistaken, for he has put the seal in the wrong impression. What he remembers is not what he just heard but quite a different thesis: Knowledge is of the knowable, and the knowable is that which has or admits of a *logos*, while the unknowable does not. *Logos* here cannot mean proof; it is merely in opposition to name (201d3). Theaetetus is daydreaming. He has put together two things which do not belong together. His present experience has stimulated an old memory which only looks as if it were the same as his present experience. He has remembered an "atomic theory," which the body-people he so much disliked propose. They now have their revenge on his fastidiousness. But Theaetetus has nonetheless made an important advance. For the first time he gives the objects of knowledge along with his definition of knowledge.

The first things are like simple sounds, about which nothing can be said except their conventional names. Each of the first things is a proper noun. Nothing else can be said about them without violating their uniqueness. They are wholly heterogenous; each is its own class, and it cannot be explained why these are the first things and not others. What they have in common is their mode of recognition; they are perceptible. The model the speakers of this dream have in mind is the alphabet. In the Greek alphabet, seven letters are vowels, and these are perceptible by themselves. The other seventeen are consonants, nine of which are not perceptible, while eight are just about perceptible by themselves. If we disregard this last refinement, we can say that the alphabet finds a perceptible representation for the consonants that puts them on a par with the vowels. The name for the long vowel O in Greek is the sound itself (ô), but the name of the consonant S is sigma. The vowel does not need to be represented— think of the nonvocalized scripts of several languages—but the consonant does. The sound ô gets as its representative Ω; it has not been in any way altered, for the representation is pronounced ô. The sigma, on the other hand, has never been heard by itself but always in conjunction with a vowel. The syllabic sound sô gets transmuted through the dropping of ô and the isolation of what remains as Σ. It is now as perceptible as Ω. The difference between Σ and the sound sô is as great as that between the oblong number 12 and its image as a square. The squaring of an irrational (*alogon*) is exactly the same as the alphabetization of a consonant. It is no wonder that Socrates recognized it as Theaetetus' dream.

Knowledge consists in the representation of the unknowable. This representation is arbitrary (the shapes and names of letters) but not entirely. It results from the breaking down of the perceptible into a perceptible and nonperceptible element. This breakdown, in turn, allows for the working out of all possible syllables or compounds. The compounds, all of which are knowable, yield the possible objects of experience. Their elements, however, are divided between possible objects of experience and impossible objects of experience, all of which are unknowable. The impossible objects of experience correspond to the atomists' void. Socrates implies that none of the elements is ever found in isolation; so the simplest of all beings is compounded of two elements, only one of which is even in principle isolatable. *Logos*, whose being (*ousia*) is the weaving together of two names, has its image in the syllable. The syllable, in turn, because it joins a consonant with a vowel, images the conjunction of atom and void in a being. Void and

atom, each of which is never apart from the other, are the two principles of being. Being and *logos* are thus interchangeable, for only the
rational "is." The being which has a *logos* has it in just the way in
which the knower has it. The *logos* the knower gives for showing that
his opinion is true is the *logos* by which the being itself is. The proof
for the knower is the cause for the being.

Socrates distinguishes between the definition—what could knowledge still be apart from *logos* and right opinion?—and the "physiology." The ingenious part of the physiology displeases him: the
unknowability of the letters and the knowability of the class of syllables. Why does he not speak of the class of letters? When Socrates
asks Theaetetus for the *logos* of sigma, Theaetetus says: "But how will
one say the elements of the element? The reason is, Socrates, that the
sigma belongs to the voiceless; it's only a sound. It's like when the
tongue hisses. And of the beta in turn and most of the elements as
well there's neither voice nor sound. The saying therefore holds good,
they're without speech (*aloga*), since the most vivid of them are the
very seven that only have voice and no speech whatever." Theaetetus
makes a threefold classification; he does not regard this as a *logos,* nor
even speak of it as a classification. He divines without comment that
an account in terms of efficient cause—the hissing of the tongue—is
not a *logos.* To state the class to which an indivisible belongs is not a
logos. "One" has no *logos;* only the countable has a *logos.* Theaetetus
has returned once more to his first answer, but he now is in a bind,
since there is obviously knowledge of the countable class of vowels
even if not of each vowel separately (cf. 206b7). Theaetetus says that
there are seven vowels because there are seven letters for vowels. But
that is a convention which is not always true, for there are either only
five or ten—five if one disregards the difference between long and
short, ten if one introduces that distinction everywhere. Moreover,
there are only that many vowels in Greek; the seven conventional
vowels belong to a continuum which admits of an uncountable number
of vowels. The stops a language puts into one and the same continuum
are conventional, and though there is a limit of discrimination for the
human ear, there is no real limit in itself. The class of vowels, however,
is wholly distinct from that of the consonants. The class is by nature,
while every articulation within the class is conventional. Theaetetus
does not listen to his own voice. He dreams better than he knows.

The paradigms of the physiology are neither more nor less than
the syllables and letters of writing. Everything that is true of writing
must hold for the physiology of knowledge. Writing is not an image;
it is a sample of the thesis. Socrates and Theaetetus hold this sample
like a hostage. A hostage is meant to serve as a guarantor for the good

behavior of others: the letters are meant to guarantee that all the beings are knowable and unknowable in the same way. Are letters, then, the best possible hostages? Does everything we know have the same character as our knowledge of letters? The model for prescientific knowledge is illiteracy. That which is the condition for rapid progress in the sciences is the goal of the sciences. The sciences have looked at a social characteristic of themselves in order to determine what science is. Writing is an advance over the beautiful wax block in the soul, for it replaces the private with publicity. The seals of perception are now of science's own devising, limited in number and wholly corrigible should any mistake occur in their combination. *Logos* puts its own stamp on the beings. We know a priori that KPG does not exist.

There are three levels of "reality": the finite atomic letters, the finite molecular syllables, the infinite number of syllabic complexes which most things/names are. Theaetetus is asked for the first syllable of Socrates. He says sigma and *ô;* he does not say *ô* and sigma (cf. 206a8). The *logos* of the syllable must specify the order of the elements as well as the fact that they must be uttered without "and." "And" is the expression of their being bonded which disappears when they are bonded. This "and" is the same as the "and" of the sum of seven and five. "A conjunction makes many one."[38] To say "twelve" is the correct way of saying seven and five together, just as "ΣΩ" is the correct way of saying sigma and *ô* together. If it were true that every even number is the unique sum of two prime numbers, the *logos* of twelve would be seven and five.

Letters and numbers seem to be in competition with one another for being the model of knowledge. The commutability of certain mathematical operations would, if applied to letters, make ΣΩ and ΩΣ fundamentally the same. The perceptible would thus be merely an initial guide to the symmetry of what is. Letters, in contrast, have the advantage of finiteness. Euclid's proof that there is no greatest prime number puts a limit on the intelligibility of what is. Either not everything with a *logos* could be known or if what is, is finite—this could not be known through numbers. Letters, however, no less than numbers seem unable to handle meaning. Theaetetus had distinguished between the illiterate's seeing the shape and color of letters and the literate's reading of them. The reading of them is the reading of them in a *logos:* "Socrates sits." Nothing corresponds in letters to the gap between Socrates and sits. SOCRATESSITS, which is how it would appear when written in Greek, would be a name/thing different from but somewhat alike to SOCRATES. Theaetetus' physiology, which asserted the otherness of "Socrates sick" from "Socrates healthy," reappears in another guise. It is unfortunately no more plausible, for it entails that every complex is in principle infinite and necessarily linked with every other complex. There are no separate names/things. The private atomicity of Theaetetus' physiology now becomes a public atomicity in which all things are together.

Socrates offers Theaetetus the choice of saying that the syllable is all its elements or that when the elements are put together some single whole comes to be. Theaetetus chooses the first possibility; he had formerly agreed that in the case of perceptions there must be some single whole to which they as a manifold pertain (cf. 184d6, 203e6). He therefore tacitly acknowledges that there are two kinds of beings, one of which is most manifest in a number, all of whose parts are the whole number, and another most manifest in soul, whose unity does not consist only in its parts. It is unclear to which kind the syllable belongs. Socrates quickly shows that the syllable cannot be known if its elements are unknown and proposes that they consider the alternative, which he reformulates: "We should not have perhaps set down the syllable as its elements, but some single species that has come to be out of them, with its own single look and other than the elements." The syllable as a single kind with a single look can no longer be known as merely that out of which it comes to be. Material causation does not suffice. The syllable is opposed both to a hybrid like the mule, with its single look but doubleness of kind, and a single kind with a variety of looks like the human face. That it could be a third kind seems doubtful. It seems to be as much a hybrid as the mule—donkey and horse are like consonant and vowel—and as various in looks as the face. If ΣΩ is taken to mean the written letters, there is a wide range of deformation open to it without its losing its recognizability, though there might be a perfect ΣΩ as invisible as the perfect triangle; and if ΣΩ is the sound, it too allows for a range of variations within which one can still hear it as *sô*, to say nothing of the difference between its accentless form Σωκράτησ (nominative) and the effect the accent has on it in Σώκρατεσ (vocative).

If we allow Socrates for the sake of argument to gloss over these difficulties, the new thesis says that there are two kinds of knowledge, of wholes and of parts, and that knowledge of parts does not yield knowledge of wholes. Theaetetus, however, does not notice that Socrates slips in a new consideration when he repeats the thesis: "The syllable comes to be one look out of those several elements that fit together." Knowledge of the syllable must include knowledge of those elements which do not fit together. Knowledge of what is not is part of the knowledge of what is. There is room for nonbeing in knowledge even if not in being. Socrates then shows that the syllable could not have any parts, for the whole is all its parts, but Theaetetus wants to distinguish between whole and all: the single kind that comes to be from all its parts is other than all its parts. Theaetetus' instinct in all its rashness is sound, but not as he understands his answer. Σ and Ω when they are apart from $\Sigma\Omega$ are not parts of $\Sigma\Omega$.

Socrates asks whether there is any difference in our saying one two three four five six; twice three; thrice two; four and two; or three and two and one. Socrates implies that to speak is to count—to be a teller is to tally—and therefore to ask for a *logos* that does not enumerate is impossible. But if a speech is a summation, it can only be told if it is tellable, that is, articulated into a tellable form, which must be there before it is told. The manifold must already be there as a manifold, for otherwise there is no end to the tale. Socrates gives three ways in which the tale can be told, only one of which—twice three or thrice two—includes the operation as part of its telling. The summation with "and" can be read as either two separate groups (four and two) or three (three and two and one) which are not to be summed. Socrates has reimported the notion of numbers in themselves and disregarded the perceptible character of the syllable, as well as the difference between the consonant Σ and the vowel Ω. In the first telling, moreover, one two three four five six, the teller must not repeat himself but gather up in each successive telling the former tale. The soul of the teller which is invisibly present in the telling does this gathering. The hearer cannot tell whether he means six or twenty-one. Theaetetus is too adept in mathematics to hear what Socrates says in any but a mathematical way. His beautiful speech, in which he recognized the soul as a whole in itself, has run away. He would never have come to recognize it at all, if Socrates had not enslaved him to the illiberality of precise speech.

The difficulty with which Socrates confronts Theaetetus concerning whole and part, is independent of the restriction that the whole be knowable and the part not. That restriction forced Theaetetus to distinguish all and whole in an artificial manner and therefore to overlook the more obvious—that if the parts of six are expressable in more than one way, its parts are not always elements, and when they are all elementary, they are all the same. Five is as much a whole as six, and four as five, and so on; at each summation there is completion, the sign of which is the asyndeton between the numbers of the series. The sound *sô*, on the other hand, determines from the initial hearing the phonetic shape of its every bit, apart from which it is not a syllable.[39] Indeed, one can go further and say that the vocative Socrates as a whole controls the enunciation of its first syllable, but six has no effect on the counting of two. Wholes becomes most manifest as wholes when there is something missing from them (cf. 186a4), but numbers are never caught short. Counting has the double character of always being complete and never being complete. To begin to count is never to stop and already to stop counting. Theaetetus, therefore, cannot avoid agreeing that whole and all are the same, for at any moment the number is a total, and just as in a whole nothing is missing.

What, then, is the problem of whole and part?[40] If Σ and Ω are each a part of the whole speech (*logos*) ΣΩ, and no part can be a part unless it takes part in a whole, then Σ takes its character as a part of the speech from the whole speech ΣΩ, and likewise Ω. Σ and Ω, therefore, have each as its own speech the whole speech; but then each speech of each part doubles again, and an unending duplicity results. The doubleness of part, itself and of the whole, cannot be handled, as Plato's Parmenides says, by the distinction between same and other (146b2–5). Parmenides shows their difference in the two-fold structure of his first hypothesis, the first five sections of which deal in sequence and as if deductively with part-whole, beginning-end, figure, place, motion-rest, while the last five in turn seem to be in the deductive sequence of same-other, like-unlike, equal-unequal, older-younger, being as time. The second section contains no mention of whole and just one of part (140c9), but the first section cannot dispense with same and other. Socrates does not give Theaetetus the proper tools for dealing with the problem of whole and part, which he presents, like all the problems of the dialogue, solely in terms of same and other. He does not give them because Theaetetus does not yet know that being is a problem apart from time.

XVI. Speech
(206c1–208b10)

To ask what is knowledge is to ask what is the most perfect or complete knowledge (cf. 206a10, b9). It is not to ask what kind of knowledge we have or can have. Theaetetus is wholly unaware of the difference between these two questions. Socrates has been trying to make him see that difference. He proposes that they explore what could be meant by *logos* in the definition of the most perfect knowledge as the addition of *logos* to true opinion. Socrates seems to want the *logos* of *logos* (cf. 208b12). If *logos* means proof, he cannot want the proof of proof, but an accounting of proof: What constitutes a proof? We usually say "It does not follow" when there is a gap of some sort in an argument, something which is not explicitly listed but nonetheless assumed to be true, and which if made explicit would at once appear doubtful. To raise to the level of *logos* what is only a silent opinion is to make the opinion known. Socrates opines that *logos* can only mean one of three things according to the present definition of knowledge. He does not prove that there are only three possibilities. After he has shown that *logos* adds nothing to true opinion, he has not shown that knowledge cannot be true opinion with *logos*. But if he is correct in saying that there are only three possibilities, he has shown that knowledge cannot be of such a sort, though he himself has only true opinion without *logos*.

His proof by *logos* yields the knowledge that knowledge is not true opinion with *logos;* but it is not truly knowledge, for he does not know why there cannot be another sense of *logos* which could save the definition. True opinion cannot be known as true opinion unless there already is knowledge. If the meaning of *logos* were self-evidently an either/or proposition, Socrates could have proved conclusively that the definition of knowledge is false. He leaves out of his accounting his own counting. His accounting partakes of all three definitions: he speaks, he goes through the elements of speech, and he seeks to find the difference between true opinion and true opinion with *logos*. His failure to find the difference could be, for all we can know, due to his failure to go through all the elements of speech.

To speak is "to make evident [to another] one's own thought (*dianoia*) through sound with words and phrases, just as if it were into a mirror or water one was striking off one's opinion into the stream through one's mouth." The stream is Heraclitean. It constantly changes its quality and its place; it must be both before one starts and after one stops speaking, for otherwise one would always run the risk of not impressing either the first or the last edge of one's opinion on the stream. One's opinion is in words and phrases; it is a translation of one's thought, which can be revealed in the opinion more or less plainly. The words and phrases appear as sounds; if the words and phrases were the thought, the thought would be like letters on a page of writing, and there would be no difficulty in reading the silent writing aloud, and Socrates could not speak of the difference between Parmenides' thought and its expression. Thought must be truly silent; it cannot be silent while being potentially audible. Silent thought can only be like the consonants, not audible until they are inserted into the variable stream of vocalization. Thought therefore can never become manifest except in the company of that which is not thought. Mistaking, both on the part of the speaker and the listener, can thus easily occur.

Socrates likens the stream of sound to a mirror; he calls our attention to the reversal thought undergoes in becoming audible. The reversal perhaps consists in the denial of the priority which thought has to sound. That which is not thought looms larger than thought in speech. Not to correct for this reversal would be to speak thoughtlessly. If, moreover, speech is the image of thought, as Theaetetus says (and as the example of the mirror implies), the pointing out of speech would consist in making images. The knower par excellence might therefore be the best image-maker: whoever could image his thought in speech with the greatest clarity would know perfectly. Unless, however, one said that he who had false opinion could never image his thought with the greatest clarity, the knower would be indistinguishable from the sophist. But perhaps one could say this: The greatest clarity of an image is the revealing in the image that it is an image. Perhaps Parmenides was not the best image-maker.

Socrates exemplifies elemental knowledge with a quotation from Hesiod. Socrates and Theaetetus know only five pieces of a wagon; Hesiod says there are one hundred. The wheelwright must know the hundred pieces, but the wheelwright's superior—whoever knows what kind of wagon the circumstances require—does not need to know anywhere near that number. Socrates might casually be adding a meaning of *logos*, which either could not have been meant as that which changes true opinion into knowledge or, if meant, leaves his examination of *logos* unfinished. *Logos* in this sense has obviously something to do with wholes, but since whole has been equated with the sum total of parts, such a *logos* could not be part of the definition of knowledge. Socrates can thus survey completely the meanings of *logos* only by omitting any consideration of completeness, and he does this despite the fact that the elemental knowledge of something needs a proof that it has gone through the whole of that something (cf. 207c3–4, 208c6). A proof of this kind cannot be self-evident unless everything we know is what we make. Socrates' example was an artifact, the number of whose parts was known to the poet (maker) Hesiod. The image making implicit in ordinary speech stands right beside a making that illustrates the second definition of *logos*.

Socrates distinguishes between the syllabic and the elemental knowledge of Theaetetus' name, but it seems absurd to say that the syllabic knowledge of his name is inferior. Syllabic knowledge is knowledge of how to pronounce the name as a whole; it knows that it is a proper name, and that its syllables are meaningless separately. There are four perceptible parts to Theaetetus' name (THE-AI-TE-TOS), all of which are in Theaetetus' name exactly what they are in its knowledge; but the elemental knowledge knows nine parts, not one of which is in its knowledge just what it is in Theaetetus' name. "A" is a part of the grammarian's knowledge in a way in which it is not part of the spoken name. Not his scientific knowledge, but his prescientific true opinion tells him that "A" and "I" are one sound. The syllabic knowledge is a part of the elemental knowledge, but the elemental knowledge adds nothing to the syllabic knowledge, which remains as a part what it was by itself. Knowledge therefore is two and not one. As a whole it is true opinion, in its parts a *logos*. *Logos* is the analytical content of true opinion, without which it would know everything possible but nothing actual.

This twoness yields the following paradox. The man with true opinion or prescientific knowledge never makes a mistake (220e4); but the man who is on the way to scientific knowledge can make mistakes. He will at times write Teodorus instead of Theodorus, but the illiterate always says Theodorus. Socrates here points to the difference between knowledge and to know. In knowledge there are no mistakes, but the knower can make mistakes. There are two kinds of mistaking. Either the same is believed to belong to the same and the other, or the other and the other are believed to belong to the same. In terms of letters, whoever mistakes in the first way writes D at the beginning of both THIS and DOES, and whoever mistakes in the second, writes D at the beginning of DOES and T at the beginning of DOZE. Theaetetus, it seems, made the first mistake when he said knowledge was true opinion, and he made the second when he said knowledge was true opinion with *logos,* for this was the same as true opinion.

In writing DIS incorrectly but DOES correctly, one's mistake is to take DOES as a paradigm for THIS. In writing TOZE and DOES, one's mistake is not to take DOES as a paradigm. Knowledge therefore must consist in knowing what paradigm to use in any particular case. Theaetetus' first mistake was due to his believing that all knowledge is immediate—his paradigm was perception. His second mistake was due to his believing that all knowledge is deduction—his paradigm was mathematics. In his first mistake he misread his own soul, in the second he forgot it. The atomists assumed that their paradigm was simple, but if they discerned correctly that letters were the model— the difference between literacy and illiteracy was manifest—then no knowledge of paradigms would seem possible. We should not hit upon, except by luck, which paradigm was to be used when, and for what purpose. If, however, paradigmatic knowledge were possible, and we had obtained it, we would know how to select from the proper paradigm (as D from DOES) just that element which recurred some-how in that which we wished to examine.[41] Plato presents Socrates as the master of paradigmatic knowledge. Its indispensable guide and companion is Socrates' knowledge of soul. The Eleatic stranger tries to instruct Theaetetus and young Socrates in paradigmatic knowl-edge,[42] but he does not succeed so well in instructing either of them in knowledge of soul. Perfect knowledge, then, is the unity of paradigmatic knowledge and elemental knowledge. But we do not know what could bring about this unity, for elemental knowledge, proceeding as it does on the basis of true opinion, cannot supply a proof of its own completeness; and paradigmatic knowledge, since it looks at one thing to know another, can always be mistaken. Paradigmatic knowledge can inadvertently become image making, elemental knowledge a making.

XVII. DIFFERENCE
(208b11–210d4)

Socrates has so far considered two possible meanings that "with speech" can have in the definition of knowledge as true opinion with *logos*. The first was speech as the reporting to another of one's own true opinion (intersubjectivity); the second was that speech split up into its parts what was already known as a whole. If, however, the definition of knowledge is true, it must have the same character as any other kind of knowledge. The definition consists of two parts; so *logos* must be the addition of something not already present in true opinion. *Logos*, therefore, must mean a speech which tells what something has which distinguishes it from everything else. Only this characterization of *logos* strictly conforms with the definition of knowledge. The two other meanings are possible and in fact seem to contain glimmerings of the truth, but not for the proposed definition. Only with this meaning can Socrates strictly prove the redundancy of "true opinion with *logos*;" for with the first and second meanings, the would-be knower might not know perfectly, but he knows something which the man with true opinion does not know (cf. 208b8–9). Socrates had to disqualify the deaf and dumb in equating true opinion with public speech (206d9). Theaetetus was really dreaming when he remembered this definition. He meant that knowledge was elemental knowledge, but he said that it was knowledge of difference. He did not express his thought.

Elemental knowledge and knowledge of difference are not incompatible with one another; indeed, the Eleatic stranger combines them in his dichotomies, for he begins with a whole like art or science, articulates the whole into its parts, and ends up with an indivisible form, which is the distinctive *logos* of whatever he is seeking. Whether this combination meets Socrates' separate arguments against each of them can for the moment be left aside, but their juxtaposition does illustrate a perplexity which, Socrates says in the *Phaedo*, put him on the trail of "ideas" (96e6–98b7). Socrates began with a search for causes, why each things becomes, perishes, and is, but he became puzzled by the fact that the causes of the coming to be of two were two and contrary to one another. If a two comes to be when one and one draw near to one another, and their coming together, which consists in their juxtaposition, is the cause of their becoming two, Socrates was amazed that if one splits a one in two the cause of their becoming two should then be this splitting.

Division and addition have the same result. Division is the second meaning of *logos,* and addition the third. Theaetetus' very first definition of knowledge, that knowledge is the arts and sciences, is an additive definition and as such, redundant: Knowledge is knowledge and the knowledge a, b, c, d, etc. (cf. 146d2). Socrates' counterdefinition, in contrast, is divisive. If Socrates had gone on dividing knowledge as if it were mud, he would presumably have comprehended every member of the single class of knowledge, and the result would have been Theaetetus' enumeration of the arts and sciences. His alphabet of knowledge might have been more detailed and complete than Theaetetus', but no better. None of his letters could tell us what a letter is. Both the additive and divisive answers have to fall back on what each of them started with, true opinion. Prescientific knowledge, like mud, is right before us (cf. 147a2, 170b6). It is one. Scientific knowledge is two or more than two, the cause of which multiplicity we do not know. We could well ask, therefore, whether the *Sophist* and the *Statesman,* the two dialogues Plato devotes to answering the *Theaetetus'* question, are two by juxtaposition or by division.

Socrates gives an example of speech as the interpretation of difference: The sun is the most brilliant of things in the sky that go around the earth. The speech of correct opinion would presumably say that the sun was one of the things that go around the earth. Socrates, however, rejects this understanding when he cites his own recognition of Theaetetus. If a correct opinion about Theaetetus will suffice to make Socrates recognize him tomorrow, a correct opinion about the sun will make him recognize it tomorrow. Socrates' exemplary speech, then, is the speech of correct opinion. Whatever else we added to it would not improve our capacity to recognize the sun. Is Socrates belittling astonomy (cf. 145d1–5)? Perhaps, but his speech is not as concise as it might be. As far as recognition goes, "the most brilliant" would suffice,[43] but as Socrates presents it, the sun's difference is embedded in an astronomical speech, which asserts that the sun moves, the earth is round, and something—lightning perhaps—is more brilliant than the sun. Socrates seems to be indicating that true opinion is not as available as Theaetetus has been led to believe.

Socrates' recognition of Theaetetus is equally perplexing as an example. Recognition of Theaetetus through perception would be far more infallible than any speech could possibly be. Theodorus, at any rate, could not make Socrates recognize Theaetetus through his speech. Socrates thus suggests the following distinction. Whoever has an impression of Theaetetus, which a speech about his difference does not accompany, can only recognize Theaetetus when he sees him again, but the knower, who has this speech, can present Theaetetus to himself even in his absence. This speech is what the dialogue itself has conveyed to us. As a speech, it is potentially universal. It does not improve our ability to recognize this Theaetetus, but to recognize all other Theaetetuses, who just because they are before us might be invisible to us. Speech makes for the proper distance (cf. 208e7–10). One would hesitate, however, to call this speech anything more than true opinion. Socrates says it is a very noble blindness to demand to take up those things we have "in order that we might learn or know what we opine." A taking up of this kind is not as idle as Socrates makes it out to be. No one fails to recognize laughter, but a speech that distinguishes it from everything else is not to be despised. Everyone knows what mud is, and Socrates' speech is just the content of true opinion, but as a speech it suddenly becomes capable of being paradigmatic. If the *logos* of mud is taken by itself, it ceases to be a paradigm and sinks to the level of the trivial; and if Plato's presentation of Theaetetus is isolated, as if it were an overelaborate way of remembering Theaetetus, it too becomes no better than the dialogue Euclides thought he wrote.

Socrates, in poking fun at a definition of knowledge which reports what already is present to true opinion, obscures the speech of true opinion. With an "unwonted discursiveness,"[44] Socrates seems to imitate the uninformative lengthening of which he accuses the definition. His first sentence is a fitting conclusion: "Of those things of which we have right opinion, by which they differ from everything else, [the definition] urges us to take in addition a right opinion of those things by which they differ from everything else." But then Socrates begins to waffle on his own: "Compared to this injunction, the twirling of a *skytalê*, a pestle, or whatever name it goes by, would be as nothing in point of nonsense." The proverb Socrates has in mind—the turning round of a pestle—means to go round in circles and accomplish nothing. Socrates seems to have himself gone round in circles in his groping for the right expression. And yet he cannot help saying something new while awkwardly attempting to repeat himself.

A *skytalê* was "at Sparta a staff or baton, used as a cypher for writing dispatches, thus: a strip of leather was rolled slantwise round it, on which the dispatch was written lengthwise, so that when unrolled they were unintelligible: commanders abroad had a staff of like thickness, round which they rolled these papers, and so were able to read the dispatches."[45] We ambush a Spartan messenger; his dispatch is in code. Since we read all the letters, we have a correct opinion about them and would not mistake the dispatch for another, but since we cannot read the dispatch, we do not know the *logos*. The jumble of signs on the dispatch becomes a *logos* as soon as we use the *skytalê*. Socrates has assumed throughout the argument that true opinion is necessarily in order, but he should have asked what puts the manifold of perceptual signs into their proper order. The addition to true opinion which makes for greater knowledge is not *logos*, which is rather the result of the ordering, but the *skytalê* of soul. He himself has called this *skytalê* thinking (*dianoeisthai*). The Eleatic stranger pretends that he knows of an automatic *skytalê*. It is dichotomy.

Socrates has clipped Theaetetus' wings. He has made him as barren as he himself is. He has tried to place Theaetetus on his own ground. It is unclear, however, whether he has handled Theaetetus in the best possible way. Theaetetus has less than a day to understand what he has experienced before the Eleatic stranger puts him through another kind of course in the *Sophist*. The stranger agrees with Socrates that Theaetetus is not as unassuming as Theodorus believes him to be, but he does not deflate Theaetetus by suddenly confronting him with the disparity between the brilliance of his visionary's dream and the semidarkness of Socratic wakefulness; rather, he accepts Theaetetus' assumption that the true beginning is completely known, and they can deduce everything from it. He shows Socrates that if one encourages Theaetetus in this illusion—Socrates had tried to encourage Theaetetus while disillusioning him—Theaetetus can advance much further. The stranger draws up a powerful indictment of Socrates' maieutics; that is, at any rate, the impression everyone has of the *Sophist,* and which Socrates confirms when he thanks Theodorus for his acquaintance with Theaetetus only after he has heard him in conversation with the stranger. In the *Theaetetus,* however, Socrates consoles Theaetetus. At worst, he will be less harsh to his associates—Theodorus is mistaken even on this point—and with a greater tameness will not in his moderation, the only mention of moderation in the dialogue, believe he knows what he does not know. Socrates' art can do no more. He has obtained it from a god to practice on all the noble and beautiful young. And yet despite the impasse they have reached, Socrates only goes away because he must now answer Meletus' indictment; tomorrow at dawn, he tells Theodorus, they should meet again at the same place. Socrates is not easily discouraged. Only here in the Platonic dialogues does Socrates make a definite appointment which he keeps; he does not now say, as he did once, in putting off the importunity of others, that he will meet them "if a god is willing."[46] Socrates seems to divine that the Eleatic stranger is coming.

The *Theaetetus* is the *logos* of Socrates. It is that by means of which Socrates can be recognized and known. He is, however, negatively determined, for he is not anyone Theodorus would call a philosopher. It is in light of this that the two main conclusions of the dialogue have to be understood: the soul and its experiences cannot be the truth of all things, and the soul and its experiences cannot be understood mathematically. The first conclusion is connected with the attempt to separate Socrates' maieutics from Protagoreanism, that is, from the improvement Socrates made in the thesis of Protagoras himself, and the second is connected with Socratic ignorance, whose character resists any attempt to understand it in arithmetical terms. It might seem, however, that these conclusions are a function of the peculiar circumstances of this dialogue and do not pertain to the truth of Socrates in himself. The *Sophist* and the *Statesman* are needed to show that the *Theaetetus'* negative determination of Socrates obtains of necessity for the philosopher simply. This universalization of Socrates as a problem thus brings in its train the problem of being. The discovery through the perplexity of nonbeing of the equal perplexity of being is the *Sophist'*s equivalent to Socratic ignorance. Being, too, is not wholly countable.

Notes

Dialogue

1. Euclides and Terpsion appear without speaking in Plato's *Phaedo* 59C. They belonged to the Megarian school of philosophy of which Euclides was the founder. They denied potentiality and had recourse only to *logos* in rejecting all phenomena.
2. The date of the battle in which Theaetetus was wounded and possibly died afterward was either sometime between 390–387 B.C. or in 369 B.C., when the Athenians and Spartans combined against the Thebans under Epaminondas. The earlier date would seem to condense Theaetetus' achievements into too short an interval.
3. Erineos is on the border between the Megarid and Attica, a distance of some ten miles from Megara. It was on the Cephisus, and Persephone was said to have been snatched by Hades there.
4. In a papyrus fragment of an anonymous commentary on the *Theaetetus,* written sometime in or before the second century A.D., there is the following (3.28–34): "It is reported that there is a different prologue, rather frigid, and consisting of an almost equal number of lines; its beginning is: 'Are you bringing, boy, the speech about Theaetetus?' " Cf. *Anonymer Kommentar zu Platons Theaitet*, Berliner Klassikertexte II, ed. E. Diels and W. Schubart (Berlin, 1905).
5. Theodorus of Cyrene (a Greek colony in Libya) was a younger contemporary of Socrates (b. ca. 460 B.C.). Theaetetus (414–369 B.C.) was most famous for showing that only five regular solids could be constructed; he also analyzed the various kinds of irrationals.
6. Wisdom (*sophia*), whose identity with knowledge is later denied by Socrates' Protagoras (166D), does not occur in either the *Sophist* or the *Statesman*. After 150C it has become tainted: "sham-wisdom" (*doxosophia*) occurs at *Sophist* 231B.
7. Pollux (IX.106) describes the game. A ball was tossed against a wall and the number of bounces before it was caught was counted; the loser was

called the ass, the winner the king, and he could order the loser to do whatever he wanted.

8. "Agreeable" (*prosêgoros*) could also be a mathematical term, "congruent"; cf. *Republic* 546B.

9. For a plausible account of Theodorus' individual proofs and why he got stuck at 17, see W. R. Knorr, *The Evolution of the Euclidean Elements* (Dordrecht-Boston, 1975), pp. 21–96, 170–93.

10. Cf. *Protagoras* 335E–336A.

11. "Noble and farouche" also occurs together at *Republic* 535B. "Farouche" (*blosuros*) is a rare word, whose tone is not exactly known; cf. M. Leumann, *Homerische Wörter* (Basel, 1950), pp. 141–48; P. Chantraine, *Dictionnaire étymologique de la langue grecque* (Paris, 1968–1980), s.v.

12. Cf. *Meno* 79E–80B.

13. Socrates indulges in a series of alliterative puns that this is meant to reproduce: *alokhos ousa tên lokheian eilêkhe*. *Alokhos* ("unallied") elsewhere means spouse, but Socrates takes it as an alpha-privative formation with the stem cognate with *lokheia* ("lying-in").

14. For the likely and the necessary, see *Symposium* 200A; *Laws* 656A–B.

15. The text is uncertain here, but the sense is not.

16. For Socrates the pimp, see Xenophon *Symposium* iii.10, iv.56–64.

17. Socrates' *daimonion* is referred to by Plato in the following passages: *Apology of Socrates* 31C–D; *Euthydemus* 272E; *Republic* 496C; *Theages* 128B–131; *Phaedrus* 242B–C. The word itself is difficult to translate since, as Socrates indicates in the *Apology* (27B–28A), it could be understood as either the diminutive of *daemôn*, which in turn has no fixed distinction from "god" except that it is usually nameless, or a neuter substantive from the adjective *daimonios*, "that which pertains to the more than human."

18. "Divinely-speaking" (*thespesios*) is a poetic word.

19. "Wind-egg" is an unfertilized egg, which was extended to mean fruitless and vain.

20. This sentence occurred in Protagoras' book *Truth*. Another book, *On Gods*, stated that he did not know whether the gods are and what sort they are; it is alluded to at 162D–E.

21. "Appearance" (*phantasia*) is not a separate faculty as it is in Aristotle, and which it may be at *Sophist* 260C, but merely the substantival equivalent to the verb *phainesthai*. Outside of *Republic* 382E the word occurs only in the *Theaetetus* and *Sophist*.

22. "Converge" is meant to convey the pun on the original meaning of *sumpheromai* "move together" and its extension "agree." The word occurs in the fragment of Heraclitus that the stranger quotes at *Sophist* 242E.

23. Epicharmus (540?–443? B.C.) wrote comedy in Doric. He lived most of his life in Sicily (Megara and Syracuse). The extant fragments contain passages that read like Platonic dialogues, but their genuineness has been doubted.

24. *Iliad* XIV.302. It is spoken by Hera to Zeus with the intent of deceiving him as to her purpose, which she says is to reconcile Oceanus and Tethys but in fact is to seduce Zeus. Cf. also in the same book line 246.

25. The passage alluded to is at the beginning of the eighth book of the *Iliad,* where Zeus threatens all the assembled gods: "Come, gods, try it, in order that you all may know, hang from the sky a golden chain, and all you gods and goddesses attach it, but you would not draw to earth out of the sky Zeus the highest, the wise, not even if you should wear yourselves out with toil. But whenever I should wish to draw it, I would draw it along with earth and sea, and then I would tie the chain around the ridge of Olympus, and everything would be up in the air; it's by so much that I am superior to gods and human beings" (18–27); cf. *Laws* 644E–645A.

26. Euripides *Hippolytus* 612: "The tongue has sworn, the mind (*phrên*) is unsworn." Hippolytus says it to Phaedra's nurse after he threatens to divulge Phaedra's passion though he had sworn unconditionally not to repeat anything he heard from the nurse.

27. "Hallucinations" (*phasmata*) is perhaps a slight overtranslation: *phasma* literally means an appearance or sight, usually sudden, as in "portent."

28. In Hesiod's *Theogony*, Pontus bore Thaumas (237), and Thaumas married Electra who gave birth to Iris (rainbow) and the Harpies (265–68).

29. The use of parentheses around "is" and "are" in this passage is meant to indicate the extent to which the Greek avoids it.

30. *Pheromai*, the middle of *pherô* ("carry"), means to move locally (sometimes translated as "sweep"), but the active can mean to bring to birth (particularly of plants); since the surrounding language suggests a pun, the "e" in borne is put in parenthesis. For the pun see *Republic* 546A.

31. The name-day for Athenian children was called the *Amphidromia* (Run-around). A week or so after birth, a child was carried around the hearth and presented to the family and their guests who witnessed the naming.

32. The proverb literally is "If it's dear to you, it's not even hateful to me."

33. According to the scholium "not worth even a single one" is a term from dicing, where one is the lowest score.

34. *Eikosi* could be the dative plural of either *eikos* (likely) or *eikôn* (semblance).

35. "Monster" (*teras*) is anything put together out of disparate parts, or a prodigy of some kind.

36. Socrates' confrontation with Protagoras took place at Callias' house in Plato's *Protagoras;* it is also the setting of Xenophon's *Symposium.* For the family of Callias and their wealth, see J. K. Davies, *Athenian Propertied Families* (Oxford, 1971), 7826, pp. 254–70.

37. "Truths" seems to be a necessary correction for the manuscript's "true," which involves an impossible placement of a connective. But "truth" is nowhere else in Plato in the plural.

38. Sciron was a robber who waylaid travelers on the road between Megara

and Athens; he forced them to wash his feet, and while they were doing so pushed them off a cliff. He was killed by Theseus. Antaeus was the son of Poseidon and Earth and lived in Libya; since his strength was derived from his contact with the ground, Heracles lifted him into the air and crushed him.

39. The tragic man, Socrates says in the *Phaedo* (115A), would use the word "fate" (*heimarmenê*).

40. *Odyssey* XVI.121. Telemachus tells the disguised Odysseus that he has very many thousands of enemies in his house; at line 236 the revealed Odysseus asks for an accurate count.

41. Another reading is possible which would imply that those who deny natural right are more extreme than the Protagorean position as improved by Socrates, but this seems to be a misunderstanding of pre-Socratic philosophy.

42. *Daimonie* is a not uncommon form of address from Homer onward. In Plato, perhaps because of Socrates' *daimonion*, it is usually spoken with a sense of surprise at the addressee's prescience; cf. *Crito* 44B.

43. "Practices of philosophy" (*philosophiai*). The plural of "philosophy" is rare and does not recur in Plato. Isocrates has it thrice. Wisdom (*sophia*) is plural at 176C.

44. The speakers in court had to speak within a given time, which was measured by a water clock (*clepsydra*).

45. The manuscripts have after "outline" the clause, "which they call an affidavit"; it is usually held to be interpolated.

46. An expression for the uncountable and immeasurable.

47. Pindar fr. 292S. It is not quite clear how much is Pindar's own words; "exploring" could also be his. "Under the earth and the planes" became a proverbial expression for a busybody.

48. "Mickle" translates Madvig's correction (*taü*) for the manuscripts' *t' au* ("and in turn"), which if genuine implies a separate quotation ("and possessing in turn gold") with no connection in the context.

49. Cf. *Iliad* XVIII.104: "I sit by the ships a vain burden of the field." Achilles says it to his mother after the death of Patroclus. Socrates quotes it in *Apology of Socrates* 28D.

50. "Sweeping being" (*pheromenê ousia*) recurs as "sweeping becoming" at *Sophist* 246C.

51. "Yes, by Zeus, my good man" occurs in Aristophanes *Clouds* 1338 as well as elsewhere in his work, but nowhere else in Plato.

52. The text seems not to be sound here, and the clause ("or rather . . .") has been held interpolated, but it's probable that Theodorus' indignation has got ahead of his grammar.

53. Cf. Aristophanes *Clouds* 942–44. Unjust Speech is talking: "And then I'll strike him with my arrows of fresh phraselets and thoughts."

54. A problem (*problêma*) is a mathematical term for the setting out of a construction of a figure.

55. Cf. *Protagoras* 316D.

56. This line is also cited by Simplicius, but it is not known where it fits into the poem; it resembles fr. VIII.38 "(Destiny fettered it) to be whole and immovable; therefore everything (mortals laid down) will be a name," since "whole" (*oulon*) looks like "such" (*hoion*), for which Simplicius apparently read *oion* ("alone").

57. The game is described by Pollus IX.112. Two groups of boys tried to pull over to their own side the members of the other group one by one.

58. "Arresters" (*stasiôtai*) brings out the pun in the word, which otherwise means seditionaries.

59. "To move the unmovable things" is a proverbial expression for a violation of the sacred.

60. The scrutiny (*dokimasia*) was an examination of elected magistrates to determine whether they met certain qualifications for public office.

61. *Poiotês* ("sortness" or "quality") became the standard substantive for the pronoun for "sort" (*poios*), but here it is clearly not meant to imply a substance with a quality.

62. Cf. *Timaeus* 50A–B.

63. Socrates first phrases the conclusion with the verb "be" and then corrects it out of deference to the Heracliteans with "become."

64. "Dialect" (*dialektos*) is the same word translated as "conversation" at 146B.

65. The scholium offers two explanations for the proverb. Either it's an invitation to compete, issued to those who are better than you are, or an invitation to those who want to anyway.

66. *Iliad* III.172. Helen says it to her father-in-law Priam, as the Trojan elders are surveying the marshalled troops of the Achaeans.

67. Such a use of "depth" is not common in prose. Herodotus speaks of "ways deeper than the Thracians" (IV.95.1), and Socrates is said to have remarked that Heraclitus' writings need for their interpretation a Delian diver (Diogenes Laertius II.22); cf. *Laws* 930A.

68. The quotation marks around "the same" are meant to represent the double article of the Greek (*to tauton*); it indicates that "the same" is being used as a universal (sameness). The device recurs at *Sophist* 254E.

69. For the phrase, cf. *Phaedo* 65C.

70. Campbell suggests assigning "And either together or in turn?" to Socrates, "Most beautiful" to Theaetetus, and "But . . . do?" to Socrates.

71. These possibilities can be represented as follows. Let a rectangle and a triangle represent two seals, and when perceived or known in the memory let their lines be solid, and when neither perceived nor known dotted. The first four cases in the block of wax are these, in which error is impossible:

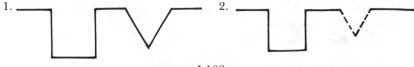

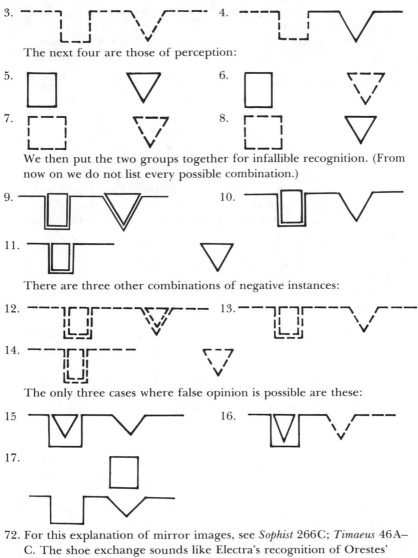

3.

The next four are those of perception:

5.   6.

7.   8.

We then put the two groups together for infallible recognition. (From now on we do not list every possible combination.)

9.   10.

11.

There are three other combinations of negative instances:

12.   13.

14.

The only three cases where false opinion is possible are these:

15   16.

17.

72. For this explanation of mirror images, see *Sophist* 266C; *Timaeus* 46A–C. The shoe exchange sounds like Electra's recognition of Orestes' footprints in Aeschylus' *Choephoroe* 205–10.

73. *Kear* or *kêr* is a poetic word for heart (*kear* among the tragic poets, *kêr* in Homer); cognate with it is the ordinary word for heart (*kardia*).

74. "Casts" (*ekmageia*) is the same word in the plural that had been used for the wax block itself (*ekmageion*).

75. "Shaggy heart" occurs at *Iliad* II.851; XVI.554 of Pylaemenes and Patroclus respectively. Achilles has a shaggy breast at I.189.

76. "Ring-dove" or "woodpigeon" (*phatta*) is a species of wild pigeon.

77. A proverbial expression for those things only known from experience.

78. "Advocates" translates *dikanikoi,* which had previously been rendered "shysters" (175D).
79. "Knowable" (*epistêta*) is being signaled as a new word; the ordinary word would be *gnôsta,* which Socrates uses at 202B and everywhere else.
80. Cf. *Symposium* 202A.
81. All the words in double quotes are to be found in the previous sentences; 'this' is an addition.
82. Omega is not the Greek name for the long O sound; it along with epsilon, upsilon, and omicron had its sound for its name (cf. *Cratylus* 393D).
83. There are seven vowels in the Greek alphabet (alpha, epsilon, eta, iota, omicron, upsilon, omega), eight semivowels (zeta, lambda, mu, nu, rho, sigma, ksi, psi), and nine consonants (beta, gamma, delta, theta, kappa, pi, tau, phi, khi). Semivowels and consonants are sometimes counted together.
84. "The same result" is that "not a whole" is equivalent to "not an all:" "out of the same" is that "whole," as that from which nothing is missing, is equivalent to "all."
85. Hesiod *Works and Days* 455–56: "A man rich in his own opinion talks of putting together a wagon, the fool, he doesn't know, but the timbers of a wagon are one hundred."
86. The Mysians were proverbially the lowest of the low (cf. *Gorgias* 521B); so "most remote" would ordinarily have meant the bottom of the barrel.
87. The proverb "twirling of a pestle" means to do the same thing again and again without accomplishing anything.
88. Theaetetus is probably referring to Socrates' question at 209A.

COMMENTARY

1. Aristocles *De philosophia* VII (Eusebius *Praep. Ev.* XIV.17.1).
2. Aristotle *Metaphysics* 1046b29–1047a7.
3. *Statesman* 257a1–2.
4. *Statesman* 258a3–6.
5. *Republic* 487a2–6
6. *Philebus* 55e1–56a2; *Statesman* 284e11–285b6.
7. *Parmenides* 130c1–e4.
8. *Republic* 408c5–409e3.
9. Xenophon *Memorabilia* I.vi.13.
10. *Sophist* 246a7–b1; *Republic* 509d3.
11. *Republic* 527a6–b2.
12. Aristotle *Metaphysics* 1010b10–11.
13. *Republic* 436a8–437a10.
14. *Timaeus* 91d6–e1.
15. *Laches* 187e6–7; *Apology of Socrates* 30a4; *Sophist* 265a2; *Hippias Major* 304d3.
16. *Parmenides* 132d2.
17. *Apology of Socrates* 38a1–6.
18. *Republic* 340a9–b8.
19. *Republic* 530b6–c1.
20. *Statesman* 257b7–8.
21. *Odyssey* 4.12.
22. *Parmenides* 128a4–e4.
23. *Republic* 507c1–2.

24. *Republic* 352e5–8, 518c5.
25. *Republic* 582d7–14.
26. For this use of *kalon,* see *Gorgias* 454d1–4.
27. *Meno* 92b7–c7.
28. Aristotle, *Metaphysics* 1051b24–25.
29. *Republic* 381e4; *Laws* 959b1.
30. *Parmenides* 136e9, 164d2, 165c7.
31. *Parmenides* 143c4–8.
32. *Republic* 516b9–c2.
33. *Charmides* 159a2; *Republic* 490a8–b7.
34. *Republic* 496b5–6.
35. This sort of nominalism is discussed by Aristotle *Posterior Analytics* 71a30–71b8.
36. *Sophist* 241d1–242a4.
37. *Symposium* 202a5–10.
38. Aristotle *Rhetoric* 1413b32.
39. Aristotle *Metaphysics* 1041b11–33.
40. What follows is an adaptation of the argument at *Parmenides* 142d6–143a3; cf. Aristotle *Physics* 185b11–16.
41. *Republic* 368d1–369a3.
42. *Sophist* 253d1–3.
43. Xenophon *Memorabilia* IV.vii.7.
44. L. Campbell on 209e5. *The Theaetetus of Plato* (Oxford, 1866), p. 209.
45. *A Greek-English Lexicon,* compiled by H. G. Liddell and R. Scott, 7th ed. (Oxford, 1882), s.v.
46. *Laches* 201c4–5.

Selected Bibliography

BIBLIOGRAPHIES

Brisson, L. "Platon, 1958–75." *Lustrum* 20. Göttingen, 1977.

Cherniss, H. "Platon, 1950–57." *Lustrum* 4, 5. Göttingen, 1959–60.

McKirahan, R. D. *Plato and Socrates: A Comprehensive Bibliography, 1958–1973.* New York, 1978.

EDITIONS, TRANSLATIONS, COMMENTARIES

Allen, R. E. *Studies in Plato's Metaphysics.* New York, 1965.

Apelt, O. *Platonis Sophista.* Leipzig, 1897.

————. *Platons Dialog Politikos oder vom Staatsman².* Leipzig, 1922.

Bluck, R. S. *Plato's Sophist: A Commentary,* ed. G. C. Neal. Manchester, 1975.

Burnet, J. *Platonis Opera I–V.* Oxford, 1901.

Campbell, L. *The Sophistes and Politicus of Plato,* with a revised text and English notes. Oxford, 1867.

————. *The Theaetetus of Plato,* with a revised text and English notes. Oxford, 1871.

Cornford, F. M. *Plato's Theory of Knowledge: The Theaetetus and the Sophist of Plato,* translated with a running commentary. London, 1935.

Diès, A. *Théétète.* Vol. 8, part 2 of *Platon oeuvres completes.* Paris, 1924.

————. *Le Sophiste.* Vol. 8, part 3 of *Platon oeuvres completes.* Paris, 1925.

————. *Le Politique.* Vol. 9 of *Platon oeuvres completes.* Paris, 1935.

Klein, J. *Plato's Trilogy.* Chicago, 1977.

McDowell, J. *Plato's Theaetetus.* Oxford, 1973.

Manasse, E. M. *Platons Sophistes und Politikos: Das Problem der Wahrheit.* Berlin, 1937.

Miller, M. H. *The Philosopher in Plato's Statesman.* The Hague, 1980.

Skemp, J. B. *Plato's Statesman.* New Haven, 1952.

Taylor, A. E. *The Sophist and the Statesman,* ed. R. Klibansky and E. Anscombe. Edinburgh, 1961.

Vlastos, G. *Plato: A Collection of Critical Essays*. Vol. 1: *Metaphysics*. Notre Dame, 1971.

ARTICLES

The items are keyed to the sections of the *Theaetetus* and *Sophist* in the commentary.

Theaetetus

146c7–147c6

Bierman, A. K. "Socratic Humour: Understanding the Most Important Philosophical Argument." *Apeiron* 5 (1971): 23–42.

151d7–157a7

Bluck, R. S., "The Puzzles of Size and Number in Plato's *Theaetetus*," *Proceedings of the Cambridge Philological Society*, n.s. 7 (1961): 7–9.

162b8–171e9

Lee, E. M. "Hoist with His Own Petard: Ironic and Comic Elements in Plato's Critique of Protagoras (*Tht.* 161–171)." *Phronesis Supplement* 1 (1973): 225–61.

183c5–187c6

Bondeson, W. B. "Perception, True Opinion, and Knowledge in Plato's *Theaetetus*." *Phronesis* 14 (1969): 111–22.

Burnyeat, M. F. "Plato on the Grammar of Perceiving." *Classical Quarterly* 26 (1976): 29–51.

Cooper, J. M. "Plato on Sense-Perception and Knowledge (*Theaetetus* 184–186)." *Phronesis* 15 (1970): 123–46.

187c7–190e4

Ackrill, J. "Plato on False Belief (*Theaetetus* 187–200)." *Monist* 50 (1966): 383–402.

Fine, G. J. "False Belief in the *Theaetetus*." *Phronesis* 24 (1979): 70–80.

90e5–196c3

Deicke, W., "*Theaetetus* 192c10." *Phronesis* 9 (1964): 136–42.

196c4–210c7

Lee, H. D. P. "The Aviary Simile in the *Theaetetus*." *Classical Quarterly* 33 (1939): 208–11.

200c8–206b12

Burnyeat, M. F. "The Material and Source of Plato's Dream." *Phronesis* 15 (1970) 101–22.

Hicken, W. F. "Knowledge and Forms in Plato's *Theaetetus*." *Journal of Hellenic Studies* 77 (1957): 48–53.

Meyerhoff, H. "Socrates' Dream in the *Theaetetus*." *Classical Quarterly*, n.s. 8 (1958): 131–38.

Rorty, A. O. "A Speculative Note on Some Dramatic Elements in the *Theae-tetus.*" *Phronesis* 17 (1972): 227–38.

206c1–206b10

Bondeson, W. B. "The Dream of Socrates and the Conclusion of the *Theae-tetus.*" *Apeiron* 3 (1969): 1–13.

Fine, G. J. "Knowledge and Logos in the *Theaetetus.*" *Philosophical Review* 88 (1979): 366–97.

Sophist

226a6–231b8

Booth, N. B. "Plato *Sophist* 231a, etc." *Classical Quarterly,* n.s. 6 (1956): 89–90.

Gooch, P. W. "Vice Is Ignorance: The Interpretation of *Sophist* 226A–231B." *Phoenix* 25 (1971): 124–33.

Kerferd, G. B. "Plato's Noble Art of Sophistry." *Classical Quarterly,* n.s. 4 (1954): 84–90.

Skemp, J. B. "Plato *Sophistes* 230e–231b." *Proceedings of the Cambridge Philo-logical Society,* n.s. 2 (1952–53): 8–9.

231b9–236c8

Bondeson, W. "Plato's *Sophist:* Falsehoods and Images." *Apeiron* 6 (1972): 1–6.

239b1–241b4

Kohnke, F. W. "Plato's Conception of *to ouk ontôs ouk on.*" *Phronesis* 2 (1957): 32–40.

Peck, A. L. "Plato and the Megista Gene of the *Sophist:* A Reinterpretation." *Classical Quarterly,* n.s. 2 (1952): 32–56.

250d5–259d8

Ackrill, J. L. "Plato and the Copula: *Sophist* 215–259." *Journal of Hellenic Studies* 77 (1957): 1–6.

Gomez-Lobo, A. "Plato's Description of Dialectic in the *Sophist* 253D1–E2." *Phronesis* 22 (1977): 29–47.

Lee, E. N. "Plato on Negation and Not-being in the *Sophist.*" *Philosophical Review* 81 (1972): 267–304.

Waletzki, W. "Platons Ideenlehre und Dialektik im *Sophistes* 253d." *Phronesis* 24 (1979): 241–52.

259d9–264d9

Bluck, R. S. "False Statement in the *Sophist.*" *Journal of Hellenic Studies* 77 (1957): 181–86.

Lorenz, K., and Mittelstrass, J. "Theaetetos fliegt: Zur Theorie wahre und falscher Sätze bei Platon (*Soph.* 251d–263d)." *Archiv für Geschichte der Phi-losophie* 47 (1966): 133–52.